LATINO CULTURAL CITIZENSHIP

Latino Cultural Citizenship

CLAIMING IDENTITY, SPACE, AND RIGHTS

EDITED BY
William V. Flores AND Rina Benmayor

Beacon Press
BOSTON

Beacon Press
25 Beacon Street
Boston, Massachusetts 02108-2892

Beacon Press books
are published under the auspices of
the Unitarian Universalist Association of Congregations.

Printed in the United States of America

Gracias to José Montoya for permission to reprint an excerpt from his poem "El Louie."

02 01 00 99 98 8 7 6 5 4 3 2

Text design by [sic]
Composition by Wilsted & Taylor Publishing Services

Library of Congress Cataloging-in-Publication Data

Latino cultural citizenship : claiming identity, space, and rights / edited by William V. Flores and Rina Benmayor.
p. cm.
ISBN 0-8070-4634-5 (cloth)
ISBN 0-8070-4635-3 (paper)
1. Hispanic Americans—Ethnic identity. 2. Hispanic Americans—Social life and customs. 3. Hispanic Americans—Cultural assimilation. 4. Citizenship—United States. I. Flores, William Vincent. II. Benmayor, Rina.
E184.S75L356 1997
305.868—dc21 97-5518

IN MEMORY OF OUR *COMPAÑERA, AMIGA, Y COLEGA*

Rosa Margarita Torruellas

(1957–1993)

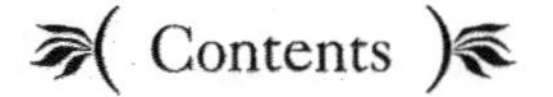

Contents

INTRODUCTION
Constructing Cultural Citizenship
William V. Flores with Rina Benmayor
1

PART ONE
CULTURAL CITIZENSHIP: THEORY

ONE
Cultural Citizenship, Inequality, and Multiculturalism
Renato Rosaldo
27

TWO
"The World We Enter When Claiming Rights": Latinos and Their Quest for Culture
Blanca G. Silvestrini
39

PART TWO
CULTURAL CITIZENSHIP ON THE GROUND: ETHNOGRAPHY

THREE
Identity, Conflict, and Evolving Latino Communities: Cultural Citizenship in San Jose, California
Renato Rosaldo and William V. Flores
57

FOUR
Citizenship, Culture, and Community: Restructuring in Southeast Los Angeles
Raymond Rocco
97

FIVE
Aesthetic Process and Cultural Citizenship: The Membering of a Social Body in San Antonio
Richard R. Flores
124

SIX
Claiming Cultural Citizenship in East Harlem: "Si Esto Puede Ayudar a la Comunidad Mía . . . "
Rina Benmayor, Rosa M. Torruellas, Ana L. Juarbe
152

SEVEN
Mujeres en Huelga: Cultural Citizenship and Gender Empowerment in a Cannery Strike
William V. Flores
210

EPILOGUE
Citizens vs. Citizenry: Undocumented Immigrants and Latino Cultural Citizenship
William V. Flores
255

NOTES · 279

BIBLIOGRAPHY · 291

CONTRIBUTORS · 307

ACKNOWLEDGMENTS · 309

INDEX · 313

INTRODUCTION

Constructing Cultural Citizenship

William V. Flores with Rina Benmayor

THE LONG AND complicated path that the Latino Cultural Studies Working Group began in late 1987 has produced something quite different from what any of us envisioned when Renato Rosaldo first introduced the term "cultural citizenship." The essays in this book reflect how, after nine years of collaboration, we have come to approach this open-ended but immensely productive concept. Cultural citizenship names a range of social practices which, taken together, claim and establish a distinct social space for Latinos in this country. Latino social space is evolving and developing new forms, many of them contributing to an emergent Latino consciousness and social and political development.

Early on in our work as a group we voiced concerns about the way that discussions of race in the United States tend to be cast in terms of a white and black dichotomy, eclipsing the complexities of the Latino experience, an experience which is racial, cultural, and linguistic. Latinos, after all, are a historical fusion or mixing of racial and ethnic groups, from indigenous native groups to African, European, and Asian. Unlike other "immigrant" groups, for Latinos, the American continent is a homeland that precedes the arrival of Europeans. At the same time it is inextricable from the epoch of conquest and colonization, as well as from that era's continuing contemporary forms. Increasingly, however, Latinos are outsiders in their homeland. They are considered foreigners and immigrants, even when they hold legal citizenship by birth or, as in the case of Puerto Ricans, by decree.

Still, borders, real and symbolic, jut seemingly ever higher and wider to encapsulate the United States against the perceived threat of cultural invasion from Latinos. So Latinos, even those who trace their ancestry and citizenship in the United States back for many generations, often feel rejected as full and equal citizens of the country in which they were born. This book examines how various Latino groups are claiming membership in this society as they struggle to build communities, claim social rights, and become recognized as active agents in society. Our approach to cultural citizenship represents an ongoing dialogue among Latino scholars over how Latinos are incorporating themselves into U.S. society, while simultaneously developing specifically Latino cultural forms of expression that not only keep identity and heritage alive but significantly enrich the cultural whole of the country.

In the course of our discussions, research, and writing over these last nine years, other national events and social debates shaped our work. During the Los Angeles riots and rebellion of 1992, which followed the acquittal of the police involved in the beating of Rodney King, the country's media and many intellectuals centered their discussion of racial conflict on whites versus African Americans. Some addressed the conflicts between African Americans and Koreans. But very little was mentioned regarding Latinos, in a city where Latinos represent the dominant ethnic group and where Latinos were widely affected by the rebellion. Again, during the so-called trial of the century, the murder trial of O. J. Simpson, discussions of race centered only on whites versus African Americans, as if other groups had no views on the trial or were simply bit players in the central conflict of white versus black. Proposition 187 changed that picture, as television advertisements depicted hordes of undocumented Mexican immigrants transgressing national borders and invading California. The message was clear. Immigration from Mexico and Latin America posed a threat to the economic, political, and cultural character of this country.

Bilingual education, too, has come under attack as an "obstacle" preventing Latino and Asian immigrants from learning English and from fully assimilating into U.S. society. Xenophobia and cultural arrogance have gone so far as to introduce "English-only" legislation throughout the country. Ironically, English-only efforts derailed conservative attempts of the Statehood movement in the "Free, Associated State" of Puerto Rico, an island where the people are Spanish-speaking and yet are U.S. citizens. For Puerto Ricans, holding U.S. citizenship is not insurance against racism. As U.S. citizens, their presence in this country may not face the open legal attacks and harassment of other Latino immigrant populations. However, Puerto Ricans are still treated as second-class citizens. Viewed as "foreigners," they receive the same harsh anti-immigrant treatment as other Latinos. Moreover, the strength and continuance of Spanish in Puerto Rican communities, and cyclical and circular labor migration patterns back and forth between the island and the United States, are issues commonly invoked by assimilationists and conservatives as explanations for persistent poverty and as justification for persistent "othering" and exclusion.

This book is particularly timely in the context of the current political and social debates raging in this country over its identity and direction. The unifying concept of cultural citizenship which we have embraced sharply contrasts with dominant notions of "America," particularly those reflected in nativist laws and policies that seek to eliminate affirmative action and drastically restrict the rights of immigrants. California's infamous Proposition 187, the 1996 Federal Welfare Reform Act, and the 1996 Immigration Reform Act, among others, prohibit or severely limit access of immigrants to medical and social services, while beefing up the

Immigration and Naturalization Service (INS) and U.S. Border Patrol to increase arrests along the border with Mexico. The Republican-led counter-revolution and right-wing hysteria that swept this country in the 1994 elections have railed over perceived threats to the social and cultural configuration of society. In the Orwellian doublespeak of the right, California's Proposition 209, adopted in the 1996 elections, proclaimed itself as the "California Civil Rights Initiative," while eliminating affirmative action in state and public agencies. The measure, overwhelmingly supported by white voters, transposes Martin Luther King's Dream into a nightmare. While raising the banner of creating a society free of racial prejudice, proponents of Proposition 209 actually sought to eliminate the very social practices that have provided economic and social opportunities for minorities and women with concrete steps to reduce discrimination and prejudice. Many Latinos feared Proposition 209 would further restrict their efforts to make social and economic gains in society. Like Proposition 187, Proposition 209 spurred record applications of Latinos for U.S. citizenship and voter registration. Consequently, over two-thirds of Latino voters rejected the measure in the polling booth.

Intellectuals have also shaped the contours of these policy debates. Early in the decade, Arthur Schlesinger (1991, 1992) decried multiculturalism that, in his opinion, results in the "disuniting of America," threatening its social fabric and core values. William J. Bennett (1992) charged that a "cultural elite" of academics and liberal policy-makers "de-value America," and he called for a "cultural war" to return to traditional values. Peter Brimelow (1996) argued that the United States is in danger of becoming an "Alien Nation" overrun by immigrants from Asia and Latin America, who inflict a "demographic mutation" on the national character of the country. Brimelow fears that Latinos have emerged as "a strange anti-nation in the United States" and embody the "American anti-ideal" by their refusal to "Americanize" and be absorbed as "Americans" (p. 218).

Even old ideas of genetic heredity have resurfaced in repackaged forms. The infamous *The Bell Curve* by Richard Herrnstein and Charles Murray (1994) became a political flashpoint. Once again proferring the argument that race and genetics determine intelligence, they called for an elimination of affirmative-action policies and government aid to minority communities as futile policies leading only to social decay.

Cultural citizenship brings a different perspective to these debates. In our perspective difference is seen as a resource, not as a threat. The essays in this book all rest on a common premise—that this country is strengthened, not weakened, by the vibrancy brought to it by immigrant and nonwhite communities. The United States has thrived not because of its efforts at cultural homogenization, but despite them. What is more, rejection of difference prevents us as social scientists and as citizens from understanding the highly complex world in which we reside. Rather than "disuniting America" or tearing apart its "social fabric," difference produces new cultural forms that, in fact, help define America—and have done so throughout its history. African Americans, stifled in racialized ghettos and confronted with Jim Crow segregation, nonetheless have made significant contributions to education, science, the English language, and popular culture. If we consider the realm of music alone, African Americans have produced the genres of blues, jazz, soul, and more recently hip-hop that define modern American music on a global scale. Similarly, through poetry and fiction, visual and public art, film and theater, music and dance, Latinos tear down borders that are both geopolitical and cultural. Scores of Latino musicians and entertainers have not only crossed over into mainstream acceptance, but have brought distinctly Latino idioms into the popular culture and daily life of the United States. In music, the most current contributors include Gloria Estefan, Los Lobos, Rubén Blades, Linda Ronstadt, Selena, and many Afro-Cuban, Latin jazz, and salsa musicians. In theater, the plays and sketches of the Teatro Campesino have been produced on Broadway, while comedy groups like Culture Clash have appeared on national television, illustrating a distinctly Latino flavor of humor and satire. Films like *Zoot Suit*,

La Bamba, *El Norte*, *Stand and Deliver*, *American Me*, and *Mi Familia* are standard stock in video stores, and actors such as Raul Julia, Jimmy Smits, Edward James Olmos, and Andy García are well known to all Americans. Significantly, these crossover artists have neither abandoned nor forgotten the cultural heritages that nourish them.

Our intent in this project is to better comprehend how cultural phenomena—from practices that organize the daily life of individuals, families, and the community, to linguistic and artistic expression—cross the political realm and contribute to the process of affirming and building an emerging Latino identity and political and social consciousness. As scholars engaged in advancing a new cultural understanding of Chicano and Puerto Rican experiences in the United States, we intuitively recognize the explanatory power of this paradoxical juxtaposition of culture and citizenship in the notion of cultural citizenship. The juxtaposition cautions us against assuming that either culture or citizenship is all-encompassing and urges us, instead, to look at how and to what extent these concepts act upon each other. Culture interprets and constructs citizenship, just as the activity of being citizens, in the broad sense of claiming membership in the society, affects how we view ourselves, even in communities that have been branded second-class or "illegal." Thus we must ask, "What role does culture play in citizenry movements? How are cultural practices political? And to what extent and in what ways do social movements affect and influence culture?"

An Intellectual History of the Project

In many respects, the collaboration represented in the chapters that follow is unique. Usually within social science research, national studies utilize a common methodological format. Research teams in various sites, using the same instruments or methodological approaches, study a specific research question. We proceeded on a very different track. First, the Latino Cultural Studies Working Group that produced this book has been interdisciplinary from its inception, including anthropology, education, political science, history, literature and cultural studies, community advocacy, and law. Second, we did not proceed from a common methodology. Each of us was already immersed in a particular community, studying dramatically different settings in San Jose, Watsonville, Los Angeles, New York City, and San Antonio, with different lenses and varying techniques. Nor were the populations the same. Rather they are reflective of the complexity of the U.S. Latino experience. The New York study centers on cultural affirmation of Puerto Rican women through popular education. The San Jose studies examine Chicanos, undocumented Mexican immigrants, and Puerto Ricans, in three separate articles. The Watsonville piece centers on Mexican immigrant women. The San Antonio essay examines Chicanos and the Los Angeles study looks at the new Latino immigrant groups.

What united all of us was our search for a theoretical concept that would move us beyond the frustrations commonly felt with existing theoretical models. Another point of connection was our mutual commitment to ethnographic research in Latino communities. Despite the fact that we were each working in cities and towns that, at least on the surface, had little in common, we found that the insights we were gaining from our various investigations had strong mutual resonance. Moreover, each of us was actively engaged in cities that provide considerable insight into national trends affecting Latinos. New York and Los Angeles are political centers of the country. What happens to Latinos in those cities has national impact.

New York, loosely termed, is "the other island" for Puerto Ricans and El Barrio the largest and oldest Puerto Rican community in that city. Today, more than two million inhabitants of metropolitan New York are Puerto Rican and Dominican. Adding Cubanos, Mexicanos, and Central and South Americans, New York Latinos easily top the three-million mark. New York is a bilingual city, as Spanish is daily currency in street life, in business, in public and social services, in schools, and in the home. Through redistricting, Brooklyn in 1996 elected for a second term Nydia Velázquez, the first Puerto Rican woman in Congress. The more than one million Dominicans who now call Upper Manhattan home have begun to flex their political muscle, electing the first Dominican to the city council, Guillermo Linares. Los Angeles is home to the second-largest Mexican population in the world, following Mexico City. Hundreds of thousands of Central Americans and South Americans are also now living in Los Angeles. Latino immigrants have changed the demography of Southern California, with formerly white suburbs transformed into predominantly Latino communities in the past twenty years. As illustrated by the recent victory of Loretta Sánchez in Orange County over right-wing Congressional incumbent Bob Dornan, this transformation is also beginning to change the political landscape of Southern California as well. San Antonio, the site of the infamous Battle of the Alamo, is also a historic settlement of Mexicans that precedes and symbolizes the annexation of the Southwest by the United States. San Antonio emerged as a political center for Latinos with the election of Henry Cisneros as mayor, who served as U.S. Secretary of Housing and Urban Development under President Clinton. San Jose is the center of Silicon Valley and the heart of this country's move to an information society. Like San Antonio and Los Angeles, the Mexican community there traces its roots to Spanish and Mexican rule, yet has a large and growing Latino immigrant population that includes Puerto Ricans, Central Americans, and South Americans. Watsonville, a rural community in Northern California, is also a significant case, as it is there that Chicanos in California challenged and won the right to district elections based on the Voting Rights Act (W. Flores 1992a). The study in this case examines Mexican and Chicana women whose activism in a labor strike coincided with and influenced the political activism of the Chicano community.

As discussions of our work unfolded and as our comprehension of social processes deepened, the concept of cultural citizenship also evolved, taking shape as a theoretical tool to help us better understand the dynamics of social change we were all studying. We focused on a common concern: that theoretical concepts used in social sciences, such as multiculturalism, assimilation, acculturation, and even broad concepts of citizenship and social rights, somehow missed the point of the dynamic processes taking place within Latino and other "minoritized" communities, which were sites not only of contestation, but also of affirmation and cultural production.

Assimilation tended to devolve into absorption, assuming disappearance of ethnic and cultural identity. Clearly assimilation does not describe present realities. In fact, many conservative forces in the country fear that the country is being overwhelmed by immigrants and is unable to absorb or "Americanize" them (e.g., Brimelow 1996). Similarly, we found discussions of a pluralist society and liberal multiculturalism lacking in that too often they assumed a stable and basically unchanging country where immigrants add color and spice. Thus, analogies of a "salad bowl" picture minorities as condiments or additives to the basic ingredient of lettuce, but fail to consider a whole new salad (perhaps bean or teriyaki chicken).

Pluralism, for all its power, does not go far enough and suffers from several serious flaws. While pluralism allows for private and even some public celebration of difference, it tends to be the celebration of difference in publicly sanctioned settings of special holidays, parades, and social events, where we are permitted to be Jewish, or Italian, or Polish, or to claim any other ethnic heritage. Pluralism implies that in our private lives we can possess and exhibit different cultural identities, but that in the public sphere, except in these sanctioned displays of ethnicity, we must put aside those identities and interact instead in a culturally neutral space as "Americans." By taking for granted that public space can be and is culturally neutral, pluralism endorses the dominant culture as normative. More serious is pluralism's silence on inequality and power relations in the country. While expression of difference is permitted, challenges to power relations are suppressed.

In fact, even some proponents of pluralism, like Schlesinger, now express concern over its contemporary implications. What Schlesinger, Bennett, and others fear is the loss of a common ground of shared values that in their view defines "America." While this country certainly has a long and proud history and values that should be retained, Schlesinger and others wrongly assert that we have a singular "common history" or master narrative that captures "the" American experience. Clearly the experience of the African slave was very different from that of the white slave master. Although both shared a "common" history, insofar as the slave master could not exist without the slave, they most certainly did not live that history in the same way. The voice and narrative of the slave produces a very different understanding of America than does that of his or her master. Master narratives ignore how the country has been divided along lines of race, class, gender, religion, and sexual preference. Schlesinger and others mistakenly assume a linear and singular process of social integration, rather than one that contests and renegotiates power relations or examines and contests the existing social contract based on those power relations. By contrast, Benjamin Ringer's important volume, *We the People and Others* (1983), presents a less mythical take on U.S. pluralism by articulating how the racial divide and second-class citizenship were structured into the very founding legal convenants of the country.

In approaching this project, then, we sought alternative voices and the alternative conceptions of "America" that they inscribe. This book does not assume that a single national community exists, but rather seeks to uncover how Latinos perceive their communities and how they perceive themselves as part of the larger society. Methodology also became important as we used life histories, ethnographic interviews, participant observation, and textual analysis to explore the shape and context of Latino communities, their voices, and their claims.

Citizenship, too, was not a simple matter. Latinos, we felt, were treated as second-class, even when they were born in this country. Puerto Ricans, for instance, are not distinguished by many Americans from Dominicans, working-class Cubans, Central Americans, or Mexicans—they are seen as simply another Latino immigrant group. Certainly the traditional legal definition of citizenship, a status conferred upon individuals by place of birth or by decree of the state and implying membership, with all of its accrued rights, benefits, and responsibilities, was too narrow for our purposes.

Instead, we found the sociological and political notion of citizen as political subject a broader and more useful concept to describe the current realities of Latino communities. In this way, immigrants who might not be citizens in the legal sense or who might not even be in this country legally, but who labor and contribute to the economic and cultural wealth of the country, would be recognized as legitimate political subjects claiming rights for themselves and their children, and in that sense as citizens.

Renato Rosaldo, who in 1987 was working on his book *Culture and Truth*, suggested that we consider what he termed "cultural citizenship." The two terms taken together, while seemingly incongruous, imply an interaction of culture and claims placed on the broader society in which Latinos, or for that matter other marginalized or excluded groups, live and interact. Rosaldo had already circulated his brief but fundamental essay, "Assimilation Revisited" (1985). In that piece, he criticized the assumptions of many social scientists who have assumed that Latinos necessarily assimilate as a consequence of intermarriage (what he terms "biologism"). Such "biological" models posit that Anglo society necessarily absorbs intermarried Latinos and their offspring. In fact, in many instances, the assimiliation is in the opposite direction. That is, the non-Latino spouse (who may or may not be Anglo) and children resulting from such marriages often identify as Latinos, even when they do not speak Spanish. Similarly, Rosaldo noted that modernist constructs pervaded these writings, so that, "instead of considering actual practices in a manner that highlights innovation and change, scholars have indulged in a primitivism that regards culture as a relic, an inert heirloom handed down wholecloth from time immemorial" (ibid., p. 2). The direction and dynamics of real cultural change, especially in Latin America and the Caribbean, were systematically misrepresented by these assumptions.

Our collaboration as the Latino Cultural Studies Working Group of the Inter-University Program for Latino Research (IUP) developed in stages. In October 1987, Renato Rosaldo and William Flores took steps to reconvene a group of Latino scholars studying culture and politics. This group had first come together in 1984 at the founding meeting of the IUP. Rosaldo and Flores produced and circulated the beginnings of a concept paper on cultural citizenship. This concept had at its heart "agency, particularly social reproduction and mechanisms for the production of new cultural forms" (Rosaldo and Flores 1987). In December of that year, we held the first meeting of what would become a cohesive working group. Along with Rosaldo and Flores, it included Rina Benmayor from the Centro, and Richard Chabrán and Raymond Rocco, both from the Center for Chicano Research at UCLA. This meeting produced the first collective effort, the IUP Cultural Studies Working Group's "The Concept of Cultural Citizenship" no. 1 (IUP 1987). This concept paper explicitly linked the processes that we were beginning to define as cultural citizenship to a progressive concept of empowerment. In early 1988, Rosaldo, Flores, Benmayor, Rocco, and Pedro Pedraza met in New York at the Centro de Estudios Puertorriqueños and formalized the IUP Latino Cultural Studies Working Group. By mid-1988 others became part of the group, including Rosa Torruellas, Ana Juarbe, Pedro Pedraza, and Antonio Lauria (all from the Centro de Estudios Puertorriqueños), Blanca Silvestrini (Stanford and the University of Puerto Rico), Richard Flores (University of Texas at Austin), and Luis Rubalcalva (California State University, Northridge). In addition, a great number of graduate and undergraduate students participated in and contributed to the research and theoretical discussions.

In one of our first meetings, we addressed the relationship of cultural citizenship to empowerment. Often empowerment describes authorization to power through electoral or other institutionalized processes, but it does not imply challenging existing power systems. Using a more radical construct, we hypothesized that "empowerment is a process of constructing, establishing and asserting human, social and cultural rights. These values and rights organize individual and collective identities and practices. We are describing this process and practice as the expression of 'cultural citizenship'" (IUP

1988). Agency is critical to the concept of cultural citizenship: it reflects the active role of Latinos and other groups in claiming rights, "of claiming what is their own, of defending it, and of drawing sustenance and strength from that defense." Thus, "a key element of cultural citizenship is the process of 'affirmation,' as the community itself defines its interests, its binding solidarities, its boundaries, its own space, and its membership—who is and who is not part of its 'citizenry'" (ibid.).

In May 1988, we held a Mini-Conference on Cultural Citizenship at UCLA, bringing together twenty Latino anthropologists, sociologists, sociolinguists, and educators from all over the country to discuss the broad topic of cultural citizenship. Each drafted reactions to the concept paper and to a panel of papers presented by the IUP Latino Cultural Studies Working Group. Among those attending that conference were Carlos Vélez-Ibáñez, Patricia Zavella, María Torres, Ana Celia Zentella, Sylvia Rodríguez, Michael Kearney, Clara Rodríguez, Antonio Lauria, and the principal investigators of each research team. The critiques of the concept paper and the broad discussion that followed underscored a concern among Latino scholars that cultural citizenship, while embracing acts of political contestation, should not be limited to the broad manifestations of organized social movements, but rather should include more subtle cultural practices that nonetheless play an important part in creating social and cultural identity. We began to think of cultural citizenship as a broad continuum of social practices ranging from everyday life activities to broad social drama. Moreover, following the mini-conference we began to explore ways that cultural claims might result in social conservatism as well as social change.

Through sustained support from the Inter-University Program for Latino Research/Social Science Research Council, and taking advantage of professional conferences, we held more than a dozen joint meetings over the years. We regularly communicated on our projects and provided one another with valuable feedback on methodology and initial findings, cohering as a group along the way. We have presented papers on cultural citizenship in such conferences as the American Studies Association, Law and Society, the American Anthropological Association, the National Association for Chicano Studies, the Puerto Rican Studies Association, the Oral History Association, the Latin American Studies Association, the American Folklore Association, and international conferences on nationality and identity held in Mexico and Puerto Rico, among others. The valuable feedback which we received has greatly improved our early thinking on the subject.

Discussions of "new citizens" and social movements in Britain and in Latin America, particularly Brazil and Mexico, resonate with our thinking and experience and locate our work in a broader global context. Stuart Hall and David Held (1990) and Néstor García Canclini (1995a) express efforts similar to ours in examining the politics of citizenship in the context of urban migrations, new identities, and new claims for rights in Britain and Mexico, respectively. Speaking to the transnational concern for this subject, a thematic issue on "cidadania" (citizenship) of the Brazilian *Revista do Patrimônio Histórico e Artístico Nacional* (1996) includes British, U.S., French, and Latin American perspectives on new citizenship. In addition, Evelina Dagnino, professor of culture and politics (Universidade Estadual de Campinas), who participated in our group in 1991, offered us particular insight into the Brazilian context where claims for "new citizenship" have come to the fore with the resurgence of mass movements among blacks, gays, and women. As in the United States, migration to urban centers, and demands for equity, inclusion, and full participation in civil society frame what is now a rich empirical and theoretical literature on new citizenship. Dagnino pointed out that in countries formerly ruled by military dictatorship such movements often begin with a struggle for "the right to have rights" (Dagnino 1994). The Latin American and black British experience echoes that of Latinos, African Americans, and other marginalized groups in the United States. Struggles for civil rights in this country have been closely connected to broader struggles for human rights—that is, the right to be seen and treated as human beings. In such contexts, notions of human rights remain fundamental to how Latinos in the United States conceptualize and act upon social demands, just as they have been and are fundamental for poor and marginalized populations worldwide.

Communities, Space, and Rights

In our opinion, what makes cultural citizenship so exciting is that it offers us an alternative perspective to better comprehend cultural processes that result in community building and in political claims raised by marginalized groups on the broader society. Unlike assimilation, which emphasizes absorption into the dominant white, Anglo-European society, or cultural pluralism, which conceives of retention of minority cultural traits and traditions within U.S. society, but nonetheless privileged white European culture and history and assumes retention of existing class and racial hierarchies under the pretense of political equality, cultural citizenship allows for the potential of opposition, of restructuring and reordering society.

Cultural citizenship can be thought of as a broad range of activities of everyday life through which Latinos and other groups claim space in society and eventually claim rights. Although it involves difference, it is not as if Latinos seek out such difference. Rather, the motivation is simply to create space where the people feel "safe" and "at home," where they feel a sense of belonging and membership. Typically, claimed space is not perceived by Latinos as "different." The difference is perceived by the dominant society, which finds such space "foreign" and even threatening. Space, of course, as Mark Gottdiener explains, is not merely a physical location. Rather, "space . . . represents a multiplicity of socio-material concerns. Space is a physical location, a piece of real estate, and simultaneously an existential freedom and a mental expression" (Gottdiener 1985: 123).

The notions of community and belonging are central to social debates in this country and have a long tradition in its social theory. But recent discussions of belonging to America, such as *Habits of the Heart* by Robert Bellah et al. (1996) and *Belonging in America* by Constance Perin (1988), which discuss the decline of civic membership in America, focus on middle-class, white America and are strikingly silent on the experiences of Latinos, African Americans, or other minority groups. Bellah's study identified a "crisis of civic membership." According to Bellah, strong individualism in America has led to a crisis in civic identity and the decline of commitment, community, and citizenship. Similarly, Etzioni's (1993) advocacy for "communitarianism" decries the "severe case of deficient we-ness" in America (p. 26) and implores us to adopt "a set of social virtues, some basic settled values, that we as a community endorse and actively affirm" (p. 25).

The policial landscape that these authors describe in many ways would be difficult to comprehend, and might even be difficult to recognize, from the perspective of Latino America. Told on the one hand that the society suffers from a lack of community, Latinos are criticized for making efforts to retain community. Latinos find themselves in a situation similar to the plight of blacks in the United Kingdom described in Paul Gilroy's *There Ain't No Black in the Union Jack* (1987), where discussions of Englishness, even from the left, excluded nonwhites from consideration. As Rosaldo and W. Flores point out in their essay in this book, one is led to ask, "Who is the 'we' referred to in these studies of belonging?" America in those conceptions is most comfortably contained as a white society with shared values. By contrast, the essays in this book and the perspective of cultural citizenship allow for excluded groups to establish themselves as distinct communities with distinct social claims, while still situating themselves in the broad context of continental American society.

For Latinos, community is essential to survival, not only in terms of neighborhood or geographic locale, but also in terms of collective identity. The struggle for the right to control space and to establish community is a central one. Manuel Castells argues that modern city dwellers "need, more than ever, to reconstruct a social universe, a local turf, a space of freedom, a community" (1983: xviii). This has been especially true for Latinos, whose neighborhoods are routinely cut up by freeways or demolished under the aegis of redevelopment. And Latino struggles for community go beyond the geographic, to include bilingual education in the schools or issues of cultural identification, as in the case of Puerto Ricans in the United States, who maintain a strong cultural and political identity as a "nation." Under such conditions, Latinos have organized by barrio or on a city-wide basis for cultural identity, group survival, and political representation.

The Essays

The first two essays in this book address the theoretical issues of citizenship and social rights. Renato Rosaldo's chapter, "Cultural Citizenship, Inequality, and Multiculturalism," reconsiders the notion of citizenry and the dissident traditions underlying the history of this country's struggles to expand citizenship. For Rosaldo, "the new social movements have expanded the emphasis on citizens' rights from questions of class to issues of gender, race, sexuality, ecology, and age. In effect, new citizens have come into being as new categories of persons who make claims on both their fellow citizens and the state." Rosaldo urges cultural studies not only to consider agency and hegemony, but also to include the voices and perspectives of Latinos and other subordinated groups. It is not enough to describe structures of power or to identify counter-hegemonic veins in everyday life. If one seeks to renew one's social vision, one must attend to the voices and visions of those who have been marginalized.

Blanca Silvestrini approaches culture and citizenship somewhat differently. In her chapter "'The World We Enter When Claiming Rights': Latinos and Their Quest for Culture," she notes that the U.S. legal system has a very difficult time in understanding cultural claims. Proceeding from the specific instance of Puerto Ricans in San Jose, California, Silvestrini addresses the issues of cultural rights as seen in a legal context. In San Jose, Silvestrini shows how Puerto Ricans found it very difficult to obtain space for meetings or public events. She found that Puerto Ricans as a group were not perceived to exist as a legally chartered formal organization, and as such, in the eyes of the legal system, had no "rights" that were violated when they were denied use of a public facility. Cultural claims and rights are inextricably linked. She writes, "Latino communities thus claim a cultural citizenship distinct from their legal citizenship." Silvestrini emphasizes that vernacular conceptions of rights precede legal concepts of rights. Groups perceive rights that have not yet been recognized in the courts or legislatures. That does not mean that the rights do not or should not exist. In fact, the struggle to recognize those rights often reshapes the law or forces its reinterpretation.

Examining Chicano community formations in San Jose, Rosaldo and W. Flores note that communities need not be geographic in locale. In their chapter, "Identity, Conflict, and Evolving Latino Communities: Cultural Citizenship in San Jose, California," they found communities established by intricate networks of family, church, and work that crisscross the city and even the Bay Area. At the same time, they describe the construction of "sacred places" that over time acquire a special significance to a group or distinct generation of Latinos and that, even after they are demolished or destroyed, live on in the collective memory of the community. Their essay examines the generational and ethnic differences that emerge in ethnographic interviews on the effects of downtown redevelopment. Significantly, their interviews found not only sharply contrasting views of redevelopment, but also a distinctly Latino utopian vision for creating a very different downtown from the one that exists. Thus, "whether activist or not, professional or working class, the interviewees felt an unfulfilled longing for community in strikingly similar ways" in hoping to create an environment for cultural and educational activity. Rosaldo and W. Flores feel that such desired space provides insights into how Latinos imagine America and, in the process, help to revisualize and recreate it.

Like Rosaldo and W. Flores, Raymond Rocco's chapter, "Citizenship, Culture, and Community: Restructuring in Southeast Los Angeles," found that networks as well as neighborhoods play an important role in the formation of Latino communities. Rocco examined several suburbs and small cities—Huntington Park, Bell Gardens, South Gate, and other communities—that have all undergone rapid demographic shifts in the past few decades as a result of severe economic restructuring in Los Angeles and the loss of high-paying jobs. White working families, economically displaced by the forces of restructuring, left the area. Land values declined and Latinos, attracted by lower rents and home prices, settled in the areas.

As the Latino populations have grown, Latino enclaves have formed with what Rocco terms "a virtual explosion of neighborhood clubs, night clubs, and restaurants promoting music ranging from the *quebradita* and *cumbia* to *roc en español*." The clubs and restaurants are as likely to be Peruvian, Colombian, or Central American as Mexican, reflecting the increasing diversity of Latinos within Los Angeles. Nonetheless, the various Latino groups share common interests and have begun to ally in defending those that affect all Latinos, such as California Proposition 187. As Rocco notes, these various groups all indicate a strong sense of membership in a larger Latino community that has the right to have access to major institutions, to being given a fair and equal opportunity for social and economic mobility, and to practice and maintain a strong continuity with the culture of their country of origin. Rocco feels that these Latino immigrants are claiming membership and entitlements in the larger society based on their economic and social contributions to society, what he terms "social" citizenship, that is, "rights to benefits based on the fact of contributing to the welfare of the community." For Rocco, "the most useful way to understand the thorny issue of citizenship is to situate it as part of a configuration of issues defined by the intersection of the themes of citizenship, community, democracy, and empowerment."

In an illuminating study of the troupe of Los Pastores, a religious play in San Antonio, Richard Flores offers us a sense of how efforts to retain past traditions serve to "re-member" the group and shape the collective identity and experience of current generations. In "Aesthetic Process and Cultural Citizenship: The Membering of a Social Body," R. Flores describes how this traditional Christmas play, acted out since the settlement of the Spanish in Texas, has nonetheless changed in recent years. The inclusion of women in key roles, and the efforts of the city and church to appropriate the event as a tourist spectacle are different examples of contested re-creation of tradition. As R. Flores notes, "the significance of 're-membering' as a social process can only be recognized when it is negated, trivialized, or, as in the case of the Mission event, contrasted with 'dis-membering.'" He argues for "a processual relationship or link, one that connects political performance within the larger social and historical drama of a community over the long duration." In his sense, the play, acted out and retained in a community setting, both reconnects to the past and reforms and re-establishes, "re-members," the collectivity. Thus, "the continuation of these performative events is itself a political act that resists social fragmentation and effects forms of cultural citizenship that wrest a realm of freedom from necessity."

Moving to New York's El Barrio, Rina Benmayor, Rosa Torruellas, and Ana Juarbe provide us with an understanding of how Puerto Rican women develop community and common sets of interests through their daily interactions in an educational center. In chapter six, "Claiming Cultural Citizenship in East Harlem: Si Esto Puede Ayudar a la Comunidad Mía . . . ," Benmayor, Torruellas, and Juarbe examine how culture, national identity, gender, and class intertwine to affect Puerto Rican migrant women's image and presentation of self, of what they can and have accomplished, their roles and expectations, and their resulting sacrifices. These Puerto Rican women had long histories of wage work in the garment or other light manufacturing industries, only to find themselves displaced from wage labor at the time in their life cycle when they were raising small children. The women sharply rejected the debates raging in Congress and the media about the "underclass" and "welfare dependence as deviant behavior." In fact, Benmayor, Torruellas, and Juarbe discovered that the process of providing adult Spanish literacy and popular education in El Barrio, combined with life history, or testimonial research, contributed to individual and collective affirmation by the women of their social and cultural rights in the home, the community, and in the larger sphere of civil society. Moreover, the collective experience of empowering education built and reinforced a collective national and gender identity that expressed itself in the collective action of building "comunidad" in the literacy program itself. The El Barrio Popular Education Program became a space where memory and affirmation came together. Thus when, through familiar and not-so-familiar actions, the women rallied to the defense of the literacy program after its funding was jeopardized, they were indeed affirming cultural citizenship.

Benmayor, Torruellas, and Juarbe found that activism could not be contrived or imposed from the outside. Rather, through interaction and common experience, the women themselves identified issues that were paramount to them. The authors note, "it is essential to provide physical and discursive spaces through which people can engage in public dialogue and actions. . . . The El Barrio Program provided a forum for the women's participation in activities outside their normal, daily sphere and familial roles. These experiences expanded their frames of political reference." Through their study (see also Benmayor et al. 1992) the authors learned "how essential it was that people themselves define their issues in accordance with their own analysis of needs; that in doing so, people are exercising their own sense of membership and rights, their cultural citizenship; and that these identified issues have to be addressed through culturally rooted practices."

Like the women in El Barrio, William Flores found that Mexican women in the canneries of Watsonville, California, began to develop a social and political consciousness through their own common experiences during a labor strike. In "*Mujeres en Huelga*: Cultural Citizenship and Gender Empowerment in a Cannery Strike," W. Flores traces the class, racial, and gender segregation that existed in the industry and the union prior to the strike. In the course of the 1985–87 strike, the women slowly claimed leadership of the struggle as they challenged the power of the union and of the city. Cultural claims were essential in the process as the *huelga* (strike) became a means by which the Mexicana strikers could regain *respeto* (respect) and *dignidad* (dignity). Prior to the strike, female workers, many of whom had worked for the company for over twenty years, were fired when they could not keep up with speed-up and new quota demands. As one worker related, they were treated *como animales* (like animals). By their involvement and leadership in the strike, the women began to make claims on the union, demanded greater participation in union meetings, and eventually took charge of day-to-day tactics to win the strike. The gains of the strike caused the women and the Latino community generally to expand the struggle to gain control of the local school boards and city council, eventually resulting in the election of a Latino as mayor of the city.

The last chapter in this book returns to San Jose. William Flores examines the emergence of the undocumented as political actors and the cultural performance of citizenship. According to W. Flores, the Chicano social movement has created a social space for the participation of the undocumented in unions, in parent struggles, and in community empowerment efforts. Focusing on the performative aspects of expressive culture, W. Flores provides insight into how counter-discourse and counter-ideology have emerged from the Chicano community to redefine so-called illegal immigrants as part of the Chicano-Mexicano community. Flores maintains that the social movement not only created space for activism of the undocumented but claimed the right to define community membership in an inclusive way, incorporating the undocumented. Thus, in some instances, Chicano activists provided shelter and sanctuary for undocumented residents. In others, the undocumented struggled side-by-side with Chicanos.

In one case examined by Flores, a Chicano *teatro* incorporated undocumented children and parents along with Chicano activists both to agitate against the INS deportations and to facilitate community organization efforts. For Flores, the undocumented "are emerging from the shadows as new subjects with their own claims for rights. These claims are given space by Latino social movements and by counter-ideology that stresses unity between Latino citizens and the undocumented based on commonality rather than difference."

Flores reminds us that in certain respects the world that Latinos envision is more inclusive and more egalitarian than the "America" that exists today. The struggles of Latinos for inclusion and for greater democracy in society, similar to the contributions of the African-American movement, are transforming this country for the better. He explains, "As Latinos 'imagine' and set out to construct their vision of society, as they create space to live it, claim rights and entitlements based on it, and, through their daily life practices construct it, they are not only 'imagining' America, they are recreating it. . . . They offer a potential for reordering, restructuring, and renewal." It is in this spirit that we offer this book.

Part One

Cultural Citizenship: Theory

ONE

Cultural Citizenship, Inequality, and Multiculturalism

Renato Rosaldo

THE CULTURAL CITIZENSHIP project involves research teams that have worked in California, Texas, and New York. The project's central focus has been a set of social processes that we have chosen to call cultural citizenship. In defining cultural citizenship, a phrase that yokes together terms usually kept apart, I should like to begin with reflections on the component "citizenship" and then discuss the implications of "cultural."

Citizenship

Citizenship is often understood as a universal concept. In this view, all citizens of a particular nation state are equal before the law. A background assumption of our work, by contrast, is that that one needs to distinguish the formal level of theoretical universality from the substantive level of exclusionary and marginalizing practices. Even in its late-eighteenth-century Enlightenment origins, citizenship in the republic differentiated men of privilege from the rest: second-class citizens and noncitizens.

In France the people who gathered in public squares were putatively all equal. They were *les citoyens*, the citizens. Certain contemporary thinkers propose that we should return to the model of the public square, to the situation of the citoyens who were supposedly all equal. The public square, they argue, was the democratic space par excellence, and it should be adopted as the model for the late-twentieth-century civil society.

Such thinkers thus affirm that there were no distinctions among citizens who gathered in public squares. These gatherings were a significant step forward in the process of democratization, no doubt, particularly in comparison with the tyranny of excessive social distinctions that reigned during the regime dominated by the monarchy and the aristocracy. One cannot but agree, at least to a point, that the universal notion of citizen was a significant step toward democracy in relation to the ancien régime that preceded it. Nonetheless, at least from the present standpoint, the public square is not the final goal, but only a point of departure for democratization.

In this respect, I differ with commentaries that stress the central importance of developing urban spaces where people may form face-to-face civil societies in sites of public gathering. Such spaces appear to certain thinkers as a solution to problems of contemporary urban life where corporate takeovers and the Foucauldian disciplining of subject populations have replaced what was once relatively unregulated social life in parks and public squares. In this view, the very notion of the public in late-twentieth-century urban spaces begins to shrink as stadiums replace parks and shopping malls replace public squares.

Consider, however, the inequalities that operated in the public squares of the romanticized past. Begin with differences of gender. Can women disguise their gender in the public sphere? If they must appear as women, and not as universal unmarked citizens, then one can ask, who has the right to speak in public debates conducted in the square? Are men or women more likely to be interrupted with greater frequency? Are men or women more likely to be referred to as having had a good idea in these discussions? As much recent sociolinguistic and feminist research has shown, one must consider much more than whether or not certain categories of persons are present in the public square. One must consider categories that are visibly inscribed on the body, such as gender and race, and their consequences for full democratic participation. The moment a woman or a person of color enters the public square both difference and inequality come to the surface. It is difficult to conceal differences of gender and race, and given the prejudiced norms under which we still live, inequities will come to the surface.

Following Enlightenment ideals, the language of the U.S. Constitution granted universal rights to its citizens. It declared that all citizens are equal (implicitly assuming, of course, that the condition of their equality is their sameness in relation to language and culture). In this sense the question of citizenship is bipolar and simple: either one is a citizen or one is not, and that is that.

In the beginning the U.S. Constitution declared that citizens were white men of property. And indeed, as has often been remarked, the stipulation can be read the other way around: that is, the Constitution disenfranchised men without property, women, and people of color. These exclusions derive from discrimination based on class, gender, and race. In the long run, these forms of discrimination defined the parameters of dissident traditions that have endured into the present. The dissident traditions so engendered have involved struggles to be full citizens in ways that were set in motion by the Constitution's original exclusions.

The dissident traditions of struggle for first-class citizenship have achieved a great deal, even if much remains to be achieved. The struggle for women's suffrage (which did not succeed until 1920) was the first step in a historical process whose present phase is contemporary feminism. Issues of women's rights have moved beyond the vote to sets of practices where, in spite of formal equality, one notices such forms of marginalization as systemic differences in pay and subtle mechanisms for not attending to what women say. Similarly, the legacy of antislavery movements has moved through civil rights to the new social movements that encompass African Americans, Asian Americans, Native Americans, and Latinos.

The long history and the success of these dissident traditions of struggle grants a certain depth and legitimacy to their successors in the present. Slavery and formally disenfranchised women are obsolete as social institutions in the late-twentieth-century United States. Debates about race and gender today often invoke that history of abolition and suffrage.

While emphasizing the continuity of dissident traditions in the United States from the nineteenth century to the present, social analysts such as Stuart Hall and David Held (1990) have discussed the new politics of citizenship in the 1990s. They assert that "from the ancient world to the present day, citizenship has entailed a discussion, and a struggle over, the meaning and scope of membership of the community in which one lives" (1990: 175). For them, the key innovation has been an expansion of the definition of citizenship and the base upon which rights are demanded:

> A contemporary "politics of citizenship" must take into account the role which the social movements have played in *expanding* the claims to right and entitlements to new areas. It must address not only issues of class and inequality, but also questions of membership posed by feminism, the black and ethnic movements, ecology (including the moral claims of the animal species and of Nature itself) and vulnerable minorities, like children. (1990: 176)

The new social movements have expanded the emphasis on citizens' rights from questions of class to issues of gender, race, sexuality, ecology, and age. In effect, new citizens have come into being as new categories of persons who make claims on both their fellow citizens and the state. For Hall and Held, the rights of citizenship have expanded in a quantitative sense, but I should like to note that the shift is also qualitative.

In this qualitative shift one can identify two dimensions of change. First, one can think of the redistribution of resources. This dimension refers, above all, to class and the struggle for economic democracy. The second dimension of change could be called recognition and responsiveness. For example, one can consider gay and lesbian rights as an area where issues of the redistribution of resources may be less central than issues of recognition and unbiased treatment in the workplace and other institutional contexts. Such issues range from blatant to subtle matters of second-class citizenship. If issues of class and the equitable distribution of resources were resolved, matters of recognition and fair treatment in the face of bias regarding sexuality, gender, and race would still remain.

A case in point for the politics of recognition would be the current situation of Latinos in the United States. A significant number of people in the United States, for example, have come to question the citizenship of Latinos by declaring undocumented workers to be "alien" or "illegal." By a psychological and cultural mechanism of association all Latinos are thus declared to have a blemish that brands us with the stigma of being outside the law. We always live with that mark indicating that whether or not we belong in this country is always in question. The distortions here are twofold.

First, the term "illegal" misleads because it suggests that undocumented workers are illegal in the sense of failing to obey and living outside the law. On the contrary, they obey the law more punctiliously than most citizens because they know that the punishment for the slightest infraction is deportation. In this respect, they tend to be more law-abiding than citizens with legal documents. Undocumented workers deserve to be treated in accord with universal human rights.

Second, the icon of the Latino illegal alien suggests, again obliquely but powerfully, that all Latinos in the United States are immigrants, most of whom came under questionable circumstances. A young Chicana poet expressed the real situation succinctly when she said, "*No crucé la frontera, la frontera me cruzó a mí*" (I did not cross the border, the border crossed me). After the War of 1848, Mexican territory became part of the United States and Mexican citizens in that territory found that the border crossed them as it moved from north to south. In other words, many Chicanos lived within the present territorial borders of the United States before the first northern European settlements were established in the New World, certainly well before Jamestown. These early settlements contained Spaniards, Indians, and Africans. Increasingly the mestizo and mulatto blends became evident. Far from being newcomers, Latinos are oldtimers in the New World. It is not difficult to document the continuous presence of Chicanos within the present territorial boundaries of the United States.

The mass media often present sensational views of Latinos as new immigrant communities with the consequence, intended or not, of questioning our citizenship and hardening racialized relations of dominance and subordination. Cynical politicians have used such ideologial maneuvers to secure the approval of such legislation as Proposition 187. The tactic divides the Latino community against itself and separates Latinos from dominant white groups.

Culture

By way of moving on to the question of how culture intersects crucially with citizenship today, I now should like to make some themes concrete through a series of examples.

PUBLIC AND PRIVATE

In his memoir *Hunger of Memory* Richard Rodríguez asserts that Spanish is a domestic language; it is, he says, fine for expressing feelings, but it is no good for thinking. It is good for family life, but it has no place in school, politics, and the workplace. He thus opposes public bilingualism. In other words, he claims that racialized ethnic culture can thrive only within the domestic rather than the public sphere. Rodríguez is no doubt being true to his experience, but I would argue that he ignores the social and ideological factors that have structured his experience.

Rodríguez's perceptions do not, I think, belong to him alone. This is a case where ideology colors personal insights about culture. The segregationist ideology of white supremacy is speaking through Rodríguez, and one should not blame either the author or the Spanish language. A day in Mexico, elsewhere in Latin America, or Spain should suffice to make it clear that the linguistic limitations Rodríguez experiences are built into social arrangements, not the language. If the United States has placed a taboo on the use of Spanish in public life, it derives from prejudice manifest in legal and informal arrangements and not because of the language. In Mexico and Puerto Rico Spanish is the language of both the heart and the mind, domestic and public life.

BORDER THEATER, BORDER VIOLENCE

The U.S.–Mexico border has become theater, and border theater has become social violence. Actual violence has become inseparable from symbolic ritual on the border—crossings, invasions, lines of defense, high-tech surveillance, and more. Social scientists often think of public rituals as events that resemble formal rituals separated from daily life in time and space and marked by repeated formal structures. In contrast the violence and high-tech weaponry of border theater is at once symbolic and material. Social analysts need to recognize the centrality of actual violence and the symbolics that shape that violence.

The new technologies of violence were tested in the Gulf War and in the staged television coverage of smart missiles and precision mayhem. These technologies are now directed at unarmed Mexicans as they enter the United States in search of work. The risk they run is real; the threat of death can readily be delivered. For North American politicians, however, the key element is theatrical, a cynical work of lethal art that they offer to their voters with an invocation of previous wars, not only the Gulf War but also the Vietnam War (thus the U.S.-Mexico border becomes a DMZ, a Demilitarized Zone). They attempt to stage the vulnerability of North American citizens who are at risk because of the "illegals" (read: outlaws) invading their land. They of course add that the government is using all means at its disposal to protect citizens from the brown invaders from the south.

VOTING

The vote is the citizen's most sacred right/rite. Yet in California statewide initiatives provide citizens with an occasion for voting their prejudices. Proposition 187 was arguably in large measure an expression of white supremacy. Proposition 209, the so-called California Civil Rights Initiative (CCRI) that appeared on the November 1996 ballot, actually dismantles affirmative action programs and thus opposes civil rights in a manner manipulated by self-serving politicians in order to deepen racial cleavages in the state. The CCRI was explicitly designed to be a "wedge" issue that would divide Democrats and increase the chances of Republican presidential candidate Robert Dole. Indeed because of its popular referenda California has become a testing ground for hot-button conservative political issues at the national level.

The study of voter behavior requires analysis at the symbolic cultural level. Arguably, such referenda manifest legal-juridical violence against Latinos, African Americans, Asian Americans, Native Americans, and women. The workings of such electoral violence cry out for an understanding of a voting subject who is quite unlike the rational choice-maker who is favored by political scientists who regard voter behavior as if it were the same as the consumer's market behavior. The people who voted for Proposition 187 and the CCRI are engaged less in a rational calculus than in expressing their inner prejudices and fears.

QUETZALCÓATL IN SAN JOSE

My final example concerns the unveiling of a statue of Quetzalcóatl, the Aztec divinity of urban civilization, about a year ago in San Jose, California. The unveiling was marred by controversy and by protests from anti-abortion activist Evangelical Christians. The Evangelical groups inspired fear because they had been involved in militant actions at abortion clinics. For the eve of the unveiling I had been asked to give a talk at the San Jose Museum of Art on the cultural and historical significance of Quetzalcóatl. As I prepared to leave my house to go and give the talk, I felt anxious because I feared the worst, particularly from the Evangelical groups. Just before I left the house my daughter Olivia wrote and gave me the following poem, called "Remember," which she dedicated "To Dad and Quetzalcóatl":

Remember
who, how,
Remember who you are.
How did I get here?
Remember your descendents.
Remember your language.
Remember who you are
even where there's prejudice
of who
and what you are.
Remember.

What I did not know as I left was that I would find, in addition to the Evangelicals I feared, an audience composed of public officials, militant Chicano brown berets, and Native American and Chicano costumed dancers from as far away as Mexico City, Texas, and New Mexico. Once I arrived and scanned the audience I felt secure and confident. I was present as a cultural interpreter at an event that had clear political as well as cultural meanings.

The examples just discussed—Rodríguez's view of Spanish as a domestic (not a public) language, border technology as cultural theater, referenda as expressions of prejudice, and the community event surrounding the unveiling of the Quetzalcóatl statue—are all instances of how we need to understand the way citizenship is informed by culture, the way that claims to citizenship are reinforced or subverted by cultural assumptions and practices. In addition, each of the four cases contains a methodological principle critical to studies in cultural citizenship.

Rodríguez's example stands as a methodological caution against relying uncritically and exclusively on personal testimony, and as a reminder of the impact of larger structural factors on local situations. He sees English as the only language of citizenship in contrast with Spanish, which he sees as the language of the heart and of domestic life. He is true to his experience but, in a way made classic by the phrase internalized oppression, he studiously pays no heed to how his experience has been structured by larger forces of domination and white supremacy.

The U.S.-Mexico border theater underscores the tenet that all human conduct is culturally mediated and that cultural citizenship studies, in everyday life, forms of exclusion, marginalization, and enfranchisement in modes that require joining together cultural meanings and material life. The way force is deployed at the border expresses dominant Anglo cultural views of limited Latino rights to full U.S. citizenship. The physical border has become a line of demarcation enforced by staged high-tech violence that is no less violent for being symbolic and vice versa—no less suffused with cultural meanings for being lethal and material.

The referenda of recent California politics underscore the way that cultural citizenship research seeks out cases that have become sites of contestation, negotiation, and struggle over cultural meaning and social violence. California referenda can productively be understood as ways of voting prejudices and fears. Unarmed Mexicans working in the United States have, for many voters, become objects of fear and hatred that require exceptional legislative action. This example emphasizes the psychological mechanism of projection, whereby people attribute their own feelings of hatred to somebody else and then in turn fear their own projected feelings.

For the Latino community of San Jose, the events surrounding the unveiling of the Quetzalcóatl statue were a classic act of cultural citizenship, using cultural expression to claim public rights and recognition, and highlighting the interaction between citizenship and culture. The artistic and cultural event of the unveiling was clearly seen as an important public statement both by the Evangelicals and by a number of distinct elements of the Latino community. In this struggle over the placement and meanings of public art, more was at stake than "culture" in a narrow sense. The Evangelical community clearly saw the cultural expression as a claim to rights in the public square.

My own reactions to the evening reflected the larger dynamic. I went as cultural interpreter, but initially felt disenfranchised as a citizen by the prospect of potential violence. When I saw the remarkable and varied Chicano community presence at the rally—costumes and traditional dance reinforcing the group ties—my own sense of isolation evaporated. I found myself transformed from voiceless vulnerable individual to full-fledged citizen.

Cultural citizenship operates in an uneven field of structural inequalities where the dominant claims of universal citizenship assume a propertied white male subject and usually blind themselves to their exclusions and marginalizations of people who differ in gender, race, sexuality, and age. Cultural citizenship attends, not only to dominant exclusions and marginalizations, but also to subordinate aspirations for and definitions of enfranchisement. In her book on writing, Anne Lamott has eloquently described the hopes of cultural citizenship as virtually universal in the United States:

> Writing can be a pretty desperate endeavor, because it is about some of our deepest needs: our need to be visible, to be heard, our need to make sense of our lives, to wake up and grow and belong. (1994: 19)

The universality of cultural citizenship aspirations most probably reflects the historical experience of civil rights and suffrage struggles. In this vein, our research has found that Latinos are conscious and articulate about their needs to be visible, to be heard, and to belong.

The notion of cultural citizenship challenges social analysts to attend with care to the point of view from which they conduct their studies. Too often social thought anchors its research in the vantage point of the dominant social group and thus reproduces dominant ideology by studying subordinate groups as a "problem" rather than as people with agency—with goals, perceptions, and purposes of their own.

Inequality and social position are critical to studies of cultural citizenship. Social position is a reminder that people in different and often unequal subject positions have different understandings of a given situation and that as they make claims to proper first-class treatment they operate with distinct definitions of such treatment. Chicana poet Lorna Dee Cervantes (1981) sums this insight up in her poem entitled "Poem for the Young White Man

Who Asked Me How I, an Intelligent, Well-Read Person, Could Believe in the War Between the Races." The young man sees peace and prosperity in his land; the poet sees a war being inflicted on her people in the "same" land. Cervantes derives this difference of perceptions from the stark fact that those conducting the race war are shooting at her, not him.

Cultural citizenship thus argues that analysts need to anchor their studies in the aspirations and perceptions of people who occupy subordinate social positions. This research demands studies of vernacular notions of citizenship. In this collection the term *respeto* (respect) has appeared frequently as a requirement of full citizenship for Latinos in the United States. Bridging the discourses of the state and everyday life, of citizenship and culture, the demand for *respeto* is a defining demand of cultural citizenship. As all the chapters in this book reveal, it is an ongoing, contested, and—for the participants—urgent process.

TWO

"The World We Enter When Claiming Rights": Latinos and Their Quest for Culture

Blanca G. Silvestrini

In this country you have to confess first, and then you can claim a right," explains an experienced Latino teacher in San Jose, California. "You have to come in front of a group and explain that you don't speak English; then you get translation at the back of the room. You have to admit that you are an inappropriate provider for your family; then you get lunch service for your children. You have to declare first that you don't belong, to then gain a place. . . . There is always an assumption that you are an inadequate person, that something is missing, that you don't belong, that as a person you have a disability. . . . In other words, you are requested to erase the past, to relearn the ways you deal with siblings, neighbors, friends, acquaintances, and outsiders . . . to celebrate in a different way. It's like being asked to be born again to participate." What is the plight of this woman? She wants to be respected in her difference; she wants not to be considered disadvantaged because of her difference; she wants her difference to be part of her public persona; she wants to participate fully, even in her difference.

Blanca G. Silvestrini

This essay studies the ways Latinos view their rights. It deals with the central role that culture has in their definition of the law and their relationship with the legal system. This dimension of law as experience provides an opportunity to look at ways in which Latinos' sense of justice and of participation in American society come together in their claim to culture rights. In a broader sense, it also questions the world we enter when making claims about who we are.

Culture and Cultural Citizenship

In multiple ways, Latinos give culture a central place in defining their identity, relationships with the world, and sense of rights. In 1988, shortly after I first arrived in California, I attended two events that helped me review my conceptions of culture and the Latino experience in the United States. The first was a meeting of Puerto Ricans held in San Jose, California. Puerto Ricans from California, Nevada, and Hawaii met to organize an agenda to make their voices heard. Some people were interested in education and employment, others in culture and politics. Much to my surprise, a broad array of people called themselves Puerto Ricans. I met people who had lived in Northern California for over forty years and who considered themselves second-generation or third-generation in the United States. Some had lived in Hawaii since the beginning of the twentieth century and had come to California not long ago. Many had arrived fairly recently from the East Coast. Others, like me, had just come directly from Puerto Rico. Although only a few had known each other before the meeting, the atmosphere was one of reunion. Initially, the purpose of the meeting was not clear to me. People seemed to be having a good time together, and that was perhaps the main reason for the gathering. Something was deeply shared in spite of the varied life histories and migration experiences. Soon one of the organizers announced that the purpose of the meeting was to begin looking at the problems faced by Puerto Ricans on the West Coast. "We want to make Puerto Ricans more visible, to claim our space, to make others know that we are part of this community." Participants recognized that a Puerto Rican community exists, though it cannot be located in a particular neighborhood. At the same time they kept using the word "community" with different meanings. "Community" was used to refer to the Puerto Rican community or the Latino community, as well as to those who inhabited a particular place, such as California, San Jose, East San Jose, even the United States.

I had a similar experience when I was invited to a Latino festival celebrated in a vacant lot in East San Jose. The gathering was organized by a Protestant church, although religion as such was not involved in the activities of the day. The purpose of the festival was to "build a sense of community" rather than to convert people to a particular set of religious beliefs. The atmosphere was one of festivity and celebration. Chicanos, Mexicanos, Nicaragüenses, Puertorriqueños, Salvadoreños, among other Latinos, came together in search of their common heritage (*lazos*). Food, talk, laughter, and music provided the background for a rich cultural interchange (*vivencia*). Groups of people were sitting around talking in English or Spanish, or both. Vendors were selling tacos, *pasteles*, hot dogs, *empanadillas*, burritos, hamburgers, and rice. A booth was registering people to vote. In spite of their many differences, people were stretching to find the similarities in their cultures.

The organizers of both events faced some challenges. Their aims were clear: "Gathering makes us stronger. Not to impress others, but for ourselves, we need to come together, to talk to each other, to trust each other (*confiar en nuestra gente*). Then we can face (*enfrentar*) those who don't like us. If we don't come together for ourselves, we can't come together to struggle. And we need to make this place a better place to live." At stake was people's very sense of construction of culture and of community. Organizing these events brought up memories of past times. The organizers encountered problems they thought had already been solved. The first group had had difficulties finding a place to hold their meeting. They applied for space at the public library. Much to their surprise, they were told that they did not qualify as an organization because they did not have a charter, a board of directors, and the other formalities required. Their idea of a gathering of this nature was far from the Californians' conception of a group. In the second case, a city employee told them that religious organizations did not qualify to use the park, even when the activity was not religious. The organizers were outraged; the park was in their neighborhood and they thought they had a "right" to use it.[1] In the end, when they had worked out a way around this obstacle, the organization did not use the park because they could not post the amount required for insurance purposes.[2] So the festival was held in a vacant lot in the community.

These two seemingly unimportant gatherings and their attendant difficulties struck me as illustrative of people's construction of their sense of rights and of community. For those involved these were examples of the distinctions often made between "us" and "them." In the ways the norms were explained to the organizers of these events was an implicit assumption that these were the norms of the community (meaning really "our" community); anyone who wanted to be part of it would have to follow in the way the dominant cultural group (meaning "we") believed to be correct. In other words, the message was that outsiders have to accommodate, to manicure themselves in the way the insiders want in order to be part of the "we" dominant society.[3]

From a formal legal perspective, these events are similar to many other instances of everyday life. If the norm is applied in the same way for everybody (even if it is considered unfair by some), then no claim can be made that rights were violated.[4] Part of living in American society, thus, is complying with requirements assumed to guarantee the social good. What happens, then, when a group feels excluded because its ways of understanding the legal system are not part of or differ from the prevailing legal ideology?

The legal system is often studied from the perspective of the formal application of norms and rules that seem fixed and invariable. In this paper, I am looking at the law from the perspective of the community. What are the diverse meanings and ways to understand its application among Latinos? My initial hypothesis was that the conflicts of citizenship that Latinos experience in gaining a public space, that is, in establishing a visible public presence, affect their sense of participation in the communities where they live. Latinos draw upon their own historical paths, their distinct cultural backgrounds, and the shared experiences of living in multiethnic communities to construct their own ways of understanding the law and the norms that govern everyday life.[5] These constructions may be far different from those of the prevalent American legal system: they are based on distinctive conceptions of justice, fairness, and equality.

Culture is recurrent in Latinos' discourse on rights. "Culture gives us a sense of unity, of connectedness, a vision of our identity," explains a Latino woman who has played an active role in organizing a political group. "The difficulty is trying to pinpoint what we mean by culture. It isn't simply language, community, the arts, religion, history. . . . It is a little of each, and all at the same time. We all know what it is, but can't explain it. It makes us closer to our brothers and sisters; it makes us disregard the differences when it comes to the tough things of life; it's like a unity within the difference." Culture provides, then, a sense of belonging to a community, a feeling of entitlement, the energy to face everyday adversities, and a rationale for resistance to a larger world in which members of minority groups feel like aliens in spite of being citizens.

The definitions of culture given are very loose, fluid, multidimensional. They are understood better when seen in the particular context of experience. Although culture changes over time and with experience, it provides a common basis of understanding; it is understood as the basis of who we are.

In his book *Culture and Truth*, anthropologist Renato Rosaldo explains that a general conception exists in the United States that "cultural" means different and that to pursue a culture is to seek out its differences. In this sense "full citizenship and cultural visibility appear to be inversely related. When one increases, the other decreases. Full citizens lack culture, and those most culturally endowed lack full citizenship" (Rosaldo 1989: 198). People then face the dilemma of choosing between the possibly competing interests of trying to belong to their cultural community and national community. "It is a constant contradiction for us," explains the fifty-two-year-old Chicano. He continues, "We are American citizens; we are supposed to be part of this nation. What we want is a space, the freedom to be American citizens and still be what we are—Puerto Ricans, or Chicanos, or Latinos. We want to be able to enjoy the land that is ours." As a Chicano, this man is claiming a right to the land his ancestors possessed and that was taken from them. He also is claiming full citizenship hand in hand with an entitlement to be different.

Latino communities thus claim a cultural citizenship distinct from their legal citizenship. Cultural citizenship refers to the ways people organize their values, their beliefs about their rights, and their practices based on their sense of cultural belonging rather than on their formal status as citizens of a nation. "A key element of cultural citizenship is the process of 'affirmation,' as the community itself defines its interests, its binding solidarities, its boundaries, its own space, and its membership (who is and who is not part of its 'citizenry')," states a concept paper from the Inter-University Program for Latino Cultural Studies Working Group (IUP 1988: 3). Cultural citizenship usually has an oppositional character because it "describes the claims of social, human and cultural rights made by communities which do not hold state power and which are denied basic rights by those who do," says the report (IUP 1988: 2).

At first glance, one may think in terms of hierarchical categories of belonging—either we are loyal to our national and legal citizenship, in which homogeneity is assumed, or to our cultural citizenship. Which comes first may seem a reasonable question when dealing with specific situations like communities organized as barrios or with isolated cases of Latinos living in Anglo neighborhoods. In the barrio, bonds formed of common interests and solidarity are better understood and help define meanings and symbols within the context of a community. "Thus, if a family resists eviction from a house in a community marked for demolition and redevelopment, this act can spark response from the entire community. The house becomes something greater than a single place of residence. It comes to represent the violation of the entire community's sense of being. The symbolic import of that single house can inspire the entire community to fight the redevelopment plans" (IUP 1988: 9). In this context, people choose action within the framework of their cultural citizenship, without immediate consideration of their participation in the polis, where they often feel "treated culturally as though they belong to another species and put into the least favorable places, socially, economically, politcally" (Perin 1988: 7).

Similarly, Latinos living in Anglo suburban neighborhoods do not have many alternatives in choosing between conflicting citizenships. Although they feel the effects of cultural boundaries around them, their isolation from a "cultural community" can make it difficult for them to construe their individual claims as part of their cultural citizenship. Therefore, they frequently define themselves and choose their actions in terms of their legal citizenship, at least temporarily, until they reach again to their common bonds in a cultural community.

Today, however, many Latinos are moving out of the barrio, not necessarily to predominantly Anglo neighborhoods, but to multiethnic middle-range cities in the United States, where often they become part of invisible communities or communities without very defined boundaries.[6] Does cultural citizenship take a different form for them? What happens to people's sense of cultural citizenship when communities are dismantled or their boundaries change? Is cultural citizenship different in a multiethnic community, like San Jose and many other cities in the United States, where Latinos share their living space with many different cultural groups? In these new environments, cultural symbols, rituals, and meanings are recreated and interchanged as Latinos interact with culturally diverse peoples.[7] Interpersonal relationships are not limited to those people of similar cultural heritage. People intermarry, have neighbors, friends, employers, and acquaintances whose beliefs, affections, and behaviors are very different from their own. They acquiesce, disagree, and clash on cultural terms. New ways of constructing identities merge with the old ones. As a result of these processes, people's lives are simultaneously "lived within and against the dominant culture" (Clifford 1988: 336) and their claims and sense of citizenship also change.

Therefore, in their everyday life Latinos move back and forth from cultural citizenship to legal citizenship and from one identity to the other. Although for them this process does not necessarily represent a contradiction, the world in which they have to claim their rights does not accept this fluid state of identity. It demands a clear definition of loyalties, with corresponding consequences for the person's identity. Under the assumptions of the melting-pot theory, people from different backgrounds have to erase these differences to enjoy full participation, because homogeneity is assumed to be the basis for political stability and economic growth.

Culture Rights and the Constitution

Some of the assumptions of the American legal system about culture make Latinos' claims to cultural citizenship contradictory to legal, national citizenship. A look at the formal legal system that Latinos enter when claiming rights may help us understand the possible conflicts in conceptions of the law. Formal legal scholarship or case law in the United States has not often directly addressed the relationship between the legal system and culture.[8] This task is left to anthropologists, sociologists, and historians, or to common knowledge. Several possible explanations can be offered for this situation. Two are of particular relevance in understanding Latinos' claim to cultural citizenship. First, the legal system assumes that in spite of profound cultural differences, American society can be identified as an homogeneous entity, with shared values and beliefs (Karst 1991: 188). Second, a recognition of culture rights[9] as such is absent from the American constitutional system. In general, the prevalent doctrinal parameters within which the American legal system addresses questions of culture—religious and language rights, and race and ethnic rights—make Latinos' claim to cultural citizenship difficult to prove.

The absence of formal legal treatment of the issue does not mean that the

American legal system does not have an ingrained conception of culture. Legal scholarship and constitutional discourse have long incorporated a particular definition of culture, with its center and borderlands well defined. In the formation of the United States as a nation, agreement was reached on what Karst calls the American civic culture—a white, male-dominated ideal of individual formal equality (1991: chap. 1 passim). As part of it, "Americans came early to accept the inevitable presence of outsiders. . . . Although every citizen could claim a basic set of legal rights, some of these citizens would almost certainly remain outsiders. Actual membership was determined by additional tests of religion, perhaps, or race or language or behavior, tests that varied considerably among segments and over time. Each generation passed to the next an open question of who belonged to American society" (Wiebe 1976: 95).

Culture provides, then, the basis for shaping identity by contrasting "our" beliefs and behavior, which are examples to be followed, with "theirs," which must be avoided because they seem strange and alien. The general assumption has been that those "others" will eventually become part of the national community by joining the mainstream through a process of assimilation. "Throughout this gradual and typically painful widening of the nation's embrace, the already-included Americans have shared a sense of 'peoplehood.' Because American identity still inheres in the abstractions of the civic culture, citizens who seek a more inclusive definition of our national community can draw on two valuable resources. First, it is consistent to express both a strong ethnic identification and a strong attachment to the nation. Second, tolerance of other groups is itself proclaimed as a national ideal" (Karst 1991: 183). The rhetoric of these values—diversity and tolerance—has been historically associated with the need to incorporate newcomers into the national community and with the willingness of newcomers to become a part of that community.[10] However, the assumption always existed that eventually people would accommodate to the new cultural values and become part of the national citizenship. The process of European migration became the model—a process of accepting dominant constructs and creating some new constructs through adaptation of the old ways. If citizenship, as Karst says, means personhood, then the American legal system requires one to give up a full personhood to gain another—hence, to make a choice between national citizenship and cultural citizenship.[11] Therefore, while Latinos, as well as other groups today, are saying cultural citizenship is critical to our sense of participation, Anglo society says that assimilation is a requirement of full participation.

In her article on cultural rights in the United States, Sharon O'Brien argues that nonimmigrant minority groups have been relatively successful in their efforts "to protect their cultural rights through traditional United States constitutional doctrines" (O'Brien 1987: 287). The courts have applied constitutional doctrines of freedom of religion, equal protection, and the right of parents to educate and raise their children in various ways when faced with claims related to culture. After analyzing case law, O'Brien concludes that Native Americans have been more successful than Native Hawaiians and Chicanos in obtaining recognition of their claims. "When viewed in totality, however, it is clear that the federal government's willingness to acknowledge tribal cultural rights stems more from the tribes' political status and jurisdictional rights than from either a moral recognition or constitutional basis" (O'Brien 1987: 355). As long as Native Americans remain isolated in "museumlike reservations" (Clifford 1988: 284), the courts are willing to accept that

> tribes remain quasi-sovereign nations which, by government structure, culture, and source of sovereignty are in many ways foreign to the constitutional institutions of the Federal and State Governments. . . . Efforts by the federal judiciary to apply the statutory prohibitions . . . may substantially interfere with a tribe's ability to maintain itself as a culturally and politically distinct entity.[12]

O'Brien contends that the courts and the federal government have been prone to acknowledge the centrality of traditional religious practices in Native American culture (1987: 298). The Indian Religious Freedom Act of 1978 states that "the religious practices of the American Indian (as well as

Native Alaskan and Hawaiian) are an integral part of their culture, tradition and heritage."[13] The Act commits the federal government "to protect and preserve for American Indians their inherent right of freedom to believe, express, and exercise the traditional religions."[14] But how are these "traditional religions" understood within the context of the American legal system?

In *People v. Woody*, the Supreme Court of California examined the conviction of members of a Navajo tribe for the use of peyote in a religious ceremony.[15] While the Indians claimed that peyote was a sacramental symbol and an object of worship, the state argued that "the compelling reason for the prohibition of Peyotism lies in its deleterious effects upon the Indian community."[16] In reversing an inferior court decision, the higher court faced the dilemma of making an exception to the narcotic laws to favor "a few believers in a strange faith."[17] Once it has condemned a practice to the realm of the "strange," the court can acknowledge its appreciation for diversity:

> In a mass society, which presses at every point toward conformity, the protection of a self-expression, however unique, of the individual and the group becomes ever more important. The varying currents of the subcultures that flow into the *mainstream* of *our* national life give it depth and beauty. We preserve a greater value than an ancient tradition when we protect the rights of the Indians who honestly practiced an *old* religion in using peyote one night at a meeting in a *desert* hogan."[18]

Woody has been praised as a recognition of cultural rights (O'Brien 1987: 300). Further judicial use of the case, however, has provided its assimilationist undertones. In *Peyote Way Church of God, Inc. v. Smith*,[19] for example, while trying to make a distinction between the religious rights of members and nonmembers of Native American tribes, the court said that "religion is an integral part of Indian culture and that the use of such items as peyote is necessary to the survival of Indian religion and culture."[20] On the one hand, Native American culture is viewed by the court as something constant in time and isolated, with invariable characteristics.[21] But on the other hand, it seems as if Native American culture is expected to follow a path of assimilation similar to other ethnic groups. In that sense the court contends that "Congress has the power or duty to *preserve* our Native American Indians . . . as a *cohesive* culture until such time, if ever, all of them are assimilated in the main stream of American culture."[22] Such cultural cohesion must be determined by a "formal organization or community . . . so that it may be determined who is a member of the culture to be preserved."[23]

Wisconsin v. Yoder[24] provides a good example of ways in which the court tries to reduce its definition of a culture to some of its specific expressions. The case involved the conviction of three Amish parents for violating the compulsory education law of Wisconsin. In overturning the conviction, the Supreme Court found that the law violated the Free Exercise Clause of the First Amendment, applicable to the states by the Fourteenth Amendment. The language of the Court seems to reflect contradictory conceptions of culture. First, the Court defines the controversy in strictly religious terms, although acknowledging the significant role of the community in the religious practices: "As a result of their *common heritage*, Old Order Amish communities today are characterized by a *fundamental belief* that salvation requires life in a church community separate and apart from the world and worldly influence. This concept of life aloof from the world and its values is central to *their faith*."[25] Later, the Court explains that "Amish beliefs require members of the community to make their living by farming or closely related activities. Broadly speaking, the Old Order Amish religion pervades and determines the entire mode of life of its adherents."[26] On the one hand, the Court views the "common heritage" as producing a set of religious practices; on the other, the religious beliefs determine the mode of life of the members of the community.

The language of the Court summarizing Amish claims suggests an interesting framework within which to discuss Latinos' conception of culture.

> Amish society emphasizes informal learning-through-doing; a life of "goodness," rather than a life of intellect; wisdom, rather than technical knowledge; community welfare, rather than competition; and separation from, rather than integration with, contemporary worldly society. . . .

> Formal high school education beyond the eighth grade is contrary to Amish beliefs, not only because it places Amish children in an environment hostile to Amish beliefs with increasing emphasis on competition in class work and sports and with pressure to conform to the styles, manners, and ways of the peer group, but also because it takes them away from their community, physically and emotionally, during the crucial and formative adolescent period of life.[27]

In many ways, what the Court is construing as the claims of the "religious community" is similar to what Latinos view as their cultural citizenship—a demand to be what they are. However, contrary to O'Brien's and others' contention that the courts have construed individualistically oriented doctrines, like educational and parental rights, to implicitly protect cultural rights, I find that the courts are defining boundaries for the concept of culture. In *Yoder* the Court says that

> in evaluating those claims we must be careful to determine whether the Amish religious faith and their mode of life are as they claim, inseparable and interdependent. A way of life, however virtuous and admirable, may not be interposed as a barrier to reasonable state regulaion . . . on purely secular considerations. . . . The claims must be rooted in religious belief. . . . Thus, if the Amish asserted their claims because of their subjective evaluation and rejection of the contemporary secular values accepted by the majority . . . their claims would not rest on a religious basis.[28]

Culture as such is not constitutionally protected. But some particular instances may occur in which the courts are willing to address related claims. In *Yoder*, for example, the Court recognized a claim to a mode of life. Still, culture by itself is not construed as deserving protection; it has to be deserving by reason of its significance to a religious faith. Moreover, not all cultural-religious claims will stand the test. Some do because they have roots congruent with some basic assumptions of American culture. For example, the values of "reliability, self-reliance, and dedication to work,"[29] central to Amish culture, are construed as promoting "the social and political responsibilities of citizenship."[30] In other cases, the courts acknowledge the inviolability of a culture for exactly the opposite reason. By declaring an Indian tribe "quasi-sovereign" and culturally "foreign,"[31] the courts place culture in the context of another jurisdiction and disregard its centrality within the American legal system.[32]

Language has been a very important issue for Latinos in the United States since early in the twentieth century. The Americanization of *hispanos*, during the process of incorporation of newly acquired territories in both the Southwestern United States and Puerto Rico, depended heavily on the acquisition of English as the primary language.[33] From the other end, language has provided the basis for cultural resistance and political action for Latinos. Today, when faced with English-only propositions, the expiration of laws supporting bilingual/bicultural programs, and the development of assimilationist schemes such as the English as a Second Language programs, Latino groups still use language as the hub of their cultural citizenship claims.

The paradigm of culture revealed in legal cases involving language resembles that discussed in religious beliefs cases. Language cases, perhaps more than any others, illustrate the pervasiveness of the assimilationist position in American jurisprudence. In 1923, the Supreme Court, while striking as unconstitutional a Nebraska statute that prohibited foreign language instruction, reflected the goal of assimilation:

> The protection of the Constitution extends to all, to those who speak other languages as well as those born with English on the tongue. Perhaps it would be highly advantageous if all had ready understanding of our ordinary speech, but this cannot be coerced by methods which conflict with the Constitution—a *desirable end* cannot be promoted by prohibited means.[34]

An analysis of the language of the court in *Lau v. Nichols*,[35] which became the most important case for the establishment of bilingual education guidelines, provides an interesting background to understand the court's position in relation to language rights. The court's point of departure is the assumption that students who do not speak English have a "language deficiency."[36] To remedy the deficiency, states have to comply with federal antidiscrimination guidelines, which direct each school district to "take affirmative steps to *rectify* the *language deficiency* in order to open its instructional program to these students."[37] Showing an assimilationist intent, the guidelines require that "the special language skill needs of national origin–minority group children must be designed to meet such language skill needs as soon as possible."[38] Once again, the measures are seen as temporary, until the children become fully assimilated into the Anglo culture.

Although recently we have seen some cosmetic use of Spanish among politicians, I believe that the actual federal policy still coincides with then President Ronald Reagan's statement that "it is absolutely wrong and against [the] American concept to preserve native language and culture in school programs."[39] As the court acknowledged in *Soberal-Perez v. Heckler*,[40] "English is the national language of the United States."[41] Language is not considered an integral aspect of national origin. Therefore, without constitutional protection, language rights, one of the basic claims of the Latinos in the United States, remain uncertain. The courts seem to support what many Latino students have heard in their journeys through American schools: "If you want to be American, speak 'American.' If you don't like it, go back to Mexico where you belong" (Anzaldúa 1987: 53).

Latinos view cultural citizenship as critical to their participation in American society and to their self-identity. Culture becomes their central claim to recognition of their rights. Their quest for culture is not necessarily separatist; it is actually a quest for multiple paths, the freedom to be both Latino and American. In the long run, it is a quest to be able to have a say in the multicultural world in which they live—that is, in the world they enter when claiming their rights.

Part Two

Cultural Citizenship on the Ground: Ethnography

THREE

Identity, Conflict, and Evolving Latino Communities:

Cultural Citizenship in San Jose, California

Renato Rosaldo and William V. Flores

THE PROJECT ON cultural citizenship in San Jose, California developed over four summers (1990–1993) in coordination with research teams working on the formation and evolution of Latino communities, as well as their interaction with other ethnic groups and the larger civil society, in Los Angeles, New York City, and San Antonio (IUP 1989). The project studies how Latinos view themselves, how they constitute communities, and how they conceptualize and claim rights.

Cultural citizenship refers to the right to be different (in terms of race, ethnicity, or native language) with respect to the norms of the dominant national community, without compromising one's right to belong, in the sense of participating in the nation-state's democratic processes. The enduring exclusions of the color line often deny full citizenship to Latinos and other people of color in the United States. From the point of view of subordinated communities, cultural citizenship offers the possibility of legitimating demands made in the struggle to enfranchise themselves.

These demands can range from legal, political, and economic issues to matters of human dignity, well-being, and respect.

Claiming rights is part of the process of belonging to America (Karst 1991). Patricia Williams argues that for African Americans, being American is tied to obtaining rights afforded to white Americans. Thus, she says, "the concept of rights, both positive and negative, is the marker of our citizenship, our relation to others" (1991: 164). According to Constance Perin (1988), white middle-class Americans find a sense of belonging through their negotiated interactions in neighborhoods, schools, parks, and shopping centers. Unfortunately, her analysis takes place in class and racially segregated suburbs and, like dominant national ideology, often excludes minorities, who are treated as the "other" as opposed to white middle-class America.

As the "other," racial minorities have often been neither thought of nor treated as Americans. Historically they have by a number of legal and informal means been excluded from buying property in certain areas, prohibited from voting, and restricted as to whom they could marry. In practice, full American citizenship has been restricted to whites. Over many years of struggle, rights have been extended and the concept of who belongs to America has expanded. Even so, racial and gender discrimination continue to create real differences in opportunities and in people's perceptions of their treatment.

We focus here on Latino cultural citizenship, that is, how Latinos conceive of community, where they do and do not feel a sense of "belonging," and how they claim rights to belong to America. In our view, the process of claiming rights both defines communities (Rosaldo 1989) and comprises a renegotiation of belonging in America. Latino identity is, in part, shaped by discrimination and by collective efforts to achieve social gains and recognition for Latinos and their culture. Thus, cultural citizenship is a process that involves claiming membership in, and remaking, America.

Cultural Citizenship

For Latinos, the issue of legal citizenship is salient and often vexed. Many recent immigrants from Mexico and Central America are undocumented and thus vulnerable to multiple forms of special harassment. In this context, one should remember that Latinos range from native born (some from families resident in the present territorial United States since the sixteenth century) through U.S. citizens born in their homeland (Chicanos and Puerto Ricans), and naturalized citizens, to recent immigrants who may be either legal or undocumented. How then do Latinos, in their range of legal citizenship statuses, perceive their membership in society, and how are such perceptions related to their efforts to claim and expand rights, even when they are not citizens of the United States?

Historically, non-citizens have been disenfranchised in the United States. Yet even citizenship does not guarantee a full extension of legal rights, as American citizens of Mexican ancestry learned in the 1930s. Many were deported in that period along with their non-citizen parents or grandparents during the involuntary repatriation of over 500,000 Mexicans residing in the United States. At the present time, citizenship rights have once again been called into question. In 1993, a number of prominent U.S. politicians, including California Governor Pete Wilson, proposed revising the Constitution by denying citizenship to native-born children of undocumented immigrants (Reinhold 1993).

The concept of cultural citizenship includes and also goes beyond the dichotomous category of legal documents, which one either has or does not have, to encompass a range of gradations in the qualities of citizenship. Ordinary language distinguishes full from second-class citizens and tacitly recognizes that citizenship can be a matter of degree. The project, then, explored the qualitative distinctions in senses of belonging, entitlement, and influence that vary in distinct situations and in different local communities.

Culture in this context refers to how specific subjects conceive of full enfranchisement. It does not refer to culture as either a monolithic, neatly bounded, homogeneous social unit or a realm of art and expressive production as opposed to, say, the economy. Project interviews with Latinos and other ethnic groups in San Jose reveal differences in perceptions of rights and in the very definition of first-class citizenship. Such differences occur within as well as between groups because of internal differentiations and inequalities that roughly correspond with divergent perceptions of social reality. Similarly, the perceived elements of full citizenship can range in varying mixtures from dignity, well-being, and respect, to wages, housing, health care, and education. The definition of first-class citizenship cannot be taken as given, but rather must be a central focus of research.

Subtle and not-so-subtle differences in perceptions vary with such factors as gender, class, age, and immigration status. For example, without talking at length to a woman, a man cannot understand how she conceives of well-being or personal security. Certain men (depending on their race or class in combination with the particular neighborhood involved) may feel at ease jogging or walking alone late at night on city streets, and women may realistically find the same situation threatening. The different perceptions may follow from differential treatment and vulnerability. In this case, men cannot use introspection, based exclusively on their own experience, to discover women's sense of comfort or fear of violation.

Latinos often feel that they are denied rights and opportunities accorded to white Americans. One hears nonwhite Americans say that they are treated as "second-class citizens" or that there are two standards of justice, one for white Americans and another, inferior one for nonwhites. Several Latinos interviewed by project members spoke of being treated "*como animales*" (like animals) or "*como basura*" (like trash). The sense of relegation to lesser citizenship emerged in a number of interviews, ranging from citizens to the undocumented, light-skinned to dark-skinned, and middle-class professionals to working-class manual laborers.

In this context, communities become essential foci for solidarity and for the struggle to claim and expand existing rights. Yet Latino communities increasingly fail to fit the "barrio" model of a bounded ethnically homogeneous space. They are often deterritorialized (García Canclini 1989), broken up by freeways, and dispersed in pockets throughout the city or even among cities. Thus the very definition of community becomes a central research problem as one explores the networks of social relations that connect a series of dispersed points and enable Latinos to struggle for enfranchisement, both in official arenas and in the realms of everyday life.

The San Jose project explored vernacular conceptions of rights, entitlements, responsibilities, and citizenship. How do Latinos (mainly Chicanos and Mexicans, but also Puerto Ricans and Central Americans) perceive citizenship and how do their perceptions affect their relations with others and with the broader civil society? Extensive interviews with over fifty families represent a broad cross-section of the Latino population in San Jose. Interviewees include Latino elected officials, businessmen and women, cultural activists, educators, youth, social workers, working-class Chicanos, and recent immigrants.

Elected officials and political activists have been most concerned with political representation. By contrast, the poorest Chicanos and recent Mexican immigrants have emphasized finding work, providing for their families, education, housing, public health, and residential segregation. A minimal level of housing, food, work, and schooling is a fundamental starting point for cultural citizenship. But even in these cases, where sheer survival is at stake, the interviewees not only reflected on basic necessities, but also articulated their own vision of well-being and human dignity.

Interviews with stable working-class and lower-middle-class Chicanos revealed that the search for well-being opens up into areas less precise but of central importance for understanding cultural citizenship. These interviews framed questions in a positive vocabulary (on well-being, respect, dignity, or feeling confident) and in a negative one (on malaise, humiliation, censure, or feeling violated). Open-ended interviews explored the precise terms used and their definitions in practical everyday life situations.

Renato Rosaldo and
William V. Flores

The Research Site

San Jose, California, and the South Bay Area (widely known as "Silicon Valley") offer a number of significant issues for research. A rapidly growing region, the South Bay Area is an emergent multicultural metropolitan area that, like much of the country, is undergoing significant economic transformation.

The city of San Jose has long been a center for Chicano/Mexicano settlement. Established in 1777 during the Spanish colonial period, the first Spanish and Mexican settlement was along the Guadalupe River in what is now the downtown section of the city. After the war with Mexico in 1848, California and most of the Southwest was annexed by the United States. The Gold Rush brought an onslaught of Anglo settlers. Within a few years, the colonizing majority Mexican population, which had ruled California, became a colonized minority. San Jose briefly served as the state's first capital before losing that status to Vallejo and eventually to Sacramento. The city grew as an agricultural center in the shadow of San Francisco to the north.

By the turn of the century, Santa Clara County was known as the "Valley of Heart's Delight." The economy at the time was based on agricultural production and related industries, such as canneries, packing houses, and food machinery manufacturing, and developed through the 1930s. After World War II, San Jose began to attract defense and electronics industries and many of the orchards were increasingly converted to housing developments.

The economic boom resulted in rapid population growth, which in turn produced a demand for new housing. From 1950 to 1960, the city government approved nearly 500 annexations; it approved more than 900 annexations from 1960 to 1970. From 1950 to 1970 the city's area expanded by over 130 square miles (Trounstine and Christensen 1982: 92).

Suburban sprawl displaced fruit orchards, resulting in a rapid decline of agriculture and related industries. In the late 1940s, over 100,000 acres of

Santa Clara County land was devoted to farm production and produced 90 percent of California's canned fruits and vegetables. The Santa Clara Valley accounted for one-fourth of the country's canning and packing production. In the 1950s and 1960s, the canneries offered the main source of employment for Chicanos. In the post-bracero period, many Mexicans immigrated to the area, found jobs in the canneries, and began to reside in and around the downtown area.

Skyrocketing land values pushed median housing prices from $74,000 in 1977 to $217,000 by 1991 (McCormack and Kanda 1991). Increasing land values spurred further declines in agricultural land use as it became more profitable to sell farm lands to developers. By the late 1970s the majority of canneries in San Jose had closed or moved to Mexico and other parts of the country. In 1990 only 16,300 acres of county land were devoted to agricultural production, representing only 11,000 of the 833,400 workers in the San Jose metropolitan area (San Jose Metropolitan Chamber of Commerce 1991; E-14). Peak employment in the canneries declined from nearly 50,000 in the mid-1950s to less than 4,000 by 1992 (ibid; Zavella 1987).

Since World War II, San Jose's population has grown by more than 700 percent. In the 1940s, Santa Clara County had only 175,000 residents with 69,000 living in San Jose. By 1990, the county population had mushroomed to 1,463,530 and in 1992 San Jose had 803,000 residents. Although statistical data for the area is still linked to San Francisco and Oakland (as part of the San Francisco Standard Metropolitan Statistical Area), San Jose has bypassed San Francisco as the state's third largest city (behind Los Angeles and San Diego) and is now the eleventh-largest city in the country (San Jose 1992). San Jose has emerged as the center of Silicon Valley and the heart of the country's rapid growth in high-technology industries. The changes have transformed the city and its importance to the Bay Area, the state, and the country. It is now a major center for manufacturing production and provides important connections for trade and production to Pacific Rim countries. Santa Clara Valley manufacturers produce more than $20 billion in shipments annually and account for 22 percent of all computer storage devices and one-fifth of all semiconductors produced in the country (San Jose Metropolitan Chamber of Commerce 1991). Of the 2,500 largest electronics firms in the United States, 1,500 are located within a thirty-mile radius of downtown San Jose. High-technology industries (computers, peripherals, software, aerospace, and defense) now account for twenty-one out of the top twenty-five employers in the country.

The rapid growth of the city and suburbs required freeways and road construction to connect the homes in the suburbs with the new jobs in defense and electronics industries. Freeways were built, cutting through the downtown and displacing hundreds of mainly Latino families. Urban renewal programs, downtown redevelopment, and housing projects scattered the Chicano/Mexicano population throughout San Jose, particularly to the Eastside.

Throughout the late 1960s, shopping centers sprang up in the suburbs, pulling business from the downtown. Even the city and county moved a few miles north, outside of the decaying center of the city. By 1970, every major downtown department store had closed or had moved to the suburbs. Mexican restaurants and businesses took over the downtown, while hotels were converted to housing for the elderly. To the east of San Jose State University, located in the downtown, fraternities gave way to halfway houses and alcohol treatment programs. In the eyes of city officials, downtown San Jose was an eyesore and "wasteland" (Trounstine and Christensen 1982).

In the mid 1970s, city officials formed a redevelopment agency and targeted the downtown area. Since 1980 more than $1.4 billion have been spent on downtown redevelopment to produce a convention center, hotels, a sports arena, a high-technology museum, and a light-rail public transportation system to connect Silicon Valley and the downtown to the Almaden Valley in the south. Redevelopment tore up the downtown and pushed out many Mexican-owned enterprises.

By the 1980s, Silicon Valley industries faced a crisis owing to heightened competition from Japan, Taiwan, and Hong Kong and because of the rapid transfer of U.S. capital and assembly plants from the United States to Mexico, Pakistan, Malaysia, and elsewhere. To remain competitive, Silicon Valley manufacturers moved assembly operations to third-world countries where workers are paid as little as $2 per day. Some production remains in the area, which for the most part now houses corporate headquarters and research and development.

The disappearance of unionized and relatively well-paying jobs in the canneries coincided in the late 1970s with the closure of the Ford plant in Milpitas and the General Motors plant in Newark (which later reopened as a joint venture with Toyota utilizing state-of-the-art robotics and "team" production).

San Jose is now a "dual city" (Mollenkopf and Castells 1991) characterized by a sharp division between extreme wealth and extreme poverty. The rapid growth of high-technology industries has produced an economy that is sharply dichotomized between predominantly white, highly skilled and educated white-collar workers and a secondary labor force of Latinos, Vietnamese, Filipinos, and others competing for limited assembly and service-sector jobs.

On the surface San Jose appears to be a center of affluence. In fact, in 1991 it was the most affluent metropolitan market in the United States, with an effective median income of $42,126 (LeBlanc 1991: S-9). Although 41 percent of its households had an effective buying income in excess of $50,000 (San Jose Metropolitan Chamber of Commerce 1991: E-6), this new wealth is not equitably distributed. In 1988, for example, the Mayor's Task Force on Housing found that 31 percent of San Jose households spent over 30 percent of their monthly income on housing costs and that 19,000 homeless people were in desperate need of shelter (San Jose 1989).

A third of the region's Latino households live below or near poverty levels. According to a 1989 Employment Task Force Report of the Latino Issues Forum of Santa Clara County, "Latinos make up nearly 80 percent of all clerical workers and operators and are concentrated in marginal sectors that are growing slowly or declining or moving out of the country." Latinos account for less than 5 percent of managers and professionals in Santa Clara County (Latino Issues Forum 1989a: 7).

The expansion of Silicon Valley produced new hotels and restaurants to service visiting banking and corporate executives from throughout the world. New jobs in the service sector, however, are rarely unionized, often lack benefits, and rarely pay much above the minumum wage (Cleaning Up Silicon Valley Coalition 1991). Segregated by gender and ethnicity, jobs in the low-paying service industry, which offers employment as maids, housekeepers, janitors, construction labor, and restaurant and hotel workers, have been the main source of employment for Latino and Asian immigrants. The few remaining production jobs in electronics are predominantly held by women, especially Filipinas and other Asians. Mexican and Central American recent immigrants are also divided by gender, with men predominating as day laborers in construction and women predominating as housekeepers for upper-middle-class homes.

Segregation by class and race tends to spatially divide the region into white affluent communities versus large zones of poverty. Latinos are concentrated in Eastside San Jose, the downtown, Redwood City and small sections of Mountain View, Sunnyvale, and Palo Alto. While San Jose's average household income in 1990 was over $40,000, per capita income was only $16,904 and trails most other Silicon Valley cities. Predominantly white Palo Alto, home of Stanford University, had an average household income of $59,100, while Los Gatos and Saratoga had average household incomes of $63,500, and $91,100 respectively (McCormack and Kanda 1991: 10).

Even so, immigration from Mexico and Central America has continued. Between 1980 and 1990, San Jose's Latino population grew by 41 percent and now comprises 27 percent of the city's residents. Fueled by changes in the immigration law and by the large influx of Southeast Asian refugees, Asians from 1980 to 1990 became the fastest growing racial/ethnic minority in the city and increased by nearly 200 percent to make up nearly 20 percent of the city's population. African Americans showed relatively little change and now account for 4 percent of the city's population. Although whites are still the largest single racial/ethnic group, they now make up less than 50 percent of the city's population (Hazle 1991).

Political power, however, did not grow in accordance with demographics. Throughout the 1970s and 1980s, Latinos had only one representative on the city council and no representative on the board of supervisors (W. Flores 1992a; Browning et al. 1984). By 1990 the beginnings of political change became evident as two Chicanos were elected to the city council and one was elected to the board of supervisors. Despite the beginnings of change, project interviews show that Chicanos continue to feel that they have little influence in local government.

Research Phases

Research began in the summer of 1989 with a pilot project on inter-ethnic interactions in public spaces. In the summer of 1990 the researchers made more systematic observations in four sites: a high school in Eastside San Jose, a large outdoor flea market, a public park, and a county hospital. The researchers also attended a number of public celebrations, such as the Chicano/Mexicano Cinco de Mayo and the Puerto Rican Día de San Juan, where Latinos gathered to claim (more as renters than owners) certain public spaces as their own. The observations and initial interviews in the summer of 1990 focused on how Latinos claimed space in public and semipublic settings and how they resolved conflicts with other ethnic groups.

In the summers of 1991 and 1992 the project supplemented participant observation with open-ended interviews. The people interviewed included: Chicano elected officials, Chicano cultural activists, Chicano educators, and Puerto Rican activists and families in Eastside San Jose. The interviews also included a Mexicano family that had immigrated to San Jose during the bracero period of the 1950s. The researchers expanded on the initial interviews through a snowball technique that followed personal networks horizontally (friends, work associates, church members, neighbors, and so on) and vertically (across generations within the same family). Interviews began in three sections of San Jose: the downtown and adjacent Gardner district; the northside; and the Eastside.

The open-ended interviews concentrated on the following topics: how the interviewees or their families came to reside in San Jose (or in the South Bay Area); their experiences growing up in San Jose, particularly in schools; their relations with other ethnic groups, particularly Anglos and Asians; their perceptions of belonging and violation, particularly as illustrated and explained through specific cases; their sense of the San Jose Latino communities, especially in relation to the quality of social relations and their sense of boundaries within and between the communities; their perceptions of their rights and how they were restricted, won, expanded, or changed over time; their sense of downtown redevelopment and its impact on Latino communities; and their sense of how other immigrant groups have changed life in San Jose.

During the summer of 1992 the researchers continued observations of public celebrations, often attending events with interviewees. Such events proved critical in shaping Latino senses of their communities. In the absence of a localized barrio, Puerto Ricans, for example, found that their celebration of El Día de San Juan created a sense of community that otherwise would have been more diffuse and less visible for residents of the Bay Area.

During the summers of 1992 and 1993 the researchers continued to conduct open-ended interviews along the lines of personal networks. Research topics expanded to include the following: labor, religion, identity, youth, and new immigrants. Interviewees were extended to include Vietnamese, Native Americans, and Anglo developers. Interviews with recent immigrants focused on the experience of resettlement, cultural adjustments, perceptions of belonging in and to America, and relations with as well as perceptions of other ethnic groups. Collective and individual interviews were conducted with Latinos, Koreans, Chinese, and Vietnamese in Mountain View at an ESL/Adult Education center and at motels in Mountain View and Palo Alto. Most of the interviews with speakers of Spanish and Vietnamese were conducted in the appropriate language by native speakers.

Identity, Respect, and Rights

Through the interviews the project gained an understanding of how Latinos view their place in society and how they associate their sense of enfranchisement with cultural concepts such as "*respeto*" (respect) or "*humillación*" (humiliation). An interview with a Chicana activist may prove instructive. She has lived in San Jose for more than forty years and when interviewed was a community worker in a social service agency. In one of the interviews she explained her concept of respect and its connection to rights and entitlements. Her notion of respect began with her father:

> My father was full of wisdom. One time Dad asked me: "Do you love me?" "Yes," I said, "I really love you." "Why do you love me?" "Because you're my father." "That is the last reason you should love me. Many people should not love their fathers." When he asked me on the other days I said, "Because you're kind . . . gentle . . . understanding."
>
> About *respeto* my father gave me this advice: the first, first thing about *respeto* is to listen to the person. Second, don't tell them that they don't feel something just because you don't. Even if the temperature is 106 we can't tell you that you're not cold when you tell us that you are. Third, if you see something and they see something different, accept what they tell you. Fourth, ask a lot of questions to make sure you respect and understand. Fifth, you can be angry, but show *respeto*. Do not raise your voice, break things, or belittle the other person. Do not put yourself in a position where you have to apologize for yourself. Sixth, don't lie. All these *consejos* [pieces of advice] were taught by my father.

She conceived of respect as a series of paternal pieces of advice that underline the fact that different individuals are capable of experiencing the world in very different ways and that being respectful has to do with finding out what another individual sees and feels. This interviewee's conception of *respeto* proved representative of how Chicanos/Mexicans understand human dignity, both as conveying a sense of full citizenship and as a potential area of violation.

The interviews moved from the vocabulary and particular meanings each person gave to specific examples of how such matters worked out in everyday life. The researchers asked for concrete stories about occasions when the interviewees felt respected, humiliated, and so on. The woman who spoke about respect went on, at the interviewer's request, to tell of a concrete instance that could clarify how respect functions, not at the level of advice, but in her daily life. She answered in the following way:

> My reputation in this town is that I'm real tough. My dad taught me to be real tough. I've tangled with the [former] mayor, and with Reagan when he was governor. This was in the papers. I don't respect either man.
>
> When Reagan came into a meeting I had my feet stretched out and I didn't move them so that he had to walk over them. He looked at me real funny. I wanted him to look at me so that he would remember me when I asked him questions. I asked him, "Why are you using prison inmates to break the farm workers union?" Reagan got so angry that he broke his pencil. He asked my name. I said, "Answer my question." We went back and forth like that until he got so angry he broke his pencil. Then he said something, and I told him, "My name is Chela Ramírez. I'll repeat my name because I know you can't pronounce it." Then I spelled it. Then, when I was in Sacramento with the Poor People's March, he said, "Hello, Chela Ramírez." He did it with respect. I got more out of him by acting with respect than if I'd cussed him out.

This interplay between Chela Ramírez (pseudonym) and then Governor Ronald Reagan reflects an effort to elicit respect for those who traditionally are seen as "powerless." By refusing to move her legs or to answer Reagan's questions, she angered him, perhaps even insulted him, but she earned his respect, doing so in a way consistent with her own code of *respeto*. Not only did he finally respond to her questioning, but he also remembered her name the next time they met.

Winning respect from the powerful required resistance and fortitude; it also represented an effort to claim space within a public sphere. Ramírez was not demanding that she, as an individual, be respected, but rather that the interests and concerns of Chicanos be heard. Through her actions she insisted that the government respect Chicanos. By remembering her name, the governor was forced to remember the interests and concerns of her group. In this way, the struggle for individual respect is collectivized and enters a broader, public sphere. Many such examples appeared in our interviews.

Claiming Space

San Jose's recent waves of immigration in combination with the displacements of downtown redevelopment have resulted in a widespread, but not universal, settlement pattern of relatively small ethnic enclaves. New immigrants tend to concentrate in a number of separate apartment complexes. Japantown stands a few blocks from a concentration of Vietnamese businesses that replaced a former pocket of Mexican establishments. Chicanos predominate over larger territorial expanses, but their neighborhoods are mixed rather than exclusive barrios. Other groups, such as Puerto Ricans, Filipinos, and Native Americans, follow highly dispersed residence patterns.

Different ethnic groups often use the same public spaces, usually peacefully, but with occasional conflict. As we discuss later in this chapter, conflicts have arisen between Vietnamese and Chicanos over claims to space. Disagreements also occur within ethnic groups. For example, a dispute arose at various parks in San Jose because Chicano softball leagues and Mexicano soccer clubs wanted to use the same playing fields. Eventually the Mexicano clubs moved to other parks and to schools only to face new disagreements with youth soccer clubs.

Another downtown park displays a peaceful and tacit ethnic division of labor in the use of its facilities. Asians play tennis, Chicanos play handball, and young Chicanos and African Americans play basketball. Now rarely used, the park's lawn bowling facilities were once enjoyed by retired Portuguese and Italian men who have since moved from the neighborhood. In another small grassy sector of the park, homeless people, primarily European American and African American, often sleep on benches and station their shopping carts in a semi-circle surrounding a picnic table. Although all ethnic groups in the downtown park use the softball field and the playground, their patterns of usage tend to vary. At the playground, for example, European American parents were observed staying close to their children whereas Latino parents would sit farther away, on blankets or at nearby tables, while an older sibling supervised the children at play.

Competing and complementary claims to public space have proven significant, especially in the early research phases, but they fail to reveal the positive sense of community and belonging among Latinos in San Jose.

Changing Notions of Community

The notion of community, not unlike that of *respeto*, has proven a complex and rich topic for interviews. Life histories and memories of places, people, and events reveal the range of communities central to an individual, both through different points in time and at a single moment in time. When people discussed their perceptions of "community," they usually began with the barrio, an almost sacred way for Chicanos to name community in its double sense, as a physical place and as a set of human attachments.

Asked to be more precise, a number of the interviewees said that today the barrio is neither homogeneous nor the nucleus of their communities. One woman activist said that in taking a house-to-house survey one cannot tell beforehand who will open the door: "It might be an African American, a Vietnamese, or a person just arrived from El Salvador, or a Chicano." Whether familial, work related, or based in friendship, people's communities often derived from geographically dispersed networks of social relations rather than being contained within a well-bounded physical space. Community, in the sense of webs of significant relationships, rarely coincided with one's immediate neighborhood.

Communities derived not only from family, friendship, and work, but also from a sense of shared social and political commitments. A Chicano social worker who was born in the San Jose area said that, for him, the Chicano community consisted of people like him, other activists. He felt most at home during cultural events or at big political rallies. Such events routinely include people he dislikes or disagrees with, but he feels in his element because Chicanos are visible and "not afraid to say who we are and what we want."

A Chicana cultural activist said that she most experienced community when she attended poetry readings and *teatro* presentations. On such occasions she could spend time with people who shared her passion for Chicano artistic production. Her cultural community gathered together as a group only on the occasion of particular presentations. It did not have a continuous ongoing existence in either a neighborhood or a workplace. In this respect, shared activities and claims create collective identity as well as community.

Imagined Communities and Social Gatherings

In his seminal work on national communities, Benedict Anderson (1983) found that ethnic groups in Eastern Europe often used the print media to find one another, to form alliances, and to begin building their communities. He termed such groups imagined communities because they constructed their collective identities as if they were members of face-to-face communities (which, given their numbers, they obviously were not). In contrast, this research project found that Latino imagined communities derive less from print and other media than from such events as public celebrations and protest rallies.

Puerto Ricans represent a small segment of the Latino population in San Jose and are dispersed throughout the Bay Area. Several of those we interviewed came to San Jose from Hawaii as descendants of earlier migrations to work in the pineapple and sugarcane fields of Hawaii. Others moved to California from New York or came directly from the island. New arrivals often have difficulty locating other Puerto Ricans, who are interspersed with

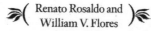

Chicanos and do not have their own neighborhood or barrio. Similar to Dominicans and Haitians who use Caribbean celebrations to create community identity (Kasinitz and Freidenberg-Herbstein 1992), Puerto Ricans utilize the Día de San Juan as a key cultural event for the development of a Puerto Rican community in San Jose.

On this day of national celebration, families from Morgan Hill to San Francisco and further north hold reunions and stake out tables and sections of the San Jose park with flags or banners proclaiming the family name or their Puerto Rican city of origin. New arrivals to the Bay Area use San Jose's Día de San Juan celebration to meet other Puerto Ricans and create networks, or to find friends and family members now living in the Bay Area.

Despite the fact that they are U.S. citizens and longtime residents of San Jose, several Puerto Ricans described the difficulties they faced in obtaining a meeting place to organize. In one instance a group's request to meet at the downtown public library was denied because the group, which had been in existence for several years, lacked a formal charter, by-laws, and a board of directors. In the eyes of the city, it was not an "authentic" organization.

In another instance, a community festival was unable to obtain use of a public park, because "religious organizations" cannot reserve public parks. Although the event was sponsored by a local Protestant church, the festival was not religious. In fact, it was also sponsored by several community agencies. Eventually, a lay committee was formed to officially sponsor the event, but could not raise the exorbitant liability insurance required by the city. Frustrated but determined, the organizers held the event in a vacant lot (Silvestrini herein).

When asked why they were unable to use the park, several interviewees told us, "They don't want us to meet." This sense of "they" and "we" recurred in the interviews and reflects a sense of exclusion (ibid.). "They" might be the city or it might be a perceived white power structure. By contrast, the "we" reflects a sense of inclusion, Latinos who share a common bond of denial of rights. Even with the obstacles, the events were held. Under such circumstances, claiming space defined a community of shared interests and served as both affirmation and defiance. Organizing the festival also helped to organize the various Puerto Ricans involved with it. Their determination to bring off the event brought them closer together and their success encouraged them to undertake other activities. Moreover, the festival itself announced the presence of Puerto Ricans in the area and made them visible to other Latinos.

Like Puerto Ricans, Chileans have also used public events to create a visible Chilean community. Chileans first came to San Jose in large numbers following the 1973 coup. They concentrated in the Gardner district, where they were welcomed by the parish priest. Since then Chileans have continued to immigrate to San Jose, but are scattered throughout the city. This community came to know itself in large measure through well-publicized public events, sponsored by the parish church, that featured Chilean or Latin American protest music. By attending the parish-sponsored events, Chilean political refugees located one another and built community in their new country.

By contrast, Chicanos are scattered throughout the city. Even the Eastside, where Chicanos are heavily concentrated, is now only 50 percent Chicano. Chicano and Mexican neighborhoods established between 1930 and 1970 have found themselves subject to a process of deterritorialization due to the city government's downtown redevelopment project and the extraordinary rise, since 1974, in Silicon Valley's housing costs. Because they cannot afford to buy homes in the neighborhoods they grew up in, children often move far from their parents and other relatives. The resulting deterritorialized communities are linked not by proximity, but by social relations maintained by periodic phone calls and visits on holidays, birthdays, and other occasions. It is through social gatherings and celebrations (each happening separately within relatively intimate circles, but all imagined with, and many in fact having, similar music, *gritos* [shouts], formality, decor, *pan dulce*, *piñatas*, *tortillas*, and *despedidas* [good-byes]) that Chicanos construct their imagined communities.

Renato Rosaldo and
William V. Flores

Sacred Places

Like others who have studied the significance of "place" (Hiss 1990; Agnew and Duncan 1989) or have found "great good places" (Oldenburg 1989), the interviewees described several places where they felt comfortable or at home. We found that a few of these places had special, almost sacred meanings (Rowe 1992), which we term sacred places. When interviewees described public places in San Jose—including churches, nightclubs, bars, and shopping areas—it soon became apparent that, in a number of cases, their accounts had a mythic or sacred significance impossible to predict beforehand. The significance of places appeared more related to their being a locus of meaningful social gatherings than to their economic or aesthetic value. A number of sacred places that had special significance over people's lifetimes no longer exist in a physical sense, but continue to live on in collective memory (W. Flores 1992b). Names of places where people met and shared special events have been passed on from parents to children in their stories of good times and bad. These stories of the remembered past, and the list of associated significant places, varied from one generation to another.

For a certain Chicano generation, a church demolished to make way for a freeway was among San Jose's most significant sacred places. A Chicano social worker described his family's pain when their parish church was destroyed in this manner:

> At the time it was the only church in the area that had a Spanish mass. It was the only Mexican church in San Jose. After it was torn down we heard that they were building a Mexican church on the Eastside, Guadalupe. That's where the Mexicans went.
>
> I remember when we learned that they were going to tear down our church. My father just shook his head. He couldn't believe it. None of us could. He just kept saying, "In Mexico, they would never do this. Imagine, tearing down a church to build a road. No, in Mexico, they would just build the road around the church. But nobody would ever tear down a church to build a freeway. Is nothing sacred here?"

The man's father was working within a Mexican scheme of values where a church would always cause a freeway to bend. A developer's scheme of cash values stood beyond the Mexican father's moral comprehension.

When Greg Mora, who teaches at the local university, took a group of researchers around an old neighborhood, he walked under the freeway, raced across one onramp, and stopped under another, where he explained: "Right over there. [He pointed]. That's where the church used to be, Sagrada Familia [Holy Family]. I was just a child then, but my parents talked about it all the time. They built the freeway; tore down our house; lots of families had to move. But, it hurt the most to lose the church. That was like cutting the heart out of the body." The excruciating pain of removing the church cannot be exaggerated. The developers probably had no idea of the pain they caused, but they did choose to dislocate a working-class Chicano/Mexicano community rather than a middle-class white neighborhood.

Generations clearly differed in their assessment of San Jose's downtown, especially in relation to redevelopment. Among people over fifty who lived downtown or in the adjacent Gardner district, the demolition and subsequent downtown redevelopment were traumatic. One woman in her late sixties said she could not go downtown anymore: "Why? There's nothing there. Everything's gone—all the stores. Even the church is gone. There's no place to meet my friends and shop anymore. We used to just go there and walk around. Or I'd meet my *comadre*[1] there and we'd shop and talk. Now, maybe I go to the center [Gardner Community Center], but the bus doesn't come and pick us up anymore. So, I just stay here. And I go to church. My daughter comes and visits. That's my community now." For her, the downtown has become a wasteland.

By contrast, her granddaughter, who is in her late twenties and performs with a local Mexican folkloric dance group, relishes the new downtown. For her, the old downtown was barren and threatening, but redevelopment now offers a place to find community. She explains: "Before it wasn't safe. Everything was torn up. The streets were dark and dirty and they had all those adult bookstores. Now, I go to clubs with my friends. We can listen to jazz, even salsa. It's much better. The streets are well-lit. I feel safer. There's people on the street, places you can have coffee or see a movie. And I like the light rail, although I never ride it. It adds a lot to the community." In part the gap in perception is widened by the grandmother's remembering the old downtown in its best times, and the granddaughter's recalling its worst times. In addition, the grandmother recalls the activities of her middle age and the granddaughter thinks of her youth as a single woman. At the same time both grandmother and granddaughter evaluate the downtown as a place to spend enjoyable time with friends and acquaintances.

Located at the corner of King and Story, the Tropicana shopping center on San Jose's Eastside was referred to by a number of interviewees as the "heart of the Eastside," and represents another such sacred place. Chicanos regard the Eastside as the barrio, the largest concentration of Chicanos/Mexicans in the city. Icons of Chicano urban cultural style, lowriders made King and Story the center of their activities as they cruised the nearby streets on Saturday and Sunday nights. Today the Tropicana has become one of the major locations for Mexican and Central American day laborers, who line up early in the morning in search of construction and restaurant jobs. The Tropicana houses a large Mexican supermarket, a Mexican bookstore that also sells herbs, compact disks, tapes, religious items, and dress clothing, a few restaurants, and a bakery that sells fresh Mexican pastry. Until recently, the shopping center was the home of the Tropicana nightclub, which is vividly remembered by many people, as in the following: "The Tropicana has moved now—downtown. But it's not the same. Not like before. The music's changed and it's not in the Eastside. People used to come from all around. You'd meet people. Dance. People even got married there. Late at night you could have *menudo* [a Mexican soup made of tripe and hominy, usually eaten after drinking]. Now, everything's gone. The shopping center's still there, but the spirit's gone." The shopping center has been diminished without its dance music and the dance music has been diminished without its location in the heart of the Eastside.

Certain places—some lost except to living memory and others emerging in the present—take on an aura because they have played a role as physical gathering points for people, themselves differently located by such factors as age, gender, generation, neighborhood, and class. It is in such sacred places that people have developed community by coming together and claiming a place of their own, where they meet friends, develop romances, and make enemies. Members of the Chicano/Mexicano community in San Jose use their social lives to create their imagined community. Loss of sacred places is felt collectively as is the desire to preserve such locales. These collective and shared experiences also shape Latino desires for a better world.

A Shared Vision

One researcher asked what turned out to be a surprisingly productive question: "If you had the power and the money, how would you change the Chicano/Mexicano community in San Jose?" Different members of the Chicano community had very similar answers to the same question, and their utopian visions contrasted with those of San Jose's downtown planners and redevelopers who, as will be seen, are intent upon building up San Jose's skyline.

Consider the case of a woman for whom the Catholic church plays a major role in her sense of community. María Pérez (a pseudonym) explained her sense of religious community in these terms:

> And of course the Church has its hierarchical structure. All male clerics, and [she lowers her voice here] the classism, and the—[you] can't say whitism [she laughs]—the racism. I feel very empowered knowing my own spirituality, my parents' spirituality. How could you give somebody else the power over your spirit? What a horrible thing. You're part of a divine energy, God, a flame, whatever, and you can sense that power within you. When you know that, you don't allow someone else to control you, to make decisions for you.

Because she suffered the double discrimination of race and gender she distanced herself from the institutional church and began to form an egalitarian spiritual community without official clergy. She insisted on not ceding control of her intense spiritual life to a stranger, much less to a person who would deny her social existence as a woman of Mexican ancestry. Her struggle with the official church hierarchy was a struggle to enfranchise herself within a meaningful spiritual community.

When the researchers asked her about her utopia, she explained that she would build schools for children, employ lawyers for the undocumented, obtain hospitals for the sick, and get work for young people. When asked, "Would religion play a role in all this?" María Pérez responded: "No, that's illegal . . . but this is utopia, so I'd have classes which use spiritual gifts. Kids would meditate, imagine being somewhere else, we'd talk about mysteries—why are we capable of love, anger, etc.? We'd teach values—of Buddha, Christ—his principles—and Indian spirituality—how to connect it with science, the stars, and the moon. We'd connect everything, there's meaning to life, we're all part of the same source." This woman's struggle to secure her well-being has to do with the yearning to live a spiritual life without suffering from racial and gender discrimination.

Interviews on the emergent or the imagined led toward an understanding of social processes in relation to human aspirations for well-being, belonging, and enfranchisement. The gap between the hope for a better world and the ordinary vices of prejudice and inequality points to directions of struggle and change as well as the realm of ethics and social justice. Because these emerging processes of change remain as yet ill-defined, they must be depicted as complex, uncertain, and unfinished at the same time that they are the very fabric of life in the present (on the emergent, see R. Williams 1977: 121–35).

Thus the interviewees talked about incomplete or uncertain processes. If one asks, "Where is such and such a school?" the world is seen in black and white because there are correct and incorrect answers. But if one asks, "Where does one find community?" when established urban neighborhoods are being deterritorialized through downtown redevelopment and rising real estate values, there is no correct answer to the question. The project thus explored the objective and subjective complexities of still open-ended social processes.

From the National Community to Local Communities

The cultural citizenship project also explored the conflictual process between the national and the local. Consider, for example, the work of sociologist Robert Bellah (1996) and anthropologist Constance Perin (1988) as a point of departure. Bellah and Perin discuss national character on the basis of their ethnographic research in a number of different places. For them, the concept of national character tacitly refers to suburban-dwelling middle-class European Americans. They portray the suburbs as if they were small, autonomous towns where everyone knows everyone else face to face. The imagined suburban community, as will be seen in a moment, is homologous with the imagined national community.

The limitations of Bellah and Perin's notions of "belonging in America" become apparent when one reflects on the point of view from which their analysis is made. From the vantage point of Chicanos, it immediately becomes evident that Bellah and Perin have described a set of norms for middle-class European Americans, and not for an increasingly large sector of the population in the United States (compare Harding 1987). In other words, their studies are not wrong, but their validity is more limited than they claim; they have overgeneralized.

Two points in particular require emphasis. First, it is necessary to recognize not only the dominant norms, but also the variety of norms prevailing in the United States. Latinos have distinctive norms that partially overlap with and partially diverge from those of European Americans. Chicanos cannot reasonably be described as failed gringos; they must be described in relation to distinctive norms and practices. Their vision of being a full citizen in the United States does not coincide with that of European Americans. Second, the nation-state attempts to produce a coercive conformity at the collective level of the national community and a uniform monoglot person at the individual level of the citizen. In ideological terms, the nation-state thus denies the very existence of polyglot citizens, notably but not only, Latinos.

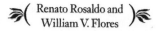

Monoglot citizens could perhaps recognize the polyglot in their own range of speech registers. In a certain sense, everyone speaks more than one language (or at least has use of more than one register). A sketch of Chicano registers could begin with so-called standard English and Spanish. For example, José Montoya (1972) begins his poem, a eulogy called "El Louie," with the sentence: "Hoy enterraron al Louie." This sentence passes muster in Los Angeles, Mexico City, or Madrid. But the poet soon changes speech registers as he tells of Louie's youth and breaks into street talk in the following:

> Trucha, esos! Va 'ver
> pedo!
> Abusau, ese!

The poet has jumped a register beyond standard speech. When the poet describes el Louie's car and his girlfriends, he playfully combines English and Spanish, both in street tones:

> 48 Fleetline, two-tone—
> buenas garras and always
> rucas—como la Mary y
> la Helen . . .

The creativity largely resides in the shifting juxtaposition of registers. When performed, the poet makes further cross-overs evident, by pronouncing English as if it were Spanish, and vice versa, or by using body language (for example, slowly moving his head back, just a little, in the silent greeting of young Chicano men).

This digression on polyglot citizens and human speech registers underscores how difficult it is for a dominant group of monoglot citizens to conceive of the very existence of Chicanos. From a Chicano perspective, the nation-state imposes its national community and its monoglot citizen in a manner that translates class and racial inequalities into linguistic and cultural hegemony. The cultural politics of domination have intensified during the Reagan-Bush period when the nation-state's coercive mechanisms were used to further consolidate a homogeneous national community.

From the Global to the Local

To understand how global forces have shaped San Jose's urban development requires a historical sketch of the political economy of Silicon Valley. In broad terms, the last hundred years of history in San Jose may be discussed in four stages, each one labeled development but in very different senses. Each stage appears quite differently when viewed from the perspective of developers as contrasted with that of Chicanos/Mexicanos.

First, around the turn of the century there was a change from latifundia to minifundia. California's large cattle ranches, the majority of which after 1848 had passed from a Mexican to a European American elite, were divided into smaller holdings and transformed into fruit orchards. Second, from 1930 to 1950, the city of San Jose was surrounded by orchards that supplied a number of fruit canneries in the city's center. Third, from 1950 to 1970, developers subdivided the fruit orchards and transformed them into suburbs with private homes for nuclear families. Fourth, from 1970 to the present, the old downtown, including predominantly Chicano/Mexicano neighborhoods, has been demolished and rebuilt in the name of downtown redevelopment. At the same time the white-dominated suburbs and hills have engaged in tax revolts and other tactics to dissociate themselves from and fend off perceived urban threats (such as crime, gang violence, drugs, and people of color in general) whereas the predominantly nonwhite suburbs in the valleys have attempted to cope with escalating real estate values by converting houses made for nuclear families into multifamily dwellings.

The stages of San Jose political economic history just outlined resemble those proposed for Los Angeles by Mike Davis in his rightly celebrated book *City of Quartz: Excavating the Future in Los Angeles* (1990). Allowing for major population differences between Los Angeles and San Jose, both cities fit the "sunbelt" pattern of urban development marked by rapid growth following World War II. The initial period of postwar growth was later sustained by the major transfer of industry from the Northeast to the South and Southwest as American capital sought relatively cheap labor in a region distinguished by its relative lack of unions, the racial segmentation of its labor force, and the significant presence of recent Latino immigrants.

In broad strokes, Mexican migration to San Jose during the twentieth century can be usefully divided into three stages. First, in the 1930s people of Mexican descent from Texas and Arizona arrived via the migration circuit for picking agricultural products. Those who managed to move from picking to the canneries established themselves as members of San Jose's stable working class. Second, in the 1950s men from the northern highlands of Mexico came to work in the bracero program. Migrants from the first two stages established predominantly Mexican neighborhoods in the Eastside and south of the downtown in the Gardner district. Third, in the 1980s and 1990s undocumented men and women came from the northern Mexican highlands and from Central and South America to work in the service sector. New immigrants have followed a distinctive settlement pattern that resembles a series of disconnected points (that is, apartment complexes). The new arrivals have not been able to afford to buy their own homes and instead have crowded into small apartments with family or new acquaintances, often but not always from their home town or state.

To return to Mike Davis's work on Los Angeles, his penetrating analysis of Los Angeles proved suggestive for our project and greatly helped us frame our own investigation of San Jose. Still, his book had limitations that the research on cultural citizenship nicely supplements. Davis's study virtually ignores the perspectives or experiences of Latinos in Los Angeles. In his first chapter, for example, he shows how Los Angeles has imagined itself through the writings of intellectuals and literary figures without mentioning a single Spanish-language source or Chicano/Latino writer. His geopolitical study of Los Angeles, whose Mexican population trails only Mexico City, presents an anlysis of the global process that focuses attention only on the movement of large capital, while losing sight of the movement of Mexican labor.

Latinos fail to enter as players in the political economic history. While Latinos do appear as threatening objects of fear in white suburbs, as gang members, and as figures in a Catholic movement, they do not enter consistently as analyzing subjects, as people with valuable perceptions about their urban situations. In general Davis remains the lone authoritative voice in his work. His authority derives, in part, from his impressive capacity to name names and to demonstrate his own insider information.

Project researchers have found, however, that a number of interviewees have analyses that sounded remarkably like Davis. One spoke, for example, about how downtown redevelopment destroyed a Chicano neighborhood in this manner:

> McHenry was mayor from 1982–1990. He started redevelopment in San Pedro Square. Then it was valued at a million dollars; now it's over seven million. Tom Jones [a pseudonym] is a good friend of McHenry's. In the Guadalupe-Azureis case Jones talked a Mexican into selling his house for $90,000 (the Mexican originally paid $9,000 for the house, so it seemed like a good deal to him). Then a year later (after the redevelopment project was announced) Jones turned around and sold the house to the city for $519,000. This house was located right where they were going to put the station for the light rail.

This informant names names and provides insider information, revealing to us what appears to be a commonly known scandal in which, in his view, a friend of San Jose's mayor swindled a poor Chicano because he knew beforehand about the redevelopment program plans. Both researchers and interviewees have proven capable of social analysis. The very notion of cultural citizenship, with its emphasis on the value of subjective understandings of well-being and full enfranchisement, calls upon authors to recognize and build upon the insights and limits of their subjects' perceptions of the world. When doing research among relatively subordinate groups, this general methodological principle becomes even more critical.

In making himself exclusive owner of authoritative knowledge, Davis ignores the fact that differently situated subjects live their social reality in different ways. In his critique of developer Alexander Haagen's shopping malls, for example, Davis (1990: 240–44) consciously borrows from Jeremy Bentham's nineteenth-century prison design (Foucault 1977) and speaks of "The Panopticon Mall." Davis, of course, is certainly right in one context: Capitalists have built shopping malls to reach consumers and not to serve as modern-day plazas. There are few places to sit, cameras to monitor "suspect" teens, and guards that restrict leafleting or public demonstrations other than petition-signing or registration of voters. They are private, not public spaces. At the same time, there are movie theaters, skating rinks, and video-game centers that attract families and youth. Davis deduces the human use of shopping malls from their architecture and from the architect's vision. His interpretation makes it evident that he, not unlike his anticipated reader, is an adult, not a teen-ager, and a critical intellectual, not an adolescent who finds shopping and "hanging out" the ultimate goals of terrestrial life.

San Jose youths, by contrast, find shopping malls a favorite place to hang out and meet friends. They do not conceive of themselves as the objects of a "panoptical vision," but instead they use the malls, in an act of cultural appropriation, as if they were plazas where the main social activity is the *paseo*, the promenade, where they greet friends, flirt, and spend time seeing and being seen. Although adult critical intellectuals may experience malls as sites of alienation, young people can clearly live another intersubjective reality. One teenage male, for example, told us, "Eastridge [a large shopping mall in East San Jose] is where you go to meet people. Sometimes we just spend the whole day walking around and getting the names of girls."

Ironically, the redeveloped downtown area has no space for the leisurely promenade, not even for adults. Pleasant places to walk or sit are scarce. Many shops in the newly-built elegant Pavilion mall across from the Fairmont Hotel are outrageously expensive and several have closed for lack of customers. As one man, a former shop owner in the Pavilion, explained:

> The city just doesn't get it. They want people to shop here. But who's going to come? The people who live in Los Gatos and drive Mercedes? They have their own shops. Why come here? There are two downtowns. The one by day that's made up of working people, secretaries and the people that ride the light rail, the Mexicans, and young people. And, there's the other downtown, made for yuppies. But they don't come here to shop. That's why so many of the stores in the Pavilion are closed. No one buys those things. The people who live downtown don't shop here. They shop at Eastridge.

The Yuppies who come at night seek elegant dining, concerts, civic light opera, and comparable fare. They do not come to hang out. They may work in San Jose, but they often do not pay taxes there. The planners have probably found it difficult, as indeed it is, to predict patterns in the use of urban space, and they probably did not have Chicanos, Latinos, and Vietnamese in mind as potential users.

Chicanos and Vietnamese

The project researchers were taken aback to hear a number of Chicanos voice strong prejudices against the Vietnamese. It was not the fact of prejudice—one would be astounded to find a human group without it—but its target, the Vietnamese, that had not been anticipated. Refugees who reached San Jose after the fall of Saigon, the Vietnamese had lived there for scarcely two decades. Naive as it appears in retrospect, at the time it seemed unlikely that such recent arrivals, coming with official welcomes and blessings, could have aroused so much ire. Chicanos explained that the Vietnamese did not wait their turn. Their short time in San Jose was part of the problem. The critics added that, as new immigrants, the Vietnamese did not have the right to get ahead of the Chicanos, especially in the economic field. Opening with a riff on language, Chela Ramírez explained the popular resentment in this way:

> I speak differently, but I have a right to speak the language as I've learned it. And we have the right to speak wherever we want. Yet I still feel that guilt when I speak Spanish in public. Before you couldn't walk outside with a taco in your hand. I'm still aware of all this prejudice against acting Mexican in public. There's a saying, I can't recall now, about speaking Spanish in an elevator. The reason for not speaking up is that the Anglos are going to think that you're talking about them.
>
> The Vietnamese haven't yet fought for what they have. They look down on our houses. They've not been here long enough. It's not their turn. They've infested the campus. They speak loudly; they shout in their language.

Aside from economic inequalities, what most hurt Chela Ramírez was the injustice that Chicanos were forbidden to speak Spanish in public and the Vietnamese speak their language wherever they want.

The Vietnamese are conscious of the Chicanos' economic resentment, but they are not aware of the linguistic resentment against them. A Vietnamese woman explained:

> Mexicans don't like us because they have a perception of us as newcomers who are already succeeding and becoming rich. They say, look at all the businesses, the universities. The keys to success, to equality, mainstreaming, and wealth are economic and education. Furthermore, all the Vietnamese restaurants hire Mexicans to do the low-paying jobs and they are resentful. But this is only a facade that makes it look like Vietnamese are doing well. If you look at the luxurious Lion's Head mall it looks like we're very rich, but we only rent. The real owners of the mall are developers from Hong Kong and Taiwan, not Vietnamese.

She explained that Chicanos' perception of Vietnamese wealth was exaggerated. In this case, Chicanos understood global forces on a human level, like the flow of Mexican labor, or the arrival of Vietnamese political refugees, but global capital, emanating from Hong Kong and Taiwan, remained invisible to them. The woman correctly recognized what Chela Ramírez and others said: that the perception of Vietnamese wealth, combined with their status as recent arrivals, led to prejudice against them.

What Chicanos failed to perceive was the Vietnamese perception that their limited economic power does not translate into political power. The Vietnamese woman explained: "The Mexicans have their representatives in the political process and are being funded at the governmental level, and in this way they are more successful than the Vietnamese." Chicanos certainly would be taken aback to be characterized as relatively effective political power brokers because their yardstick in this area has been Anglos more than Vietnamese. Nor would most Chicanos recognize the systemic bias that has kept Asian capital from being converted into Asian-American public political office.

It may be appropriate here to note that one can easily begin to imagine the tensions generated recently among Latinos in the heart of the Eastside when the Tropicana food market was purchased by an Asian American businessman. A number of interviewees have said that Asian Americans, particularly the Vietnamese, are "taking over" the Eastside and traditional Chicano haunts.

Downtown Redevelopment and the Chicano/Mexicano Community

For Chicanos of a certain age, downtown redevelopment has been a social disaster. One person said, "I don't go downtown anymore because I feel so disoriented—it's like someone has taken away my memory." For her, the landmarks of the old downtown (what above were termed the sacred places) were like mnemonics, sites in which her memories were stored. The demolition of old buildings through downtown redevelopment also erased her remembered past, leaving her disoriented.

Although the experience of memory loss and disorientation was unusual, it was quite consistent with and derived from the collective phenomenon described above of endowing certain places in San Jose with mythological dimensions. Varying between men and women, different age groups, and different historical periods, the sites that acquired such meanings were often less than ordinary in appearance. What made the places extraordinary were the human experiences that groups of long-term intimates had there. The places became larger than life through the telling and retelling of stories about "what happened the night that . . ." whenever old friends or families gathered together and recalled good and bad times from their shared past.

In comparing and contrasting Chicano and downtown redevelopment visions of San Jose one could do worse than revisit the unanticipated collective utopian vision found among a number of Chicanos who did not know one another. Their utopian vision typically began with the construction of a Chicano cultural center. One of the interviewees, for example, responded to the question, "if you had a million dollars for redevelopment, and you could do whatever you wanted with that money, what would you do?" by portraying the utopian project in this way:

> I would build a gigantic building. It would be a theater, it would have a stage in the middle and rooms in the back. It would have performing arts; it would have the best musicians and the best dancers. I would have them stay there two or three nights a week. They—the dancers, artists, musicians—would give classes to young children. Another part would be a library. There would be rooms with teachers, tutoring and classes. We would teach the parents how to teach their children. There would be sewing machines, a lot of them, to teach children. And I'd have the best fabrics, a lot of that kind of stuff. And I'd teach families how to preserve food, and what's the nutritional value of what they eat. I'd identify leadership and give training.

Her vision of culture resembles, not a quaint relic or item of folklore to be preserved, but a more dynamic and forward-looking mix of fine arts, schooling, sewing, nutrition, and leadership. The gigantic building could be called a factory for cultural reproduction and enhancement. The gargantuan scale of the cultural center seems designed to revitalize a community struggling to survive in school, work, and other environments of racial and cultural prejudice. The desire was for a sovereign space. The imagined effort to create a space within which a community can build competence, cultural knowledge, and local leadership comprises an effort to define and create well-being, enfranchisement, and respect.

The researchers asked more than thirty persons to describe how they would change San Jose if they were suddenly granted the money and power to do so. Most responded in broadly similar ways. They shared a desire to give Latinos their own institutional space within which they could create a center for cultural and educational activity. Each phrased that longing differently. One emphasized children learning the arts, another highlighted labor concerns, but all—probably reflecting distinctively Latino values—gave a central place to such expressive cultural forms as dance, theater, arts, or poetry. Whether activist or not, professional or working class, the interviewees felt an unfulfilled longing for community in strikingly similar ways.

Latino visions of San Jose differ sharply from those of developers and downtown elites. The latter have a different view of culture and appear driven to make San Jose into a city that seriously challenges San Francisco. Downtown redevelopers in part share the will to create culture, history, and community found among Latinos, but their desire becomes manifest not in utopian cultural centers, but in symbols of major metropolitan status in the realms of high culture (a civic light opera, an art museum, and a symphony orchestra) and popular culture (a hockey team, the Sharks, and a baseball team, the Giants). San Jose's cultural policies reveal its envy of San Francisco.

Downtown redevelopment has made efforts to promote Chicano artistic production. It helped fund, for example, a summer multicultural arts festival in 1992. Chicano artists rightly celebrated the event as the major breakthrough it was, but their art, dance, and mystique remained confined to the open air of Guadalupe Park and did not violate the sacred chambers of the high culture museums or music halls. From European American to African American, San Jose's rainbow coalition of popular cultural production was proudly on display in the parks, but local art has yet to enter more high-status places.

A revealing fact is that the redevelopment officials do not know the local names for the neighborhoods, like the "Gardner district," much less "Barrio Horseshoe." Downtown redevelopment officials tend to perceive San Jose as an empty space without prior history, culture, or community. When they look at terrain long inhabited by Chicanos/Mexicans and see emptiness, the vision of developers appears classically colonial (Pratt 1992). Downtown redevelopment and earlier phases of development as subdivision appear to have a certain continuity with the vision that shaped the colonizing westward expansion of the United States. It may help to borrow from Mexican anthropologist Guillermo Bonfil Batalla who characterizes the colonial project in these terms: "A characteristic of every colonial society is that the invading group, which belongs to a culture different from that of the peoples over which it exercises its dominion, ideologically affirms its immanent superiority in all areas of life and, consequently, denies and excludes the colonized people's culture" (1990: 11). Downtown redevelopment tacitly and probably unconsciously attempts to exclude and deny the cultural and historical presence of peoples of color—Native Americans, African Americans, and Mexican Americans. Within this framework, the struggle for cultural citizenship has roots in the fight against European American neocolonial domination.

From the National to the Local

San Jose has undergone a hybrid and conflicted process of social change (García Canclini 1989). On an ideological level, the nation-state has imposed a coercive conformity creating pressures toward the homogenization of the national community. At the same time global factors create pressures toward cultural heterogeneity through the movements of multinational capital and by creating a demand for immigrant labor. Consider first the pressures toward ethnic homogeneity and then those toward ethnic heterogeneity.

The intensive consolidation of the national community in the United States took place over the course of the nineteenth century. The dynamics of this process have been described, from the state's point of view, in Benedict Anderson's *Imagined Communities* (1983). Anderson argued that national communities are cultural constructs where people imagine their collective identity as if they were members of a small town where everyone knows each other face to face. Such national communities also imagine themselves as if they were internally homogeneous, territorially continuous entities with well-demarcated borders.

Despite its significant contributions, Anderson's work has two major limitations. First, it makes national communities appear static and independent from relations of inequality within the society in question. Second, he conceives of the national community as if there were a universal consensus among all its citizens. He does not recognize the contestation and conflicts that animate a hegemonic process. Anderson studies national communities from the point of view of state elites and not from that of subordinated, marginal, or excluded groups. The limits of Anderson's analysis become evident by viewing national communities from the perspective of groups subordinated by inequalities of class, race, gender, and sexual orientation (Rosaldo 1989).

The ideological efforts of the state apparatus to impose conformity conflict with global capital's press for cheap, mobile labor. The resulting implosion of the Third World into the First often follows paths opened by prior colonial relations. Recent Mexican immigrants, for example, enter former Mexican territory when they work in California, Arizona, New Mexico, Colorado, and Texas. Over the past two decades San Jose's new immigrant labor pool has come primarily from Mexico, Central America, and Vietnam. Mexican mestizos who cross the border into the United States move not only from one nation-state to another, but also from one side of the color line to the other.

The abrupt change from being a member of the majority national community to becoming a minority person might be compared to the difference in Mexico between being a mestizo and being an indigenous mixteco. However poor in socioeconomic terms, a mestizo belongs to the dominant national culture whereas a mixteco, like a person of color in the United States, belongs only in a second-class sense because of racial subordination. Subordinated by race and class, recent immigrants from Mexico find themselves classified with African Americans, Native Americans, and Asian Americans.

If their children attend school, recent Mexican immigrants will learn that their new country was formed by thirteen English colonies strung along the eastern seaboard. A nation of immigrants, the colonists enjoyed a successful revolution from England and an equally successful westward expansion. In few classrooms even today will teachers mention that mestizo settlements in what is now the state of New Mexico antedate the celebrated so-called first North American settlement of Jamestown (1609). Nor will most teachers say that the ancestors of certain Chicanos did not immigrate to the United States. Instead they stayed where they were and the border, not the people, moved from north to south as determined by the Treaty of Guadalupe Hidalgo after the war of 1848 between the United States and Mexico.

The irony of historical vicissitudes is that more or less a century and a half after the Treaty of Guadalupe Hidalgo the state of California is about to have a predominantly Latino minority population that will become a statewide statistical majority. In California today processes of transculturation have brought mutual changes to majority and minority populations alike. In struggling for enfranchisement, United States citizens of Mexican origin ask how the illusion of a democratic and egalitarian country can be sustained in a state with a dominant minority and a subordinated majority.

The New Politics of Citizenship

Not unlike a number of European countries, the United States has witnessed the recent return of citizenship as a site of political struggle. Two leaders of the cultural studies movement in England have commented perceptively on the new politics of citizenship. Paul Gilroy (1987) discusses the impossibility of becoming a first-class citizen of England, even after three or four generations, if one is of Afro-Caribbean descent. Gilroy suggests that there is an unexpected confluence between the racist extreme right and the progressive left because they agree that Englishness is a complex form of life that can only be acquired through a long period of residence in the nation. Afro-Caribbeans, however, can never, no matter how many generations they live in England, become English in the sense of becoming first-class members of the national community.

In an essay on citizenship Stuart Hall and David Held indicate that the idea of citizenship used by rightists and leftists has different definitions that arise from different political projects. They say: "A contemporary 'politics of citizenship' must take into account the role which the social movements have played in expanding the claims to rights and entitlements to new areas. It must address not only issues of class and inequality, but also questions of membership posed by feminism, the black and ethnic movements, ecology (including the moral claims of animal species and of Nature itself) and vulnerable minorities, like children" (Hall and Held 1990: 176). The new politics of citizenship arises not from abstract theoretical reflection, but from a rightist national politics bent on exclusion and from social movements determined to expand legitimate claims for rights to new forms of subordination. The cultural citizenship project attempts to analyze the possibilities for change from a progressive and more inclusive vantage point that seeks new claims for entitlements.

The central hypothesis of the cultural citizenship project has been that people in subordinated communities struggle to achieve full enfranchisement and that they search for well-being, dignity, and respect in their ordinary everyday lives. The hypothesis of a micropolitics and more internal seeking of cultural citizenship has been borne out in observations and interviews over four summers. Only time will tell concerning the eventual impact of the emergent politics already abundantly apparent in interviews and observations.

The politics of citizenship gains its force in part through its location within long-term dissident and progressive traditions in the United States. The Constitution itself defined a number of exclusions that formed the basis for social movements over the last two centuries. Perhaps this form of exclusion can be understood by imagining the revolutionary slogan, not as "Liberty, Equality, Fraternity," but as "Liberty, Equality, Sorority," Denial of the vote to women formed the impetus for women's suffrage movements in the nineteenth century and for feminist movements in the second half of the twentieth century. Denial of citizenship to slaves provided the basis for antislavery movements in the nineteenth century and civil rights movements among communities of color in the twentieth century. Their goals and strategies remade with each successive generation, the dissident traditions of the politics of citizenship have been progressive, at times radical, and have achieved certain enduring changes. Despite backlash, today only the most extreme sects would reinstitute slavery or deny the vote to women. Present-day social movements based on citizenship and civil rights have both a generally accepted legitimacy and a widely recognized political force.

Cultural citizenship is a process by which rights are claimed and expanded. It is only one process among many. But it is an important one. In an America that is increasingly diverse racially and ethnically, the manner by which groups claim cultural citizenship may very well affect a renegotiation of the basic social contract of America. These "new" immigrants are not only "imagining" America, they are creating it anew.

FOUR

Citizenship, Culture, and Community: Restructuring in Southeast Los Angeles

Raymond Rocco

THE ISSUE OF citizenship has received renewed attention within the social sciences during the last few years.[1] As some of the authors of these new studies on the issue indicate, the cause of this is not difficult to discern. They point to the fact that the dramatic changes in the traditional population base of the United States and several European countries have resulted in a strong reaction and questioning of the impact on the dominant cultures in these countries. The central urban sections in these societies are no longer primarily or exclusively European or white but increasingly are populated by immigrants from Asia, Africa, Latin America, and the Caribbean, immigrants who bring with them cultures fundamentally different from the Eurocentric tradition that has been promoted in the United States. This shift has produced a harsh politics of resentment, fueled by both economic and cultural factors. This in turn has led to a serious but divisive debate on the nature and substance of national identities, cultures, and communities. While the discourses on these concerns are varied and configured differently in different segments and locations of the societies, they have in common attempts to clarify the essential characteristics of national culture, to delineate community boundaries, and to redefine the distribution and allocation of rights, privileges, and institutional access. These are precisely the factors that constitute the defining parameters of citizenship. But because the new discourse on citizenship is in large measure a response to the large increase of non-European immigrants, the role of culture has become a central feature in the debate.

Now the kind of change in the ethnic and cultural characteristics in population that has led to the increased concern with citizenship is clearly evident in the major metropolitan regions of the United States. Indeed, one of the most obvious changes occurring in U.S. society during the last twenty-five years is the rapid growth in the size, pervasiveness, and complexity of Latino communities in many of the major urban areas of the country. And the causes and the consequences of these changes have become the subject of an increasing number of studies (Moore and Pinderhughes 1993). A fundamental cause of these changes is the large-scale immigration from Mexico, Central America, the Caribbean, and South America. The political significance of this factor surfaced clearly in the themes characterizing the anti-immigrant campaign in California around Proposition 187 in 1994, and has now developed into the arena of national policy. Although this was a central theme in the 1996 presidential campaign of Pat Buchanan, the seriousness of the reaction is reflected even more in the fact that in 1996 the House of Representatives adopted legislation that placed severe limits on welfare benefits for immigrants.

It is clear that there is a close connection between the phenomenon of immigration and the increasing concern with the issue of citizenship. But the reaction to immigration is not limited to the immigrant population but belies a more fundamental set of longstanding divisions and differences over the role and standing of the non-European "other" in U.S. society (Fuentes 1992). Thus, while citizenship is often discussed as if it were primarily about immigrants, it in fact has implications for all Latinos in the United States. I argue, then, that one of the most useful ways of explaining and understanding the political significance of the dramatic changes in Latino communities is to approach the issue through the prism of the issue of citizenship. However, approaches to and analyses of the political dimensions of Latino communities, including the issue of citizenship, are most often framed primarily in terms of the traditional focus on the nature and degree of participation in and access to the electoral system. But citizenship in the current context cannot effectively be addressed in such isolation. Instead, I propose that the most useful way to understand the thorny issue of citizenship is to situate it as part of a configuration of issues defined by the intersection of the themes of citizenship, community, democracy, and empowerment. This provides a concept of the realm of the political that is most useful for the purpose of this essay.

Several studies have provided a broader conception of the political similar to that proposed here. For example, recent works by John Friedmann (1992) and Bryan Roberts (1995), which focus on disempowered and marginalized communities, develop frameworks that attempt to demonstrate the relationship between community-level practices and political empowerment. They focus particularly on the household level as the unit that links individuals to the larger institutions where structural sources of economic, political, and cultural power are located. This approach proposes that the concept of citizenship necessarily defines a conception of community. In this approach, citizenship defines who is and who is not a member of the national community and delineates criteria for membership, along with rights, privileges, and responsibilities. And it also defines who has the right to access to the process of decision-making. Lack of citizenship means being excluded, and essentially marginalizes and disempowers those defined as non-members. This raises particular problems for societies that aspire or claim to be democratic.

Both Friedmann and Roberts therefore argue that the relationships between issues such as democracy, citizenship, and empowerment can be clarified by examining the structure and practices of communities that have a history of being on the margins of democratic regimes, those with little or no effective access to the process of collective decision-making. This approach is particularly helpful in assessing the implications and effects of the changes in Latino communities on their access to political power. Adapting from these works, this essay examines the implications for a set of communities in Southeast Los Angeles that underwent a rapid transformation from a majority Anglo population base to a predominantly Latino one during the last twenty-five years.

The Reconfiguration of Latino Los Angeles

The southeastern sector of Los Angeles first needs to be seen in the context of the broader metropolitan region. Using the notion of landscapes developed by Sharon Zukin (1991) to identify how the built environment represents symbolic, geographic, political, and economic power, even a cursory tour of Los Angeles reveals an exceedingly diverse landscape.[2] For most of the contemporary period, Los Angeles has been a city without a single dominant core. Instead there exists a diversity of sites and regions that constitute, in effect, many LA's. While these various sites and regions continue to undergo dramatic changes, they contain clear signs of both the past configurations of economic and political power and the newly emerging ones. La Placita serves as the symbolic remains of the old center of the City and as a short-lived sanctuary for undocumented immigrants, street vendors, and day laborers, while City Hall represents the official center and the space around which strategies have emerged to respond to the needs of global capital. The last agricultural sectors of the city to the northwest have been replaced by dozens of new suburban communities populated by predominantly middle- and upper-class Anglos. The regions to the south and east of Los Angeles represent a sector that has shifted from being a center of heavy industrial production to light manufacturing, the garment industry, and a host of small firms that are part of the new service economy. The concentration of high-technology firms around the Los Angeles Airport, Westlake, and Irvine made these growth areas during the 1970s and 1980s; but they are now in partial decline as the defense industry has been transformed. Hollywood represents a newly reconfigured center of the production of fantasy, images, and sounds driven by the mergers between studios and the high-technology sectors of the local economy. The rise of Los Angeles as an international financial center is visible not only in the dramatically changing skyline but also in the new configurations of transnational capital and power. And all of this is accessible to at least the middle class via the extensive network of freeways. One can now take it all in by riding the Metrolink, the mass-transit system that has adopted many of the routes used by the earlier trolley cars, which were driven out of existence by the political and economic clout of the automobile and tire industries.

But just as visible is the recomposition of the demographic landscape of Los Angeles, of who lives where. The most obvious changes can be seen in any drive through the streets and neighborhoods, where the majority is now either Latino, African American, or Asian, a stark contrast to the situation thirty years ago. And some of the greatest growth has occurred in the Latino population. But it is not the growth in absolute numbers that is significant but the fact that an extensive network of *new* Latino communities has emerged and older ones have been transformed. These new Latino communities in Los Angeles have both transformed and been transformed by Los Angeles in fundamental ways. They are both cause and consequence of a process of structural transformation in the region, including reconfigurations of the structure of social location (as reflected in the new pattern of class, racial/ethnic, and gender relations); of the demographic composition and distribution of the population; of political alignments, political actors and policy agendas; of economic and fiscal landscapes; and of spatial boundaries, including the development of new, nearly self-contained residential communities far removed from the reality of the urban core. While many have celebrated this pattern of growth and development of Los Angeles, the changing skyline and the reconfiguration of social relations signify a much different set of consequences for a majority of Latinos in the area.[3]

We get a sense of what some of this means from the following comment drawn from an interview with a Chicano resident, born and raised in the heavily Mexican community of East Los Angeles.

> I think that probably the biggest change is that now we are everywhere. When I was growing up in East L.A. in the fifties, you knew where the Mexican areas where, and when you wandered out of those, you saw very few of us in places like Santa Monica and the westside. But now, it doesn't matter where I go in L.A., there we are. It feels so different now. When I was a kid sometimes my dad would take me with him on his deliveries over in Culver City, West L.A., Santa Monica, even Beverly Hills, and I would feel kind of funny, you know what I mean? I felt out of place; I wouldn't see any other Mexicans at all. But now, hell, I feel at home almost everywhere because I know there is going to be somebody that looks like me, that talks like me, no matter where I am.

As Robert González recalls it, the Los Angeles of his youth was one where communities of Mexican origin had fairly clear spatial boundaries, with all that is implied by this type of segregation. The established barrios in the Los Angeles area of the 1950s included communities like East Los Angeles, where he grew up, and consisted of neighborhoods such as Lincoln Park, Belvedere, and Maravilla. Other important Mexican communities were located in San Gabriel, San Fernando, Wilmington/San Pedro, and a small barrio in the Venice area. The pattern of labor market segmentation, housing discrimination, and political marginalization that led to the restricted nature of these communities has been illustrated in works by Rodolfo Acuña (1988) and Ricardo Romo (1983).

But as González noted, the situation has been radically transformed, as a brief overview of the nature and degree of the formation of Latino communities shows. The official estimate of the 1990 census is that 3.3 million Latinos live in Los Angeles county, 76 percent (roughly 2.5 million) of which are of Mexican origin. The next largest group consists of Central Americans, who number about 453,000, with over half being from El Salvador. However, the Mexican American Legal Defense and Educational Fund (MALDEF) estimates that nearly 430,000 Latinos in Los Angeles were missed in that census and that is a conservative estimate. So the figure is much more likely to be more than 4 million Latinos living in Los Angeles County. Among some of the other Latino groups, the official estimate is that there are nearly 100,000 South Americans, mostly from Colombia, Peru, Chile, and Argentina, and another 90,000 Spanish-speaking people from the Caribbean countries. An important point underscored by these figures is the significant change in the composition of the Latino population since the late 1960s. Prior to that time, nearly all of the Spanish-speaking population in California was of Mexican origin. Since then, however, Latino communities have become more diverse. As the figures indicate, a large number of people from Central America, particularly El Salvador and Guatemala, now make Los Angeles home. Smaller but significant numbers have immigrated from Peru, Cuba, Colombia, Puerto Rico, and Argentina.

These figures represent the dramatic change in the population base of the region. Between 1980 and 1990, the total population of Los Angeles County grew by 1.38 million residents, of which 1.24 million, or 90 percent, were Latinos. At the same time, 360,000 Anglo residents left the county, while the African-American population increased by 20,000, and the Asian population grew by 490,000. Thus it is clear that the majority of those new to the workforce, the schools, the health care system, and the housing market were likely to be Latinos. This influx of 1.24 million Latinos to the county is obviously one of the principal causes of the transformation of communities, of the dramatic increase in the number and location of neighborhoods with Latino majorities.[4]

But these data do not reveal where these populations have established cohesive communities or neighborhoods that are integrated by a range of personal, economic, cultural, educational, service, and recreational networks. Both our ethnographic studies and a review of census tract data indicate that these populations are spread throughout the entire Los Angeles area. Entire neighborhoods have been transformed into Latino communities, in some cases from one year to the next. Latino communities with at least a minimal set of interactive networks now exist in a large number of areas of Los Angeles that previously had a very small or nonexistent Latino presence. While some of these began to form during the mid to late 1960s, others have developed only very recently or are now in the process of establishing themselves. Southeast Los Angeles is one of those regions of predominantly white working-class residential neighborhoods where the early stage of the transition to a Latino majority was visible by the late 1960s. The rate of growth here accelerated quickly during the 1970s and 1980s and these communities are now more than 90 percent Latino. The largest concentrations of Latinos in that region are in the areas of Maywood, Huntington Park, Bell, Bell Gardens, South Gate, and Lynwood. A similar pattern of growth occurred in adjacent areas, such as Pico Rivera, Montebello, Commerce, San Gabriel, and Rosemead, to name but a few.

More recently, substantial and relatively new Latino communities have also formed west of downtown, extending from the Pico-Union area to Santa Monica. An extensive barrio has developed, for example, in the Culver City–Mar Vista area of West Los Angeles, concentrated in a corridor that runs along Inglewood Boulevard, Centinela, and Sawtelle. The population of South Central Los Angeles is now at least 50 percent Latino and growing. And the percentage of Latinos residing in and close to the city of Santa Monica has increased dramatically. Whole areas of the San Fernando area have now been transformed into Latino communities, such as in North Hollywood, Van Nuys, and Canoga Park, added to the older areas such as the city of San Fernando and surrounding Pacoima.

Our ethnographic research also revealed that the dispersion and residential mobility of Latinos throughout Los Angeles is so great that many of their social networks overlap in spatial terms. Thus, for example, while there are distinct Latino areas in Southeast Los Angeles, such as Huntington Park, South Gate, Walnut Park, Vernon, Bell, and Bell Gardens, the social networks of many of the residents, which constitute the basis of community linkages, overlap and crisscross spatial boundaries. A high percentage of respondents from these communities indicated that their most significant relationships and networks were with households in sections of the San Fernando Valley, Hollywood, Orange County, and the San Gabriel Valley. Thus it is clear that the tendency to identify communities primarily or only in terms of physical spatial boundaries is of limited value. It is rather cultural space that seems to form the basis of community networks that extend over considerable distances.

While the Mexican population continues to predominate in most of these areas, in particular neighborhoods significant numbers of the other groups have established an integrated system of social relations, networks, services, restaurants, stores, medical practitioners, and cultural practices. Thus Salvadorans and Nicaraguans have established extensive networks in the Pico-Union area. Peruvians have created close-knit economic, social, and recreational networks in both South Gate and in Hawthorne. Some of the businesses, whose clients are primarily Latinos, have been so successful that they have branched out into three and four locations. One Peruvian restaurant, Pollo Inka, has locations in Hawthorne, Torrance, Orange County, the San Fernando Valley, and Redondo Beach. A Cuban restaurant is flourishing in predominantly Anglo Hermosa Beach, and yet the majority of customers are Latinos. Other businesses serving Latino customers are to be found throughout the city and in areas that as recently as two years ago had almost no Latinos. These businesses and service providers that cater to Latinos have been one of the important ways that we have identified the spatial location of new Latino communities.

And there are significant numbers and networks of Cubans, some of which control access to the distribution of Latin American music to retail outlets in Los Angeles, a business that appears to be expanding very quickly. Colombian organizations sponsor monthly dances and get-togethers that in reality serve as a major mechanism for maintaining their social networks and orienting and incorporating recent arrivals into the new environment, very often by finding both temporary and permanent housing, furniture, jobs, and so forth. *Actualidad*, published by Peruvians, and *El Colombiano*, by Colombians, are regularly circulated throughout the region through Latin American restaurants, nightclubs, record shops, and travel agencies.

Many of these types of activities, the basis of communities in formation, have been established in older Mexican communities for many decades. The publication of newspapers, a large network of voluntary and regional associations, cultural institutions, networks that provided food, clothing, shelter, and job information for recently arrived immigrants, were also part of the process of the growth pattern of Mexican communities going back more than a century in Los Angeles. In fact, many of the small communities of other Latino groups are spatially within or adjacent to Mexican neighborhoods. The pattern of interaction between the Mexican population and the other Latino groups, however, is an uneven one, and in most cases that we examined, interactions were relatively limited. Culturally, Latino communities have flourished and have established associations to ensure that there is continuity between the culture of origin and both the form and content of the social relations that are established here.

The development of these new communities, however, was not an isolated phenomenon. Their formation occurred as part of the transformation in the spatial and social landscape of the Los Angeles region (Soja 1989, 1987). As Latino immigrants moved into areas with large concentrations of African Americans, such as South Central Los Angeles, Watts, and Compton, there was an out-migration of the latter group into sections of areas further west, such as Inglewood and Hawthorne, previously populated by a majority of whites. There was also substantial movement south to previously predominantly white neighborhoods in the Long Beach area. Thus Latino migration to areas such as these, as well as communities that were primarily white before the mid 1970s or early 1980s—for example, Hollywood, Canoga Park, Van Nuys—in turn resulted in many non-Latino residents moving to outlying areas. According to some of our non-Latino respondents, this was one of the reasons for the development of new residential communities in areas such as Valencia, Saugus, and Newhall in the Santa Clarita valley, as well as other areas like Simi Valley, Calabasas, and even as far as Oxnard.

Global Economics and Local Restructuring

The driving force of this expansion and creation of new Latino communities has been the process of restructuring that began in Los Angeles since 1970 at several levels and along different axes, including economic, political, household, community, and spatial and cultural relations and patterns of practice. The basic dynamics of the economic restructuring process that has occurred over the last twenty-five years have been presented in great detail in both general terms (Smith and Feagin 1987; Sassen 1988) and in the specific form it has taken in the Los Angeles area (Soja 1989, Scott 1993). The work of Saskia Sassen, for example, has clearly identified the general global processes that are structuring the international capital and labor markets. She describes a global economy characterized by the growth of international financial markets, the expansion of the service sector, an emergence of a global network of factories, service outlets, and financial markets, and the concentration of these financial centers in a few global cities (Sassen 1991). Other works have focused on how these global processes are played out locally (Smith and Feagin 1987; Soja 1989; Zukin 1991). Some of these focus on the emergence of Los Angeles as a leading global city, noting, for example, that in 1989 Los Angeles was the headquarters to fifteen of the world's largest transnational firms. In his analysis of Los Angeles, Edward Soja indicates that restructuring conveys

> a break, in secular trends, and a shift towards a significantly different order and configuration of social, economic, and political life. It thus evokes a sequential combination of falling apart and building up again, deconstruction and attempted reconstitution, arising from certain incapacities . . . in established systems. . . . The old order is sufficiently strained to preclude conventional patchwork adaptation. (Soja 1989:159)

He goes on to demonstrate that these processes include deindustrialization and reindustrialization, internationalization of capital and labor, and capital and geographic decentralization and recentralization. The need for capital to be more mobile and competitive led to a dramatic decline in the heavy industry sector of the local economy of Los Angeles, at the same time that strategies such as subcontracting and decentralization led to a growth in light manufacturing. The result was job loss, lowering of wages, less security, deunionization, a lowering of the quality of life and a dramatic increase in immigration, particularly from Latin America and the Caribbean.

This latter has particularly affected the pattern of change in Latino community formation. Not so apparent, but nevertheless made clear by the literature on restructuring, is the direct relationship between the basic forces behind restructuring and the increase in immigration from Latin America and Asia. The connection is not one-dimensional, but is mediated through other factors as well. But clearly the restructuring process has been driven by policies adopted by global capital since the late 1960s to change its relationship to labor. This has not been a uniform process, but has taken different forms and occurred in different ways in particular countries.

The detailed analysis of this process that Sassen has carried out demonstrates that, quite ironically, the economic policies pursued by the United States itself, particularly through its basic role in the International Monetary Fund and the World Bank, have themselves actually been one of the major reasons for the rapid growth of large immigrant communities throughout the country. As Sassen indicates:

> U.S. efforts to open its own and other countries' economies to the flow of capital, goods, services and information created conditions that mobilized people for migration and formed linkages between the United States and other countries which subsequently served as bridges for migration. . . . Measures commonly thought to deter emigration—foreign investment, or the promotion of export-oriented agriculture and manufacturing in poor countries—have had precisely the opposite effect. Such investment contributes to massive

> displacement of small-scale agricultural and manufacturing enterprises, while simultaneously deepening the economic, cultural and ideological ties between the recipient countries and the United States. These factors encourage migration. (Sassen 1992: 14–15)

In addition to the displacement of traditional economic arrangements in Latin America and the establishment of strong ties with the United States, the conversion to export-driven economies decimated the middle class and lowered the domestic standard of living in these countries. Even as the overall economic output was increasing, most of it, was targeted for external markets. This contributed to the migration during the 1980s of well-educated, skilled labor, particularly from Mexico and some South American countries such as Peru, Columbia, Chile, and Argentina.

The same international economic policies and processes that were promoting investment and the expansion of manufacturing jobs in low-wage countries also directly altered the nature of the demand for labor in the domestic economy of the United States. The domestic traditional manufacturing sector went through a process of deindustrialization–reindustrialization that greatly downgraded (or "downsized," as the current corporate language calls it) the labor demand, resulting in the growth of low-wage, semiskilled or unskilled jobs. Coupled with the job growth in the high-technology sector and the great increase in subcontracting (including sweatshops and homework), what resulted was an economy characterized by very distinct and different labor markets for immigrant labor, for middle class, high-tech, and professional labor as well as a highly polarized and fragmented social fabric.

This brief review outlines some of the economic dimensions and processes of restructuring that have propelled the great increase in the Latino population and communities of Los Angeles. But while these analyses detail the changes occurring at the macro-institutional level, they tell us little about how the social, cultural, and political life of the Los Angeles region has been affected; in particular, they say little about how Latino communities have been affected by these changes.[5] The study on which this essay is based was designed to explain the relationship between these structural forces and the nature and pattern of the everyday social practices and relationships that emerge as strategies in response to the particular changes. Its findings allow us to understand not only why Latino communities have exploded throughout the region, but also help us trace the impact on the lives of families and households in the region, see how social and spatial relations have been transformed, and how the political landscape and agenda of Los Angeles have changed. And it allowed us to uncover the practices and beliefs that illuminate the relationship between issues of citizenship, community, and empowerment.

Citizenship and Ethnographic Grounding

The study focused on the region of Southeast Los Angeles, once known as the "rust belt," which includes incorporated cities such as Huntington Park, South Gate, Maywood, Bell, Bell Gardens, Vernon, and Cudahy; and unincorporated areas such as Walnut Park and parts of Los Angeles that have been designated by the L.A. City Planning Office as "South Central." This region was selected because it has undergone one of the most rapid processes of change in California. For example, the Latino population in Huntington Park went from 4.5 percent in 1960, 35.9 percent in 1970, 85 percent in 1986, to 92 percent in 1990. These changes are clearly a function of the general restructuring process, which has affected not only the area's economic profile, but its cultural, demographic and political makeup as well. Because of the very rapid rate of change, locating respondents in the area who have lived out these changes was greatly facilitated.

The degree of concentration of Latinos in this region is reflected in the data for 1990 contained in Table 1.[6]

Citizenship, Culture, and Community: Restructuring in Southeast Los Angeles

Table 1.

CITY	TOTAL POPULATION	LATINO	% LATINO
Maywood	27,850	25,900	93
Huntington Park	56,065	51,579	92
Commerce	12,135	11,042	91
Cudahy	22,817	20,307	89
Bell Gardens	42,355	37,272	88
Bell	34,365	29,554	86
Pico Rivera	59,177	49,117	83
South Gate	86,284	71,616	83

While these figures indicate the high concentration of Latinos in these communities, we need to outline what it was about the restructuring process that propelled this transformation of the area.

The specific aspects of this process as played out in this region were initially part of a more general closing of major manufacturing firms and loss of jobs in California. In the short span of three years, 1980 to 1983, 157,000 manufacturing jobs were lost in the state of California, mostly in the steel, tires, civilian aircraft and auto industries. In Southeast Los Angeles, the specifics of the economic restructuring process were a mix of large and small closures and changes. For example, some 8,000 jobs left the city of South Gate in a four-year span early in the 1980s when General Motors, Firestone Tires, Weiser Lock, and Fed Mart closed. During roughly the same period, Chrysler Credit Corporation closed three new car dealerships: Dodge, Jeep Eagle, and an outlet for Chrysler/Plymouth/Hyundai. While the number of jobs lost, 175, was significant, it was relatively small compared to General Motors. But another dimension of the effects of restructuring is illustrated in this case because the city of South Gate received 20 percent of its sales taxes from these three firms, nearly $5.6 million, and thus its ability to provide services and maintain its operation was considerably undermined.

Other plant closures and job losses included the shutdown in December 1982 of Bethlehem Steel located in the city of Vernon. Over 2,000 men and women were let go that Christmas, and the main union of steelworkers, Local 1845 in nearby Huntington Park, became a foodbank to help workers get through that period. In 1989, Dial Corporation discontinued its production of household liquid bleach at its Purex plant in South Gate and later, in December 1991, it closed all of its operations there. Oscar Mayer was another major employer located in Vernon that shut down, laying off its entire workforce, most of whom had been with the company for at least ten years or more. Some of these industrial sites had played a major role in the development of the region over a long period of time, and had established important social ties with the cities; for example, the Dial Corporation had been in the same plant for fifty years and General Motors had opened its plant in 1936. Despite this, there was virtually no consideration by management of the impact these closures would have on these host cities and communities.

But not only job loss was involved here. The nature of the labor market and labor demand were also transformed. Thus the jobs lost in this process were primarily unionized, higher-pay employment with good health, retirement, and other benefit packages. Yet during the very same period that the region was losing these high-paying, unionized jobs, other sectors were developing that employed low-wage, non-unionized, semiskilled Latino immigrant labor. Thus, although the city of Vernon lost a great number of jobs, its low-wage sector expanded by between 8,000 and 10,000, primarily in the garment industry. It now has more than one hundred garment plants, many with sweatshop conditions and all with a high percentage of immigrant female employees.

The restructuring scenario in Southeast Los Angeles was clearly driven by the dramatic change in economic profile. The closing of major plants and the resulting loss of jobs and revenue set in motion a process of rapid and complete transformation of the region that included demographic, cultural, political, and household restructuring. While Table 1 provides an indication of the high concentration of Latinos in the area, these data do not reflect the high percentage of immigrant Latinos. Although it varies by city, the immigrant population is estimated to average close to fifty percent, in a region that in the 1960s was primarily Anglo. While the restructuring process did not determine the specific processes of community transition and formation, it did create the conditions for these.

Latino immigrants came to this Los Angeles region during the period between 1970 and 1990, driven both by the economic structural changes we described but also by some of the consequences of these changes on other factors. Thus, for example, the dramatic increase of Latinos in this specific region of Southeast Los Angeles was partly caused by the decrease in property value that resulted from the loss of jobs and revenues. The Anglo working class, economically displaced by the forces of restructuring, left the area. Home prices and rents dropped dramatically; since newly arriving, economically strapped Latino immigrants must of necessity seek out low-rent areas, they gravitated toward Southeast Los Angeles. Once established as a community, of course, the area further attracted immigrants on the basis of cultural familiarity. Small commercial and retail businesses to service these new communities soon followed. In fact, this transition revitalized the economic base of the region. Thus, for example, in the vital commercial strip along Pacific Boulevard in Huntington Park, nearly 50 percent of the business sites were vacant in the mid 1970s. These were businesses that were oriented both culturally and in class terms to high-wage working-class and middle-class Anglo tastes. When that population left, the businesses collapsed. In their place arose businesses that responded to the needs and tastes of the immigrant Latinos. By the early 1980s, the strip was a thriving commercial zone with nearly no vacancies; it had become an important site not only economically but socially and culturally as well.

The specific characteristics of these dramatic changes in the configuration of communities in Los Angeles have made the issue of citizenship once again a primary policy concern. As already indicated, changes such as these have given rise to an impressive number of scholarly works focused on how best to conceptualize the relationship between citizenship and the new multicultural reality that has brought the Third World into the center of the advanced capitalist nations. The work of Will Kymlicka, for example, focuses directly on "multicultural citizenship" (1995a) and provides an approach that allows us to analyze the implications of changes in the cultural framework of urban communities for the issue of citizenship.

One of the concerns that arises from this new focus is how to think about the status of marginalized groups, particularly groups such as Latinos in the United States, who have a history of having limited access to political rights, to decision-making institutions, and to opportunities for economic and social mobility. Because of the centrality of cultural difference in this history, certain Latino cultural practices have been interpreted as undermining U.S. culture. Despite the fact that these critiques are made within a cultural discourse, they are in fact political claims being made about "appropriate" national boundaries and about what the conditions are for attaining and enjoying full citizenship. Thus it is possible to look at cultural practices of Latinos as representing, among other things, the means by which communities have both reproduced and resisted, accommodated and challenged the relations of power and domination.

What I want to focus on here are the particular local cultural practices that have developed in response to and as part of the transformation of Southeast Los Angeles described above and assess their significance for the issues of citizenship and empowerment. These cultural practices reveal the basis of a community's claiming and developing the social and cultural space within which members can and do affirm their collective sense of identity, solidarity, and common historical experience, and effectively challenge the dominant culture's interpretation of them as well as the norms and practices that reproduce their subordinate status. I also want to discuss briefly whether or not it makes sense to think of these practices as claims to "cultural citizenship," as a way to emphasize the link between empowerment, rights, and culture.

The following then, are cultural practices that emerged from our study of Southeast Los Angeles that are most relevant to the issue of citizenship, empowerment, and community. In the study, we sought to get beyond the structural and demographic changes and trace the way in which the processes of restructuring have transformed the lives of those who live in these new communities, how these changes have been lived out and interpreted at the level of everyday practices by both the immigrants as well as the older generation of Latino residents, whose lives have also been transformed in this process.[7] At this level we can uncover what the structural changes reviewed above mean for those who live in these Latino communities. Through their stories of strategies of adaptation, resistance, accommodation, and transformation—lived in and through the "mediating" institutions or sites of schools, workplaces, households, and churches—the restructuring process becomes grounded and reveals the extent to which claims of cultural space and affirmation either constitute or have translated into strategies of empowerment. The following draws on both ethnographies and participant observation in a number of community settings as well as on life-histories of men and women who live or have lived in Southeast Los Angeles, families and households that we have interviewed over a period of five years. They reveal to us some key insights about the process of community formation, the multiple ways in which the restructuring processes have affected Latinos, and the struggle, full of contradictions, to both engage and resist popular U.S. culture. At this level we found cultural practices that illustrate and relate most directly to the issue of citizenship, community, and empowerment. These fell in line with the following themes: institutional access, the concept of rights, sense of marginalization, identity, and nationalist identification. I will use some examples from both the traditional and informal economy to provide some sense of how these notions are embodied in various strategies of cultural affirmation.

Citizenship, Culture, and Oppositional Politics

As indicated earlier, the majority of the population in Southeast Los Angeles is Latino and working class, although about 20 percent have achieved a middle-class lifestyle. Thus economic survival is a major preoccupation for most households and this is reflected in the pattern of household activity as well as the commercial sectors of the area. We found that, with regard to labor market–related concerns, a clear pattern of activities among many of those interviewed reflected a strong sense of cultural affirmation. One theme that consistently arose was the adoption of forms of cultural affirmation as a response to the exploitative nature of the labor market. This ranged from developing networks to obtain work to practices within the job site. Many of the respondents had a clear sense that their limited access to higher-paying jobs, the maltreatment they felt they were subjected to on the job, and the unwillingness of the firms they worked for to provide medical and other benefits were due primarily to their being Latino. Although this feeling was more pronounced among the immigrant Latinos, it was also expressed by a significant number of those who were second, third, and fourth generation.

We noted several culturally based practices that were adopted as responses to these types of situations. For example, in several non-union sites, Latino workers supported colleagues who they perceived were unjustly penalized and/or dismissed from their jobs. The support ranged from confronting and complaining to management, work slow-downs, and providing funds to help those who were fired. In our interviews with workers who participated in these actions, we probed to see what role class identification as laborers played in the situation, but it became clear that the support was based on a sense of shared identification as Latinos; in at least three instances, there was support from those who did not even know the aggrieved individual.[8] Manuela, a worker in a radiator shop, captured a theme that we found common in these situations.

> Rafael [who had been fired] was let go because the bosses didn't care about the problems he was having with his kids. Two of them were really sick and he had to take time off to take them to the hospital, and you know sometimes that takes the whole day because the wait is so long. So they fired him. But really,

you know, that was just an excuse because they didn't like the fact that he always showed how proud he was to be Mexican. They didn't like that he organized a soccer club for the shop and then tried to get us to join a patriotic association he helped to organize. They don't like strong Mexicans, they like us to be passive, and just accept everything they tell us to do. All of us feel the way Rafael did, we just didn't do the things he did, you know, like try to organize us to do things together. I think the bosses were afraid that he was going to try to get us to form a union, which we had talked about a little a few times. Rafael got a new job right away because he knows so many people, you know, so he's alright, but we are even more determined to be ourselves, to show that we are proud of being Mexicans, and the hell with the bosses. Even some of the people who work on the other side of the shop and didn't even know Rafael, are angry about what happened to him, and have come around to say screw the bosses, . . . and you know what, they brought in some Mexican flags and a guy from Peru who works in the office has started to play different kinds of Latin music over the speakers during lunch and our breaks. If the bosses try to stop that, we all agreed we would put up a fight.

We found a different type of cultural affirmation in a different setting, a large-scale dry cleaner in a redeveloped commercial section of South Gate that has a substantial number of businesses, such as banks and insurance firms, that employ a high percentage of Anglos. Because of its convenient location on this commercial strip and because of the extremely low prices, many of these employees use this particular dry-cleaning firm, so that the clientele is about 60–70 percent Anglo during weekdays. This was one of our field sites and we observed that there were often very long lines of customers, most willing to endure the long wait because of the low prices. This firm has a retail section where customers go but it is adjacent to a larger-than-usual cleaning plant. Customers waiting in line were only thirty feet or so from the plant, and could see the twelve employees, all of whom were Latinos, at work through the glass enclosures, and through a very wide receiving doorway. The workers had set up a fairly powerful stereo system on which they played mostly tapes of different types of Latin music the entire workday. The volume was very loud so that the music could be heard by all the workers above the noise of the plant machinery and generators. But it was also heard by the customers waiting in line, and it became obvious, both through our observations and the few interviews we were able to secure with Anglo customers, that some of them were disturbed both by the loudness and by the fact that it was Latin music.

I raised this issue during interviews with some of the workers and the following excerpt from the response of the only non-immigrant employee, a third-generation forty-three-year-old Chicano, is revealing.

> Well, I'll tell you, things have sure changed a lot since I first started working at different jobs; I was about sixteen then and have worked at a lot of different things, and I've worked with blacks, whites, Chinese, you name it. But back then, the Mexicans who worked around whites especially, they always seemed to not want to act very Mexican around whites. They seemed like they were embarrassed or ashamed or something. But since I started working here about seven years ago, that——has all changed. Man, these guys don't give a——what white people think, I mean, they play all this stuff, merengue, salsa, norteño, cumbia, and some stuff I don't even know what it is, but they dig it, you know what I mean. And they can see that it pisses off some of the customers, but they don't care. They say, "——them." These guys are real proud of being Mexican and Puerto Rican and Guatemalan, we have a—— United Nations of Latin America here, man, and I guess they think this place is just as much theirs as anybody else's.

And the view of a twenty-eight-year-old man originally from Caguas, Puerto Rico, who lived for short periods in both Miami and New York, and moved to Los Angeles in 1991, directly related to the issue of cultural rights and nationalism.

> I find it strange that whites complain about our music. Look, I didn't grow up being a minority, we were all Puerto Ricans, or Dominicans or Cubans. But we were all Latinos, and this is our music. We are here and do all the work that the whites don't want, and then they don't want to let us hear our own music. I came to the U.S. when I was nineteen years old, and went to City College in New York for about a year. I learned about the history of Latinos in this country and I think that it's about time that we claimed our heritage here, because

> to my way of thinking, any group that has worked as hard as we have has a right to everything the society has to offer. I mean, we *are* this society too, right? As long as we work and make our own way, we have a right to act any way we want as long as we don't hurt anyone else. Why should anybody else be able to tell me what to eat, what to listen to, who to hang out with? No, that is my right, nobody else's. Look, we Latinos have marvelous cultures, wonderful histories, and we should never lose these things, they are ours, they make us who we are. So we live in this country! But I shouldn't have to give up being Puerto Rican. That's me, and sooner or later people are just going to have to get used to it.

These types of views were not uncommon among the people we interviewed. They demonstrated a clear sense of the right to claim their Latino identity within the workplace, and they have created spaces and practices to incorporate this as part of their work routine.

Another site where these kinds of cultural practices was clearly evident was in the informal economy. Our studies of street vendors and of swap meets discovered specific practices and views regarding citizenship rights and national identity. The street-vendor sector is significant because there are an estimated 5,000 unlicensed street vendors in the city of Los Angeles, nearly double that in the county, and 95 percent of them are Latinos, many of whom lack legal United States residency status. Street vending is illegal in Los Angeles outside of a few designated areas. Vendors are often portrayed as "illegal aliens" who litter streets, cause congestion, jeopardize the health of their customers, and threaten the viability of "legitimate" storefront businesses. In 1989, there were 2,700 arrests of vendors in the city, with nearly twice that many arrests the following year. In response, vendors formed several associations throughout the county, including the Los Angeles Street Vendor's Association (AVALA), the San Fernando Vendor's Association (SFVA), and the Huntington Park Vendor's Association (HPVA). Although these were originally created for protection, they have evolved to where they are now seeking to better their economic situation by facilitating loans and creating rotating credit unions for members.

The vendors are extremely critical of the popular view of them as a menace. Instead they argue that street vending is a respectable and legitimate means of employment that provides a needed and desired service to community members. Several vendors told us that because they can often sell items at a lower cost than local storefront businesses, they make it possible for people who might otherwise be unable to afford them to buy these products. They also pointed out that they often provide items that are not sold at local stores, and that they are therefore meeting consumer demand. They find it puzzling that their efforts to earn a living in what they consider to be a decent and honest way are met with such hostility. Most of the immigrant vendors come from countries where street vending is not only legitimate and widespread, but is also a vital part of the fabric of urban society. A common theme in our interviews with them was that the major reason they were being targeted had to do with the majority of them being Latinos. The view expressed by Carlos, a Salvadoran vendor who sells fruits in Huntington Park, clearly makes the connection between the situation of vendors, national identity, and political empowerment.

> I don't understand why people criticize us so much. We aren't criminals, we are just trying to earn an honest living for our families. Would it be better for us to sell drugs, or to steal from people, or to go on welfare? I would never do any of that. I came here to escape the violence in my country and to find a better life for me and my wife. That's all I'm trying to do. I'll bet if we weren't Hispanos, they wouldn't care so much. This is a great country, but I've learned one thing, that you have to fight for your rights. And I think that the chance to earn a decent wage is a right. I don't think anyone owes me a wage, but I do think that everyone should have the right to go and find a job. I don't belong to any organizations but I'm thinking about it because the only way we are going to get anywhere is to fight for our rights. I used to not like Mexicans when I first got here, but most of the people out here who are vendors, are Mexican and I get along fine with them. I realize now that we are all Latinos and that we need to support each other.

And Carlos's practices reflect this sense of Latino identity. He works closely with other vendors, agreeing on a weekly basis to work different areas; he attends informal gatherings of street vendors in parks and parking lots throughout the area, where a common topic of discussion is the discrimination against Latinos and the need to defend Latino culture and to make sure that their children do not lose their sense of pride in being Latinos.

At other institutional sites we found a wide range of practices and views that, like those reviewed here, were in essence claims to a Latino cultural space within the context of a belief that U.S. society has discriminated against, exploited, and otherwise been unfair to Latinos. In the arena of popular cultural practices, different Latino groups have developed networks of both commercial and informal activities based on creating and promoting spaces for the affirmation of Latino cultures and identities. For example, in Mexican communities throughout Southeast Los Angeles, there has been a virtual explosion of neighborhood clubs, night clubs, and restaurants promoting music ranging from the *quebradita* and *cumbia* to *roc en español*. Several Peruvian and Colombian and Cuban sites for salsa, cumbia, and *música tradicional* are also found in the area. In each of these, the emphasis is on creating spaces here where various aspects of their native culture can be lived out and sustained. Many restaurants serving traditionally prepared foods from throughout Latin America have added live music to their menus, and have also promoted the development of patriotic associations.

What are the implications of the types of practices described above for understanding the relationships between culture, citizenship, and oppositional practices? Clearly the themes discussed above represent practices that were part of efforts to negotiate and respond to marginalized status, discriminatory practices, and racism. Because of the specifics of this context, they represent a challenge to the dominant culture and can be interpreted as instances of oppositional cultural practices, but ones that have not resulted in political empowerment. Contrary to views articulated by scholars such as Peter Skerry (1993), who argue that the majority of Latinos are on a path to assimilation, these practices, rooted in lived experiences of struggling for equality and respect, reveal a more complex pattern of resistance and accommodation. They reveal a prefigurative element in the pattern of community networking and formation that indicates the potential for a form of politics rooted in an alternative cultural framework.

That this is the case should come as no surprise. While the context is considerably different, studies of the new social movements in Latin America have discovered a similar pattern (Eckstein 1989; Escobar and Alvarez 1992; Slater 1985). These studies clearly demonstrate the vital role of the development of a sense of collective identity in laying the foundation for the possibility of community empowerment. Summarizing a point that all these works agree on, Arturo Escobar and Sonia Alvarez state that we need to conceptualize movements for empowerment as including "cultural struggles over the production of meaning and as collective forms of cultural production" and although many of those engaged in practices such as those described in this study seem to be concerned primarily with issues of the workplace or the home, they "are also negotiating and sometimes challenging power relations in their daily lives" (Escobar and Alvarez 1992: 320).

The cultural practices in Southeast Los Angeles we focused on all indicate a strong sense of membership in a larger Latino community that has the right to have access to major institutions, to be given a fair and equal opportunity for social and economic mobility, and to practice and maintain a strong continuity with the culture of their country of origin. The majority of those we interviewed consider the United States their new home, but do not believe they must sacrifice the core of their collective identity in return. They clearly consider themselves an organic part of the larger "community," not as outsiders, but as valuable contributors to the well-being of the society. While they do not talk about these things as rights of citizenship, it is clear that insofar as being a "legitimate" member of a community implies having standing as a "public person," then the connection to citizenship is fairly clear. In his treatise on citizenship, T. H. Marshall argued for a close relationship between social, political, and civil rights. Those cultural practices we identified clearly included claims to social rights—we might say "social" citizenship—rights to benefits based on the fact of contributing to the welfare of the community. Given Marshall's analysis of the linkages between the three forms of public standing, it is difficult to see how these claims to social rights will not eventually lead to demands for both full civil and political rights, that is, claims to full citizenship.

FIVE

Aesthetic Process and Cultural Citizenship: The Membering of a Social Body in San Antonio

Richard R. Flores

AFTER SEVERAL YEARS of teaching in the upper Midwest, I returned to San Antonio, Texas, over a winter break to visit and catch up with members of the troupe of Los Pastores, a Mexican shepherd's play of the nativity. I had spent two years performing and conducting field research for a performance study in the late 1980s, and planned, during my current visit, to reconnect with many old friends and informants.

I arrived at the house of one of the elder members of the troupe where I was to meet with him and his granddaughter, Elsie, who also performed. I recalled Elsie's participation in Los Pastores quite well. She was active in several high school clubs, set her goals on attending college, and in the midst of her busy schedule still found time to dedicate numerous weekends to performing. When I queried her about her resolve to perform in Los Pastores, she replied:

> We need our traditions to be noticed here in America and here in our nation. I mean, we can't lose them along the way, you know. Striving to go forward, yes. I mean, technology brings us forward and everything, but we can't lose where we came from, it's very important, and that's why I stay, too. Like I said, it comes with education. We have to preserve what's ours. Yes, go forward and be a united nation, but also don't forget where you came from.

Elsie was instructing me on cultural citizenship. For her, performing in Los Pastores was an act of re-membering, of preserving a particular cultural practice in the face of technological advancement, of creating a space where one's identity is constructed, exhibited, and reproduced.

This essay is about the relationship between performance, as an aesthetic process, and cultural citizenship. If performance is one way people "realize" their social world, then the emerging social body evoked through performance, one that is remade with each new event, is never given, but is the locus of competing notions about the world and a site upon which social place is negotiated, constructed, and contested. As a result, cultural performance is linked to cultural citizenship: those enactments and practices that forge a sense of community and belonging, lead to renewed experiences of identity, and provide a social space for the formation of collective practice and its concomitant forms of power. Because the majority of cultural performances are public affairs, they provide an important location to investigate cultural citizenship: how communities exert and negotiate their place within the larger civic arena, an arena riddled with multiple relations that impinge on, confront, isolate, anticipate, and crystallize into various forms of power, presence, and social participation. In performance events, communities represent and explore, produce and mediate, their most elaborate notions of self and society. As such, cultural performances are expressions of "people's articulations, formulations, and representations of their own experience" (Bruner 1986: 9). But experience is never neutral: it is the product of political negotiation, ideological motivation, and human desire, underscoring the problematic and processual dimensions of social life. Life's contradictions, asymmetries, and fulfillments are not negated in cultural performances but are transposed from the quotidian to the specially marked aspects of these expressions; likewise, the disjunctures that communities respond to through cultural citizenship are not absent from performance events, but are merely reinscribed from one social field to another.

I explore the relationship between aesthetic process and cultural citizenship at two levels. First, I demonstrate that the processual aspects of performance negate any prior link between performance and the making of a political community. Performance events are negotiated and produced "on the spot," and recontextualization of an event from one venue to another produces a variety of semantic inferences and constructions.

Second, I investigate the relationship between performance and politics. Performance events are, no doubt, political affairs—their emergence from specific social conditions and historical events places them squarely in the midst of sociopolitical life. But the relationship between performance and political consciousness, action, and class-awareness is problematic. Unless performances are consciously produced to deal with particular social and political issues, the relationship between performance and politics is anything but causal. I do not suggest that the relationship between performance and politics is a dubious one, only that any such affiliation must be considered along lines that are themselves processual and emergent.

As such, this essay explores the connection between cultural performance and cultural citizenship as it emerges in the folk drama Los Pastores (its generic names are *pastorelas*, *coloquios*, or *autos sacramentales*), a nativity play performed entirely in Spanish that descends from medieval Spain. The Spanish missionaries brought this dramatic form to the New World, including the Southwestern United States, where it has flourished for over a century. The popular humor that marked this genre in Spain continued in Mexico where a similar tradition existed among certain indigenous communities, and to an extent, continues today.

The Sociohistorical Base of Performance: San Antonio's Mexican-American Community

The city of San Antonio is a thriving metropolitan area, boasting a population of over 1 million inhabitants, and internationally recognized for its "Hispanic" ambiance and historical attractions. While such charms are sure to be found in the center of town, any traveler who wanders several blocks east, west, or south of the tourist center will encounter a very different, little-known facet of the city: poverty. While the average poverty rate of the United States is 9.6 percent, San Antonio's is at 14.8 percent (Glickman & R. Wilson quoted in Cárdenas, Chapa, and Burek 1993). San Antonio's Latino community, 54 percent of the population, comprises 70 percent of those living in poverty. This large percentage of Latinos living in poverty is not a new phenomenon, but has evolved from the social and historical events that are rooted in the city's past.

San Antonio began as the site of a Franciscan mission in 1718 and soon became home to Spanish soldiers and colonists from the Canary Islands; after Mexico's independence from Spain, an influx of Mexicans, soldiers and citizens, arrived in this fledgling town on Mexico's frontier.[1] By the 1830s, however, Anglo-American colonists outnumbered Mexican citizens, resulting in both contentious relations and cooperative efforts between Anglo Americans and Mexicans. In 1836 when the President of Mexico, Antonio López de Santa Anna, annulled Mexico's constitution of 1824 and seized authoritarian power, Mexicans and Anglo Americans alike proclaimed Texas an independent republic. Men like Lorenzo de Zavala, Juan Seguín, and José Antonio Navarro played critical roles in this independence movement, working with their Anglo cohorts. But after Santa Anna's defeat at San Jacinto in 1836, just a few weeks after the Battle of the Alamo where no defenders survived, Mexicans in Texas found themselves the recipients of a vengeful backlash from Anglo Americans.

The social place of Mexicans was further eroded after Mexico lost the war with the United States and the Treaty of Guadalupe Hidalgo, which saw Texas and much of the Southwest incorporated into the United States, was signed in 1848. The period after the signing of this treaty was marked by various forms of ethnic conflict and discrimination. Beginning in the late 1850s, San Antonio's Mexicans were increasingly segregated from the growing Anglo-American population, and by 1883 San Antonio's West Side was already recognized as the "Mexican" side of town (De León 1982: 32).

Between 1880 and 1920, South Texas underwent a radical shift in economic organization that displaced many traditional Mexican families from their ranch and cattle homesteads to the agricultural fields where they found employment as wage-labor farm workers. The shift from a cattle and pastoral economy to industrial agriculture must be seen within the larger social climate in which the Battle of the Alamo and Mexico's loss of the Southwest in the U.S.–Mexican War occur. As a result, conflict between Anglo Americans and Mexicans in Texas continued into the twentieth century, adding racial and class dimensions to earlier forms of ethnic and national differences.[2] The result of this shift, David Montejano writes, was that Texas Mexicans were "reduced . . . to the status of landless and dependent wage laborers" (1987: 114).

In spite of their deteriorating social position, Mexicans in South Texas organized and responded to their plight in ways both democratic and radical. In 1911, Nicasio Idar organized the Primer Congreso Mexicanista in Laredo, Texas, where delegates deliberated over the need for bilingual education for their children, the indiscriminate lynching of Mexicans, better social conditions, and the assertion of their place in the American political system (Limón 1974). In 1915, however, Aniceto Pizaña and Luis de la Rosa took matters into their own hands, instigated a series of skirmishes with the Texas Rangers, and destroyed local bridges, post offices, and other structures affiliated with Anglo-American institutions (R. Flores 1992).

Between the emergence of a social enclave and the pressing need for unskilled, cheap labor to sustain a growing industrial sector, the Mexican population in San Antonio increased from 25.7 percent of the population in 1900 to 46.3 percent in 1940 (R. García 1991). While a number of wealthy Mexicans fleeing the political turmoil of the Mexican revolution between 1910 and 1921 adopted San Antonio as their home—and worked for political and social improvements of San Antonio's poor Mexican population, especially those living in the concentrated West Side barrio—most new immigrants were not from the elite classes. San Antonio's West Side barrio increased in size and density, and the depression-era economy caused an expansion of poverty for almost everyone in this area.

A number of reasons help explain why San Antonio Mexicanos continue to live in poverty, two of which are educational achievement and labor employment participation. According to 1980 data, 80 percent of Anglo males in the city received a high school degree, while only 50 percent of their Mexican-American counterparts could claim the same achievement (Cárdenas, Chapa, and Burek 1993). Explanations for this disparity are quite complex, but educational disparity between Mexican Americans and Anglos is surely a factor. The presence of multiple, independently funded school districts that were at one time divided along ethnic boundaries finds Mexican Americans concentrated, although not restricted to, poorer school districts with low budgets and few resources (San Miguel 1987). The effects of this practice, which continues even today, are found in discrepancies in per-capita spending per child, supplemental programming, and overall school success. The relationship between school achievement and labor participation cannot be ignored. In 1988, the ratio of Anglos to Mexican Americans in managerial and professional jobs was 4 : 1, while the ratio among laborers was 2 : 5 (Cárdenas, Chapa, and Burek 1993). Poor educational resources, a system differentiated along economic and class lines and resonating with but not entirely limited to racial boundaries, has transferred into low-skill jobs, underemployment, and poverty-level conditions for Mexican Americans in San Antonio.

To this day, San Antonio's West Side is identified as an economically poor *mexicano barrio*. It is a mixture of public housing, low-wage industry, single- and multiple-family homes, and urban renewal programs. Violence, both domestic and drug-related, is high in the area, as is unemployment. In the last twenty years, city and community leaders have targeted this area for public money to fight the ills of urban poverty. But, like many of the inner cities throughout the country, the past decade has brought only an increase in poverty and a decrease in economic resources.

In 1894, in the midst of the economic reorganization and social displacement of South Texas Mexicans, Don Leandro Granado left his hometown in Mexico for San Antonio. In 1913 he organized performances of Los Pastores from a text he memorized while still in Mexico. His performances were held in the streets, backyards, and *jacales* (huts) of the West Side, with neighborhood men like himself serving as actors. By this time, the Jesuit-run church, Our Lady of Guadalupe, was already recognized as a key barrio institution and Don Leandro used the church as the home base for his *pastorela*.

In 1949 the pastor, Carmelo Tranchese, S.J., translated and edited Don Leandro's text, calling attention to its structural, grammatical, and chronological anomalies. The priest's concern focused on the text's inconsistencies with the biblical accounts of the nativity, faulting a lapse of memory on Don Leandro's part. However, Don Leandro's performance was not solely a mnemonic act, but also one of re-membering: a performative process that "members" the social body.[3] This is an active process that draws people together through the act of performance where, as Victor Turner states, the "structures of group experience" are "dismembered, *re-membered*" and "made meaningful" (1986: 43, emphasis mine).

In spite of Tranchese's reconfiguration of Don Leandro's text, performances of Los Pastores have continued to configure the social group. This effort, however, which I will later explore as an example of cultural citizenship, does not go uncontested. Continued efforts of "dis-membering" the performance from its social ground affect the contemporary heirs of Don Leandro's *pastorela*.

The Performers

The members of Los Pastores are Mexican Americans or Mexican immigrants who either live or have lived in San Antonio's West Side barrio. Most of the performers face economic constraints similar to their predecessors': they are low-skilled workers, occupying low-wage jobs. Elsewhere (1995) I provide a more complete description of the more than twenty performers who were part of the troupe between 1987 and 1989 when I first conducted my field research.[4] Here let me briefly describe a few of the key social characteristics of the troupe members.

There are three generations of performers: elders, middle-age adults, and a group of young adults or adolescents. The elders, some of whom have been performing between twenty-five and forty-eight years, consist of men and women. Since women have only been performing in Los Pastores since the seventies, none are regarded with the same stature as the men who have been involved for a number of decades. Most of the elders are no longer working, receiving slight pensions, if any, and subsisting on their social security benefits.

Only two men constitute the adult generation, a fact often looked upon with dismay by the elders. Lack of performers from this generation is blamed on "too much television and *bailes* [dances]" by the current director, although from my discussions with troupe members, family and work obligations seem more directly related to lack of participation by this generation. On this point, the men see themselves pulled in many directions—family, work, Los Pastores, football weekends, and their own personal activities. One confided several years back that between rehearsals and performances, little time was left for anything else. I seriously suspected that he would leave the troupe, but to my surprise he was still performing in 1993.

Finally, a number of young people form a critical cadre of performers. This generation consists of high school students and young adults already employed full time. Many from this generation aspire to a more prosperous lifestyle than their elders. One young woman set her goals on joining the military, her strategy for escaping the social conditions she experienced in the neighborhood. Another was taking courses in high school that might prepare her for a job with the local police force.

As noted above, women have been performing since the 1970s, and in fact when I returned to visit the troupe in December 1993, all but one shepherd was played by a woman. Of the younger generation, women are the most active, never failing to attend an event, bringing along their children to rehearsals and performances. The one role that remains closed to women is that of a devil; the current director refuses to allow women to undertake these parts. These roles are seen as the last bastion of maleness, in what was once an entirely all-male performance genre.

Participation in Los Pastores is a labor-intensive commitment. Rehearsals begin in September and are held Sunday afternoons from two to six. In the two years I performed with the troupe, only two or three new members were added, making rehearsals as much a social as a performative affair. The actual rehearsal time, once everyone had gathered, lasted only a few hours. But the conviviality and social exchanges of this time are one of the bonding processes of this event. The performance season begins in December and extends until early February. Each performance lasts approximately three hours and when traveling and post-performance events are included could take five to six hours out of a day.

The Performance

In my two years of performing with the troupe, I participated in a number of performances. While each one was unique, especially in terms of the distinct domains discussed below, there was a constancy in each event. The following brief sketch is meant to provide a sense of the performance and its social characteristics.

After driving a short distance through pot-holed streets, the old bus squeaked to a stop. Up front, Pablo, the driver, quipped: "*Este pinche* bus . . . *casi ya no quiere correr. Tengo que hablar con el* father, and see *si nos presta la nueva*" (This stupid bus . . . it barely drives anymore. I need to speak with the priest, and see if he will loan us the new bus).

Inside, the women eyed one another's faces, checking their make-up, pulling on their sequined shepherd's cloaks. The few men on board plodded off to where the devils, having arrived earlier to set up the *infierno* or hell-mouth that kept them out of view, were gathered.

By the time I walked around the car port and made note of the physi-

cal space, the male performers, along with some of the local men, were into their second beer. As Pablo handed a cold one to me, I kept watch on the crowd entering the side door of the house. There must have been twenty people squeezed into what appeared to be a small, yet tidy, house. After a nominal time spent laughing and joking with the men, I turned and headed inside where I found most of the women, including some of the female performers. Through all the activity I could hear voices from the kitchen, actually just a few feet and fifteen or so bodies away, concerned that the amount of food might not be sufficient. "*Andale mija*, go to the *tiendita* and bring me some *arroz*," I overheard the woman of the house instruct her daughter. The patter of hands slapping flour tortillas into shape made me aware of how hungry I was.

After working my way back outside, I saw the director taking a head count, making sure enough of the performers were present to begin. It was already 5:30 in the afternoon, and he figured if troupe members had not arrived by then for the 4:30 scheduled time, they were not going to show up.

The woman who instructed the young girl was not outside, and I could see her eyeing the director. After several minutes of talk, they began to call for quiet, with the woman addressing the crowd first. Thanking everyone for their help, she turned to the subject of her *promesa* (see note 7), her mother's failing health and subsequent improvement. With a noticeable hush, the audience tuned into her introduction. Then she turned, thanked the *pastores*, and gave the floor to the director. After his usual initial remarks, he made his way to the *infierno*, and, with the statue of *el Niño Dios* in his outstretched hands, he knelt, and in the silence of the crowd, crawled to the altar that was sitting about thirty-five feet directly in front of the *infierno*. The quiet was finally broken by the lead shepherd's voice as the performance began, "*Que hermosa noche! Todo es calma y tranquilidad* . . ." (What a beautiful night! All is calm and tranquillity).

The dramatized text of the performance concerns the appearance of the archangel Michael to the resting and lazy shepherds as they keep watch over their sheep. When Michael informs them that the newborn Messiah could be found in Bethlehem, they decide to journey there, bearing simple gifts.

But their journey is anything but serene. Soon after departing, they are met by Luzbel and his legion of devils, who suspect that something is wrong in the world. During this time Luzbel attempts to sidetrack the shepherds to keep them from their destination.

One of the characters, the hermit, is the only human who recognizes the devils and he pokes fun at them, using his ludic license to provide for the humorous and picaresque moments endemic to this genre. The entire event is spoken or sung in octosyllabic verse, using forms such as couplets and decastichs. Even the hermit's comical asides and puns follow the same verbal form.

During a brief intermission, audience members as well as people from the hosting party, in recognition of the performers' efforts, pin ribbons, trinkets, and, on occasion, dollar bills on the capes of the performers. It is not uncommon for the hermit, whose verbal repartee with Luzbel keeps the crowd amused, or Gila, the only shepherd's role scripted as a female, to receive the most ribbons or dollar bills. No one, however, goes unrecognized during the break for these *madrinas* (godmothers) to offer their gifts to the performers.

After intermission there are several more routines between Luzbel, the other devils, the shepherds, hermit, and the angel. In the end, Luzbel and his cohort are sent marching into the dungeons of hell while the shepherds arrive in Bethlehem, offering gifts to the Messiah. After this, each shepherd steps up to the statue of *el Niño Dios*, and kisses it in ritual fashion. Then the audience is invited to make their adoration as well. Added to this, Gila holds a small basket in which audience members may drop a monetary offering, although none is required.

While the dramatized text outlined above remains relatively the same from one performance to another, the place of performance and the various means by which these places are negotiated provide for different kinds of semantic events.

Negotiated Spaces

In the two seasons I performed with the troupe, performances of Los Pastores were held in three distinct locations. The first official performance is at the local parish church that sponsors the troupe.[5] This event takes place on

Christmas Eve, beginning around eight in the evening and finishing just in time for people to attend the *misa del gallo*, or midnight mass. Throughout the performance season, which runs from December to early February, several other performances are held at other local churches. The majority of performances take place in the homes of people from the local barrio and are sponsored by a family, or, in some cases, several families. The final location I will discuss is a performance that takes place, as it has for a number of years, under the sponsorship of the San Antonio Conservation Society. It is held at one of the five historic missions and is well publicized, with tourists as the primary audience.

THE BARRIO

Of the different sites where Los Pastores is performed, those undertaken in San Antonio's West Side barrio are the most numerous. Families wishing to sponsor a *pastorela* at their home call the director of Los Pastores and set up the place, date, and time.[6] Little else is needed.

We arrive for a performance between thirty and forty-five minutes before beginning, although the time is quite flexible and it is not unusual to begin an hour or so late. While waiting, male members of the troupe stand outdoors talking, telling jokes, drinking beer or more *Presidente* brandy, and socializing among ourselves and the other men who are present. The women of the troupe, if not engaged in conversation with other women, are indoors talking with members of the hosting family or helping in the kitchen with the preparation of food.

The performance begins with an introduction and welcome by the host, usually a woman, although on occasion men perform this task. Many times the introduction is spent on thanking the guests, performers, and others for attending. The performance is introduced by the host in one of two ways. The most common is to speak of Los Pastores as an event that fulfills a ritual vow or *promesa*.[7] For example, at one event, the woman introducing us stated, "I had made a *promesa* three years ago to have Los Pastores here if my mother recuperated from surgery. Now that you are here I can rest assured, having fulfilled my *promesa*." The other way in which Los Pastores is contextualized is through tradition. The performance is held because it is our "traditional" way of celebrating Christmas, "the way we celebrated in the past." Barrio performances are social affairs: hosts, guests, and performers collectively undertake the task necessary for a performance to occur, a process I refer to as the "gifting of performance" (R. Flores 1994). In brief, the work of producing Los Pastores as both a social and dramatic affair is seen as the responsibility of everyone; it is the exchange of gift and reciprocal gift by a kind of labor necessary for bringing Los Pastores to fruition. This intense notion of cooperation and solidarity led one of the performers to claim: "*Yo*, anytime, *prefiero darlas en casas*" (I, anytime, prefer to give them [performances of Los Pastores] in homes).

During the performance, members of the audience sit close, bundled in blankets, sipping hot cocoa or coffee, watching and often talking among themselves. Children, while they are attentive for a while, end up wandering around, playing and enjoying themselves in other ways. While men watch the performance, it is not uncommon to find them off to one side, engaging the performance with a drink in hand. As for the women of the hosting family, they can be found inside making sure preparations for the meal are going as planned. Elderly women stay inside and help with the cooking, especially during inclement weather, while their male counterparts can be found outdoors.

Performances in the barrio are not lavish affairs. It is not uncommon to find homes in dilapidated condition, with dirt floors, poor or no heating, and leaking from rain water. Upon entering such homes, I was struck by the mixture and variety of odors: gas fumes from stoves, the mustiness of blankets and the dampness of floors, the aroma of various foods cooking, not to mention the odor of many people living in close quarters. Sponsorship of Los Pastores entails sacrifice: economic resources have to be pulled together, if available, and human resources are necessary to ensure the work gets done.

This space, then, is a scene of partial participation, conversation, movement from indoors to outdoors and back, curious spectators, and performers marching, singing, and fighting off the temptations of the devil. In all, this scene is marked by the familiar: we interact with the audience members throughout the event, laughter filtering above our voices; and visitors and family members constantly flow throughout the house as they help in the festive preparations. During the performance itself we, the actors, are more flexible, laughing at the humor of the drama, and occasionally talking among ourselves. In the barrio there is more of an inclination to shorten the performance if the weather is extremely cold or wet, to allow people to leave early or move indoors. When not performing, we are prone to keeping warm inside or gathering around a bonfire outside.

Guests and hosts react to Los Pastores with enthusiasm, contributing to the event by working in the kitchen, arranging outdoor space, or assisting in many of the minor details that need attention. On a personal level, they often recall childhood memories of Los Pastores, or previous years' performances. They see themselves as participating in an event unique to their culture and religious tradition. Talk during the post-performance festivities vacillates between humorous or memorable aspects of the performance, local and national politics, or crises in personal affairs. It is here that the introductory narrative of the performance finds its resonance with the audience: to introduce Los Pastores as a *promesa* reminds those gathered of their familial relations.

After the performance, food is served to everyone. The meal encompasses a variety of traditional South Texas festive dishes like *tamales*, *menudo*, and *buñuelos*, along with more common items like *arroz* and *frijoles*, and hot cocoa, tea, beer, whiskey, and other beverages. After the meal and more conversation and *vaciladas* (play routines), we make our way back to the bus, waiting for the trip back home, and our next performance.

THE CHURCH

My experience of performing Los Pastores in local churches is different from the home in a number of ways. The first, and predictably, is the ritual and devotional frame that contextualizes this place of performance. An official member of the church welcomes those in attendance, including ourselves, emphasizing the ritual elements of Los Pastores: its devotional aspects, elements of sacrifice on the part of performers, and the religious focus on *el Niño Dios* as the primary reason for celebrating Christmas are highlighted.

Another important difference is that of sociability. While there is still a sense of familiarity and interaction between us and the audience, it is less than what is experienced in a home. Prior to beginning, performers are less likely to interact with members of the church audience; audience members, having the church as a geographical and social focal point, are more prone to interact among themselves than with us. This place, being less familiar, is marked by a distance not experienced in the barrio. Even family members of our troupe are less likely to associate with audience members of the hosting church, both before, during, and after the event.

Related to this is the physical site itself. Church events occur in halls, church buildings, or outdoors on the property. Space in halls is usually open, less familial, and distant. There is little that marks it as particular to the community, although posters and artwork mark its religious character. Performances inside a church are usually less flexible: aisles and fixed benches restrict the use of space and movement. One advantage indoor performances have is sound, since acoustics in church buildings are usually quite good and allow voices to be heard further away. Performances outdoors on church grounds have ample space, but are marked by less sound control and more open areas. But there is also more room for people to walk about, which creates a sense of constant motion and disengagement from the performance.

Another important feature of churches is the number of people in attendance. About three hundred people showed up at one church, creating a festival-like atmosphere that is not experienced in the home event. This does not suggest that festival dimensions prevail over ritual ones. In my discussion with audience members, it was the ritual and Christian aspects of Los Pastores that informed their presence. Invariably, audience members spoke of the devotion of the performers to *el Niño Dios*, causing them to reflect on their own spiritual lives.

In the barrio we are more relaxed, jovial, and prone to forms of play while performing; at the church, however, there is a greater sense of seriousness and, inhibited by feeling "on display," we are less likely to informally interact with one another. When one of the women performers was asked to assist in taking over the lead singing for an ailing member, she grew nervous and tense and remained that way through the entire performance. Having performed in Los Pastores for over twenty years, this new role in front of a church audience was enough to change her entire demeanor. She herself admitted to me that if it had been a smaller audience and a home setting she would have had no problem.

Another distinction between the home and the church is related to the festivities after the performance. The food provided at the church, except what is served to performers, is sold. In place of a home setting where food is the product of the hosting family, the church serves food from a cafeteria, charging the audience members for refreshments during the performance and meals afterwards. The intimacy of the home table, the social nature of family cooking, and the social intercourse that produces these elements are lacking in the church. Food is served in cafeteria-style lines, with set portions, using commercial products.

The scene after the performance is also less intimate. Instead of socializing with members of the hosting family, we often sit together as a group with little or no interaction with the audience members. On several occasions, some of the performers, after eating, went and sat in the bus waiting to depart. Church members themselves are more likely to interact among themselves, but many do not stay for any of the post-performance activities, choosing instead to go home or elsewhere to eat.

THE MISSION

Since the early 1950s the San Antonio Conservation Society has sponsored at least one performance a year of Los Pastores at San Jose Mission, one of five missions from the Spanish colonial period in Texas. The San Antonio Conservation Society is a longstanding civic organization, founded in 1924, dedicated to the preservation of historic buildings and artifacts in the city. A careful examination of its 1988–89 Yearbook reveals that members of the society are, with few exceptions, from the elite classes of San Antonio. Members include former politicians or their descendants, and spouses, mostly wives, of local executives; with rare exception, none are of Latino or Mexican origin. According to the addresses given in the directory of board members, none live in the same neighborhood as do the majority of performers, but instead are from more wealthy and upper-class areas of the city.

The sponsorship of Los Pastores for a tourist audience creates a distinct performative scene. First, there is the use of an emcee, a practice initiated by the Conservation Society. Over the last decade this job has been held by a well-known local radio announcer associated with the San Antonio Missions, who has produced brief historical narratives for radio broadcast. His role is that of translator; he gives brief synopses of the narrative in English while the actors perform in Spanish. This results in people engaging the performance only partially, relying on the emcee for their specific knowledge of the narrative. While the audience may intuitively know the plot of the drama (especially those aspects related to the traditional Christmas story), the verbal artistry, specific cultural humor, and general semiotic codes pass undetected by this group. The quality of performance is also affected, since the emcee uses a microphone while the performers speak without any amplification. This creates a performance that is constantly interrupted, causing a sense of disjuncture and distance between the audience and performers.

The physical arrangement of the mission also affects the performance. While there is plenty of room to replicate the rectangular and bipolar aspects of the stage, the large open area of the mission enclosure allows people to move as far as thirty to forty yards away while still viewing the performance. The temperature in 1988 was 26° F, which also caused audience members to move to the periphery where barrels filled with burning wood kept them warm.

A key aspect of the mission performance is the presence of booths where food and drinks are sold. The San Antonio Conservation Society operates these, selling hot cocoa, *tamales*, beans, and other traditional foods to members of the audience. The booths themselves become a place where people congregate, engaging in talk and laughter, enjoying the performance from a distance.

Throughout the evening there is a constant effort on the part of the emcee to "sell" Los Pastores. He repeatedly urges audience members to buy food from the vendors or printed copies of the text sold by Conservation Society members. All this, he states, is to ensure the continuation of Los Pastores through financial support.

Related to this is the matter of money. Performers undertake their tasks freely: they receive no money or wage for their labor and do not charge for any performances. At the end of each performance, however, audience members are asked to participate in two kinds of ritual offerings. One involves the *adoración* or ritual kissing of the statue of *el Niño Dios*; the other involves a monetary offering placed in a basket held by Gila. The money goes to Our Lady of Guadalupe Church and can range from seventeen cents, collected at one barrio performance, to fifty dollars, depending on the number of people in attendance. The exception to this is the mission event. The San Antonio Conservation Society, partly from its desire to contribute to the financial security of the performance and partly because it wishes to exert some influence over the event, gives a one-hundred-dollar donation to the church in exchange for this performance. The same person who stated that he would rather perform "*en casas*" completed his statement by saying, "*Ellos . . . son muy comercial pa' mí*" (Those [performances in the mission] . . . are too commercial for me).

In sum, the mission performance is marked by a lack of interaction between the audience and performers and can even be said to constitute a social space that is at odds with the interest of the performance. If the purpose of the mission event is to preserve the historical and cultural significance of Los Pastores, this is the only location where the social relations and dynamics of performance are an issue. First, the use of the emcee who speaks over the performers' voices creates a disjuncture between the performed narrative, replete with humor, and its translation. Second, there is little interaction between performers and the audience outside the prescribed dramatic roles of the text. Audience members stay to themselves or gather around the food booths talking with vendors and other tourists; performers likewise refrain from interacting beyond their scope of friends and acquaintances who may be at the event. Finally, audience members are encouraged to buy food and books to financially support the performance. Once the event is over, both actors and audience members depart, going their separate ways.

Contextualization and the Politics of "Re-membering"

The process by which each domain of performance negotiates the rhythm and pattern of performance is a critical factor in the production of social meaning. One means of analyzing this is by focusing on the various forms of contextualization, that is, the process "of negotiation in which participants reflexively examine the discourse [drama], . . . embedding assessments" of its "significance" in the event itself (Bauman and Briggs 1990: 69). Contextualization functions as an index to competing claims on the meaning and experience of Los Pastores and a process that highlights the negotiation over cultural meaning. Contextualization is, I suggest, the process that Turner refers to when he writes of performances as "re-membering" and "dis-membering." Performative "membering" is a multifunctional process that is at the core of cultural citizenship. This is made clear when the integrative aspects of "re-membering" are contrasted with its "dis-membering" pair. Granted, to speak of contextualization and its "membering" in bipolar terms is a construct, but it is a construct that allows me to compare these places of performance and articulate the dynamic aspects of this event, revealing how Los Pastores is not merely a dramatic text, but a social event that configures social groups along lines that effect cultural citizenship.[8]

In the barrio, hosts inevitably contextualize Los Pastores as a ritual vow or *promesa*. They commence with a personal narrative, detailing the reason for the *promesa*, the person or persons involved, and their personal expectations for a positive outcome to the situation. In conjunction with the ritual vow, tradition is invoked as another means of contextualizing this event, citing how Los Pastores is "the way we celebrate Christmas."

The contextualization narratives of the hosts embed the overall performance within a highly familial and personal frame. It makes those present cognizant of their human frailty, suffering, and the universal aspects of these conditions. The weight of this action is confirmed in the emergent social body where formality is limited, if not absent, and a sense of sociability is evident. While there is no doubt that Los Pastores is understood as an extraordinary event, the level of intimacy and familiarity dominates the social scene: performers are found in various forms of verbal repartee and jocular exchange with those in attendance while the post-performance meal takes on festive dimensions. Familiarity and sociability are emergent in the event, indicated by the communal aspects of festivity.

I do not mean to suggest that the structures of everyday experience are suspended; in fact quite the opposite occurs. Stratification, especially that of gender, continues to govern this social scene. Women spend most of their time preparing the festive dishes, while at the same time attending to the construction of a home altar and other "domestic" affairs. Men, for their part, are not totally absent. Their primary contribution is to help place the *infierno* that shelters the devils in an appropriate location, place chairs alongside the performance area, and perform other tasks that require more "physical" aspects of work. In comparison to the many details that fall upon the women, men get off lightly. The role of women as hosts and organizers is significant, even if determined by culturally specific gender ideologies; their involvement follows patterns discussed by Sacks as the way "in which women's unwaged work creates community-based and class-based social ties of interdependence that are key to neighborhood and household survival" (1989: 53). Women's participation in the home is critical and essential, and without it this event would not take place. So while social disjunctures based on gender are reproduced, the overall function of women's work plays a critical part in the production of this location.

The significance of the barrio performance is related to the close-knit interaction it fosters. Contextualized as a personal affair, the performance structures the interaction between performers and audience, which leads to a sense of solidarity and sociability, and a scene where strangers are "re-membered" into the social group. This is a critical aspect of cultural citizenship where social groups experience a sense of unity and cohesion that leads to renewed senses of identity. The traditionalizing aspect of this domain signals the link of history and culture, where the past is not an absent phenomenon but a means of ordering the performance domain. To celebrate the way we did "in the past" refers not to history but to a social ordering that is reproduced in the present, an ordering based on social and communal solidarity and cultural identity. While this domain is not actively political, seeking rights in the civil sphere, it is inherently so, establishing social and communal links that are a critical aspect of community formation. To define one's past, to "re-member" the social body, to construct community, are acts of group definition and formation. A cultural practice establishes community formation.

The contextualization of Los Pastores at the church, while based on ritual, is quite different. In this domain, devotion to *el Niño Dios* is the organizing discourse. Christmas is a time to celebrate the birth of *el Niño Dios* and Los Pastores enables those present to focus special devotion and reverence on him. In most cases, church organizations or fraternities host the event and the special mission of these groups, the unique form of service or devotion they espouse, is a subtext in the contextualizing narrative.

This discourse recenters the performance of Los Pastores from a familial and personal event to an institutional and more structured one. The personal narratives that bind the members of the barrio performances have given way to an institutional and more broadly conceived ritual frame, taken from the institutional doctrine of the Catholic Church. Yet this Catholicism has a cultural emphasis since the salience of Los Pastores as a "Mexican" tradition is also highlighted.

The meaning of Los Pastores at the church turns on this dual contextualization. First, the event is presented as a Catholic celebration of Christmas, configuring the emergent social group as members of the same religious body. Second, it highlights the recent Mexican origins of Los Pastores. But this produces a less cohesive social body. One's participation and presence are not predicated on personal identification with the hosts and the human dimensions evoked through personal narratives, but on identification with the wider institution or tradition. This is seen in the social distance between performers and audience. Unless these two groups have other forums of communication, interaction between them is virtually nil. The social chasm between performers and audience marks this domain with a distinctly different type of social interaction from what is experienced in the barrio.

This also relates to cultural citizenship. The religious and ritual talk that contextualizes this event marks it as part of a religious tradition. While there is a level of "re-membering" that occurs, it highlights the religious body and not the present social group. As such, when official church members speak of Los Pastores as "our way of celebrating Christmas," they indicate the larger Christian community and not necessarily those in attendance. The "membering" that occurs, therefore, is that of a religious body—one that extends to all religiously affiliated persons regardless of ethnic identification. Institutional alliances take precedence over social ones, constituting a community that is more diffuse and less cohesive.

The mission event is quite different from either the barrio or the church. As noted above, the presence of an emcee, the amplification of his voice over that of the performers, food booths, and the tourist audience make for a different kind of performance. These elements, however, are only made possible through the San Antonio Conservation Society's contextualization of Los Pastores as an event "that will die out if not preserved." While the barrio and church performances are contextualized through ritual and tradition, the San Antonio Conservation Society produces Los Pastores as a cultural practice displaced from the social conditions and relations that are responsible for its making. In this domain, Los Pastores is enacted as a cultural event whose value and significance lie in the past. Absent are the active processes that link the past with the present, making folklore a viable social process; instead one finds the abstraction of Los Pastores from its cultural context and its production as an "artifact" of the past. The discourse of preservation that contextualizes this event frames Los Pastores as an "object" in need of saving, displacing its "cultural" value as a process of group formation and identity. As in the other two domains, the contextualizing discourse influences the emergent social body. The mission domain is a formal one, evident in the presence of an emcee and the special location of the mission.[9]

The significance of "re-membering" as a social process can only be recognized when it is negated, trivialized, or, as in the case of the mission event, contrasted with "dis-membering." At the mission performance, history is dis-membered from the present, the performers from the audience. The mission produces a Mexican tradition not in the active sense of reproducing a particular social construct from the past that functions to influence the organization of the present, but as objectifying a particular cultural form in order to preserve it. What is deemed "traditional" at the mission is not the way Los Pastores provides a frame for understanding, constructing, and organizing the present; instead its value as an object from the past is presented for touristic consumption; it is exalted as a traditional practice while the social arrangements and relations that produce it are displaced.

The Conjunction of Performance and Politics

Thus far, I have discussed Los Pastores and its relationship to cultural citizenship in terms of aesthetic process: how this event configures a social group, making members from strangers. My concern in this final section is to suggest another aspect of performance and its relationship to cultural citizenship: the formation of a political community. Before beginning, however, let me introduce my discussion with two points. First, I concur with Stanley Aronowitz that class identification in the United States has never developed to the extent that it conditions everyday practice. Instead, cultural and social affiliations (what Aronowitz refers to as subcultures) have been the sites of political group formation and activity. In a passage that resonates with aspects of my presentation here Aronowitz discusses two critical aspects of class consciousness beyond economic identification: a discursive community and political self-organization. A discursive community emerges from a cultural identity that is not "presupposed by structural unity"; political self-organization is the capability of "forming political organizations" that also "function discursively," which is to say, culturally (Aronowitz 1992: 127).

Second, in accordance with this case study, political action is never totalizing but particular and emergent. Social agents and performers choose their struggles, and to suggest that their participation is total or permanent is to misread the daily negotiation of group action, power, and identity that cultural citizenship implies. Cultural citizenship is the attempt to capture how cultural identification leads to and is influenced by practice in the civil arena. It is not merely political action nor romantic views of culture, but how a cultural community or particular cultural practices produce a collective sense of self that is the basis for political formation and action. In this context, aesthetic processes, or more specifically, how the performers of Los Pastores construct community, are an essential component of the formation and understanding of cultural citizenship. I do not mean to suggest that these performative ties signify full-blown consciousness with socially active members, only that without them the ability to act politically in the public sphere is thwarted.

Returning to Los Pastores, the question usually asked in terms of politics is: Where do we find a critical sense of civil and political practice by either troupe or audience members? Let me suggest that the question, as posed, is misplaced, not because a relationship between performance and political practice is indeterminate, but because it presupposes a causal link between consciousness and performance or performance and political action. I do not suggest that these links are impossible to achieve, only that they imply a singular understanding and relationship between performance and politics. Instead, and in keeping with the features of cultural performance itself, I argue for a processual relationship or link, one that connects political performance within the larger social and historical drama of a community over the long duration.

At this point, let me return to Don Leandro Granado, since his initial understanding of Los Pastores provides us with a critical perspective on this issue. In 1949 he bequeathed the text of his *pastorela* to the Jesuit pastor of Our Lady of Guadalupe Church, Carmelo Tranchese. Granado's letter is instructive on this point: "*En mexico comense aser Pastor en 1884 y en esta ciuidad comense aser pastor en 1913* [*sic*]" (In Mexico I began to be and perform a shepherd in 1884 and in this city I began to be and perform a shepherd in 1913). Granado's use of the phrase "*aser pastor* [*sic*]" is critical, since it indicates a kind of posture about performance that specifically relates to the notion of "membering" discussed above. To be and perform is not only to act, but to live and experience; it is to make one's self through performance. This very notion of self-making is misread by Tranchese. In the introduction to his translation and transcription of Don Leandro's text, Tranchese comments that audience members of Los Pastores do not stay for the entire performance because it is too long and complicated, but "the actors go on because for them it is an act of worship, a 'devocion' [*sic*], they call it" (Tranchese 1949). Tranchese fails to recognize in Granado's "devoción" a perspective of performance that is constitutive of community. To "*aser pastores* [*sic*]" is a communal act that constructs a performative, coherent community. This is the distinction between Granado and Tranchese: Don Leandro's *pastorela* is about the formation of a community through a religious idiom, not about religious formation. This is important since it demonstrates that the social relations of performance and the collective aspects constructed from them are not an accident of performance, but a critical component of them. While forces related to institutions, as in the church domain, and tourism, as at the mission, attempt to decenter such effects, the formation of a collectivity is one of the initial and contemporary features of Los Pastores. I do not mean to suggest that other aesthetic processes of community formation are absent from the West Side, only that none, as far as I know, have been in existence since 1913.

In terms of political action, San Antonio's West Side has long been active in efforts to improve the plight of its Mexicano inhabitants as well as to oppose the structures of the status quo. An impressive list of Mexican-American politicians and organizations has emerged from this neighborhood: Henry Cisneros was raised in this barrio, and represented the area as a councilman before becoming San Antonio's first Mexican-American mayor in modern times; the Mexican American Legal Defense and Educational Fund (MALDEF) was started in San Antonio in 1968 by a local attorney; the late Willie Velásquez founded the Southwest Voter Registration Education Project (SVREP) from San Antonio in 1974; and U.S. Congressman Henry B. González, and his politically active ancestors, have long been part of this community.[10] In the 1970s, Ernesto Cortez, after training as an organizer with the Industrial Areas Foundation (IAF), returned to San Antonio and became the first organizer of Communities Organized for Public Service (COPS), a community organization based on the Saul Alinsky model of social action, which has become an important political and social force for West Side Mexican Americans. Churches, both Catholic and Protestant, have served as local units through which problems such as poor street drainage, inadequate housing, and underfunded schools were publicly raised and brought to the forefront of San Antonio politics. COPS supported community-based needs in local elections and sought to address issues of social justice and equality for West Side Mexicanos. To this day, COPS continues to work for the improvement of this barrio, only now, after twenty years, its initial confrontational politics have given way to consultation and negotiated settlements with city officials.

Is there a direct link between the presence of Los Pastores and COPS, or other forms of political action in this community? Other than local COPS leaders being found at various performances or that Guadalupe Church has been an important supporter of both COPS and Los Pastores, such a link is difficult to sustain. However, even as I realign the relationship between performance and politics, the performers of Los Pastores remind me that a more direct articulation is also present. Recall the young woman I quoted earlier: "We need our traditions to be noticed here in America and here in our nation. . . . We have to preserve what's ours. Yes, go forward and be a united nation, but also don't forget where you came from."

Elsie was telling me that performing Los Pastores was a means by which she and others participated in the civic arena—going forward as a nation—by locating themselves in their cultural history, traditions, and performances. Los Pastores was the way she fixed herself in the present, a present established by a collective effort not to negate the past, and make herself noticed "here in *our* nation." She does not romanticize this effort, but recognizes that one must proceed and "go forward" but not at the sake of losing one's cultural self.

The relationship between the ability to constitute community at one moment and for extended members of that community to act politically at another is not coincidental; it represents an aspect of cultural citizenship. In this case, the making of a social body through performance is an effort to construct a notion of a collective self. This process clears the social ground for any future collective practice; any such practice without some semblance of communal and collective life is already too fragmented for collective action. This aspect of cultural citizenship takes seriously a community's efforts, rather conscious or not, to exert their own particular sense of self through cultural practice since these efforts are the foundation for any common action. Collective forms of cultural practice assert social rights, and, when piqued by a set of social, political, economic, legal, or other barriers, the effort to assert social rights can lead to an expanded view of communal action in the civil sphere. Such is the process of cultural citizenship.

Performing Los Pastores is the making of a cultural community, clearing the social ground for collective identity and practice. Performance, however, does not imply a priori the "re-membering" of the gathered social body in ways that lead to community formation, relations of solidarity, or assertion of civic rights. The forces of a postindustrial society that displace and dismember cultural communities and, in this case, put them on display for touristic consumption, wreak havoc on these nourishing sites of cultural formation. But clearly, without such community-making practices, performative or otherwise, collective action is nearly impossible. Finally, the continuation of these performative events is itself a political act that resists social fragmentation and effects forms of cultural citizenship that wrest a realm of freedom from necessity.

SIX

Claiming Cultural Citizenship in East Harlem: "Si Esto Puede Ayudar a la Comunidad Mía . . ."

Rina Benmayor, Rosa M. Torruellas, Ana L. Juarbe

DEDICATED TO THE WOMEN OF
THE EL BARRIO PROGRAM

"*Somos pobres pero tenemos dignidad,*" Mrs. Hernández declared. She was telling her literacy class in El Barrio about the disrespectful treatment she had received at the welfare office. She concluded in an indignant tone of voice, "We are poor, but we have our dignity." This expression, often heard in Latino cultures, contained a world of truth for Mrs. Hernández. It acknowledged that she lives in a social structure in which people are unequally and differentially treated. Through the plural subject "*somos,*" she recognized poverty as a shared condition rather than individual misfortune. It also validated her defiance. Mrs. Hernández did not see herself as passive or a victim of social circumstance. Instead, she held onto and openly affirmed more basic human values. Dignity, then, was posed as a cultural resource in the face of disempowering structural forces.

Caught in a web of persistent poverty and welfare, issues of *dignidad* (dignity), *vergüenza* (shame), *respeto* (respect),[1] and *ayuda mutua* (mutual aid) aid loom large in the daily lives of Puerto Rican women. These collective and culturally informed affirmations symbolize the main concern of this study: How do poor Puerto Rican women, marked by a history of colonialism and migration, bring cultural meanings, resources, and practices to bear in the struggle for cultural citizenship?

The El Barrio Popular Education Program in East Harlem was a native-language adult literacy and education project for Puerto Rican and Latino adults, initiated by the Centro de Estudios Puertorriqueños of Hunter College. The participants in the Program were predominantly Puerto Rican women, although there were also women from other Latin American and Caribbean countries and a small contingent of men. A core research team maintained a regular presence in the Program from 1985 to 1991.[2] This sustained presence involved participation in leadership, administration, planning, and classroom delivery; it also entailed regular classroom ethnography and in-depth life history interviews. This experience provided a wealth of understanding and knowledge about this community of women. The resulting study focused on sixteen of the women, with whom we maintained a close relationship for five years.

Cultural citizenship as a theoretical concept[3] enables a deeper understanding of the social and cultural struggles in which this particular group of poor Puerto Rican women in New York City were engaged. The sections that follow show that, although these women suffered a condition of long-term poverty, they were not inexorably locked into reproducing a culture of poverty. Drawing on what is sometimes referred to as "cultural capital" or "funds of knowledge,"[4] these women made concrete claims on the social structures that oppressed them and affirmed their own cultural codes of rights and entitlement.

Testimonio played an important role in the pedagogy of the Program. This Latin American tradition links the spoken word to social action and privileges the oral narrative of personal experience as a source of knowledge, empowerment, and political strategy for claiming rights and bringing about social change. Consequently, we use *testimonios* as primary texts in this chapter, in the form of vernacular phrases, life stories, philosophical statements, and the fuller life histories that paint the landscape of collective memory that informs our analysis. These vernacular representations of lived experience ground our understanding of cultural citizenship as a philosophical and moral framework and an expression of collective action for change.

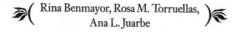

In the pages that follow, we describe the women, their history and location within the political economy of New York City, the educational context in which the research took place, and also the ethnographic methods used. We especially focus on the interplay between empowering education and the affirmation of collective practices in the struggle for cultural rights. We argue for the need to understand vernacular expressions of culture and collective agency in historical and structural context. That is, cultural claims for equality need to be appreciated from the perspective of people themselves as social agents.

The Program and the Project

THE EL BARRIO POPULAR EDUCATION PROGRAM

The El Barrio Popular Education Program was conceived as research intervention, as an opportunity to conduct research on the issue of literacy while working directly to improve educational conditions in the Puerto Rican community. Research would contribute to building a community-based program, defined and directed by its participants through a pedagogy of empowerment. The El Barrio Program became recognized as an important alternative educational program for Puerto Rican and Latino adults. Contrary to most adult literacy projects, which emphasize developing English language skills, the El Barrio Program defended the use of Spanish for teaching adult literacy to Latinos. This approach was pedagogically sound, it maintained, because people learn to read and write better in a language they already know and when their culture and knowledge is validated.

The Program started up in 1985 with two basic literacy classes. First these were held in a church and then in a local middle school in East Harlem, the oldest Puerto Rican community in New York City. Within two years, the

Program grew to offer beginning, intermediate, and advanced level classes, a beginning English as a Second Language (ESL) class, basic computer literacy, and a pre-high school equivalency class. It moved to Casita María, a senior citizen and community center in one of the Carver public housing projects on 102nd Street between Madison and Park Avenues. The classes were held three days a week between 9 A.M. and 2 P.M. The purpose of this growing program was not simply to teach the mechanics of literacy but to offer a program of general adult education in Spanish, drawing from Latin American models of educational empowerment.[5] The El Barrio Program came to be described by its participants as "*mi segunda familia* [my second family]," and "my home away from home." It became a context and a site for a collective struggle for cultural citizenship.

Participants: The annual enrollment averaged 50 to 60 participants. Consistently, 95 percent of them were women, of whom at least 75 percent were Puerto Rican.[6] They were first-generation migrants, born and raised in Puerto Rico or in other Latin American countries. With few exceptions, they were mothers, most of them single (including never married, separated, or divorced). Most fell into a thirty- to sixty-year-old age range. They were also heads of household whose documented yearly income was well below $10,000. Most of them received public assistance and had experienced both stable and fluctuating participation in the labor market. A good number of the women had no formal schooling whatsoever. Others had only been able to complete just a few years of elementary school. Several had managed to attain some high school education. Most did not have a functional command of English.

Staff and Researchers: From its inception in 1985 through 1991, the Program was directed by the late Dr. Rosa M. Torruellas, who was also associate director of the Language and Education Task Force at the Centro de Estudios Puertorriqueños. Pedro Pedraza, director of the Language and Education Task Force, played a key role in establishing the Program and fundraising. Alfredo Arango, Felix Cortés, Celestino Coto, and other progressive educators committed to community empowerment formed the backbone of the Program. A part-time counselor was also on staff. The Program also hosted many Latino student interns who gave instructional and administrative support. Researchers included the Program director, part-time classroom ethnographers, and Centro oral historians, Benmayor and Juarbe.

Leadership Development: Inspired by Paulo Freire's work in rural Brazil, this urban-based program developed an approach that drew on participants' own culture, self-defined interests, problems, and needs as conduits for learning (Freire 1972; Freire and Macedo 1987). The long-range objective was to evolve into a full-fledged community-based educational program in which participants would take increasing directive responsibilities. Structurally, participant involvement in decision-making was formalized through representation on the Program's Board of Directors and on the Steering Committee, the major directive body in the day-to-day operations. Membership in these bodies and participation in organized leadership training workshops were important first steps toward the goal of self-management. Participants gradually assumed greater roles in the planning, organization, and development of activities.

Support Services: The Program's integrated counseling services provided important support to this empowerment process. A cross-referral network helped participants obtain needed medical, legal, and other social services. Counselors worked with each participant to identify strengths and set concrete learning goals. Monthly rap-sessions were conducted, where problems affecting classroom dynamics were discussed and solutions proposed. The session always started by focusing on positive events: "Tell us something good and new in your life." This supportive participatory environment played a crucial role in promoting collective interaction and building confidence and self-esteem among the participants of the Program. This more holistic approach, also deeply reflected in the pedagogy of the classroom, ultimately differentiated the El Barrio Program from other educational programs in the community. *El programa*, as the participants called it, was more than school. It became a supportive cultural community.

Pedagogy: In the classroom, many participants found their traditional notions of education challenged. Instead of the "banking" approach to learning, in which the teacher periodically deposited information into the students' minds, the goal was to develop "critical literacy." The teachers organized their classes around socially and culturally relevant content; for example, family, gender relations, work and employment, education, housing, culture, migration, and history. They encouraged highly participatory and collective modes of interaction that helped break down traditional teacher-student hierarchies. The participants were the experts, communicating their own ideas and personal experiences. This learning environment was both exciting and challenging, since it opened avenues for development while potentially contradicting traditional roles and self concepts. Although they sometimes said that there was too much discussion and not enough "instruction," participants' discourse and practice attested to a new awareness emerging from a process of critical thought.

Writing: Writing was an important aspect of the curriculum from the beginning. As an active language skill, writing involved both rethinking and synthesizing ideas explored in class, and helped to develop a more analytical perspective. In the beginners' class, writing was also a central activity. The teacher discouraged the common practice of introducing writing through copying. Taking cues from classroom discussion, the participants learned to write key words and eventually phrases on their own. This was the first step in the process of "writing from the mind." By the time they moved to the next level, they had already established the relationship between writing and personal expression. The participants in the advanced group had literacy skills before coming to the Program. However, many did not use them frequently in their daily lives. To begin the writing process, each participant was assigned to write a life chronology. The second step was to flesh out this outline with regularly assigned autobiographical essays. In most cases, the essays were written at home and read in the classroom. In time, the participants no longer associated writing exclusively with school assignments. One of the more prolific writers explained that "now I write down everything I do not want to forget."

Testimony: In developing an empowerment pedagogy, the Program consciously placed emphasis on testimony. Testimonial literature by other Latin Americans was presented in class as evidence of the importance of sharing one's life experience in the process of searching for collective solutions and decisions.[7] Inspired by these texts, we produced a Spanish literacy reader for adults based on recorded oral history sessions with a group of women in the first year of the Program (*Aprender a luchar, luchar es aprender* [Learning to Struggle, Struggle Is Learning]). This was an example of participatory education, where students contributed to developing their own pedagogical tools. Autobiographical writings of their own provided the opportunity for students to "tell" their stories, often for the first time. *Testimonio* and autobiography helped dispel the notion, prevalent among working-class people, that history, knowledge, and writing are the exclusive domain of professionals or the rich. Similarly, by emphasizing the participants' daily lives and thoughts, the pedagogy deconstructed gendered ideologies of social roles and capabilities. As their accounts were read out loud in class, participants came to realize that their individual circumstances were not unique, accidental, or the product of their own errors or "shortcomings." From the individual accounts, a collective "story" and consciousness emerged.

THE RESEARCH PROJECT

During two years (1989 and 1990), we worked intensely with a group of twenty-three women. We collected long life histories (six to eight hours, on the average) and, through observer participation within and outside the Program, documented the women's current life circumstances. The interviews were conducted as open narratives to allow each woman to tell her story as she wanted, selecting what she wanted to reveal about her life and providing her own evaluations and reflections. In the final interview session, specific questions were posed around issues of class, gender, race, national identity, and other relevant issues.

The individual life histories, together with our observations, provided us with biographical knowledge and background to the women's present circumstances. Most important, the life histories allowed us to delve more deeply into the women's own understanding of their lives. They provided insight into how the women positioned themselves in the center, as "subjects," and how their views were embodied in social practices. While the life accounts were often contradictory and were a selected and partial representation of reality, they presented an internal point of view. This helped put into perspective externally derived assessments about the lived experience of oppressed communities. Our intent was to produce a more thorough understanding of the structural and cultural forces that organize, and disorganize, people's lives.

From the complete body of data collected, we concentrated the analysis on sixteen case studies. We found these accounts unusually rich and they covered the gamut of issues we are trying to address. They also established certain patterns of interrelationship between structural and ideological constraints and the way the women responded to such limitations.

The Historical Present: Contexts for Affirmation

Economically and culturally, the women in our project represented a sector of the Puerto Rican and other Latino immigrant community in New York City that has experienced persistent and growing poverty as well as intensified social marginalization, especially in recent decades. Most migrated to New York after World War II, some coming in the mass migration wave of the 1950s and 1960s, others in successive decades. Their life stories collectively revealed how individuals, families, and ultimately a whole community are shaped by histories of colonialism, capitalism, and patriarchy, and by the more recent postindustrial transformations of the economies of neo-colony and metropole. The women's claims for social and cultural rights—for cultural citizenship—take on depth and particularity of meaning in light of these historical experiences.

The migration and presence of Puerto Ricans in New York and in the

United States throughout this century can best be described as a planned exchange of people for capital (History Task Force 1979; Bonilla and Campos 1986). Annexation to the United States in 1898, the de-formation of the island's economy through mechanization and industrialization plans that left the majority of the population without adequate sources of livelihood, the 1917 decree imposing U.S. citizenship, and the 1952 commonwealth arrangements of Free Associated State are but the major political and economic markers that frame any informed analysis of the life history of Puerto Ricans as a people. The women in our study were born into poverty on the island. Their families, as a consequence of the tremendous upheavals in the island's economy, had become part of the rural proletariat, living on below-subsistence wages. Their fathers were seasonal cane cutters or laborers; their mothers were laundry, domestic, and garment workers; and they themselves grew up having to work in early childhood. Their families' livelihoods were shaped by the mechanization of sugar production, by the transfer from agricultural to semi-industrial and service economies, and by a sustained program of transfer payments (in the form of food coupons) to three quarters of the inhabitants of this lush, tropical island. Inscribed in all their memories was a childhood shaped by the struggle for economic survival.

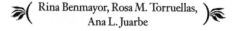

Most of the women in our study began work in girlhood. Whether in the countryside or in towns, children had to participate in the economic survival of their families. Since this was a gendered arrangement, girls were typically called upon to alleviate immediate needs on the domestic front. This meant becoming responsible for household chores, child care, sewing or embroidering for the home needlework industry, or being hired out as child domestics (González 1990; Azize 1985; Silvestrini Pacheco 1980; Benmayor et al. 1987). Educational opportunities were often extremely limited. Rural schools were often one-room structures with multigrade classes, at great distances from children's homes. Attendance was sporadic and not enforced. Although school enrollment started swelling in the 1940s, the conditions of Puerto Rico's educational system did not differ substantially from those at the turn of the century.[8] In most cases, girls were pulled out of school, if they were enrolled at all, while boys might have been allowed to continue their basic education as preparation for future employment. Significantly, this process also served to socialize girls into their future family and mothering roles. They were being prepared to carry out "women's work," whether in their own homes or for wages. Thus, these women's histories and future goals were very much shaped by the lack of education and the experience and expectation of wage work.

For the vast majority of Puerto Ricans, migration to the United States was motivated by the need and desire for jobs and economic advancement. It was facilitated by an organized state policy that provided migration offices at either end and cheap transportation. The time of the move was also a significant factor. Women who came in the 1950s and 1960s still benefited, for ten or fifteen years, from a relative abundance of factory jobs in the garment industry or in other light manufacture. They were able to earn decent union wages, with benefits, and support their families. By the 1970s and 1980s, however, these same women found themselves losing jobs because of factory relocations, an increasingly unstable job market, and the economic bottom dropping out from under them. Women who arrived in New York City during this later period—again in response to global economic shifts, disinvestment in the island, and the shrinkage of jobs for semi- or non-skilled workers—found virtually no job market for the unskilled and uneducated.

The effect has been a steady impoverishment of workers at both ends of the migration circuit. With the increasing disinvestment in manufacture in the Northeast, these women found themselves competing for disappearing factory jobs and lacking the educational, technical, and even language skills to occupy decent service jobs. At the same time, the various fiscal crises of the city, cuts in federally funded training programs, the technological and telecommunications revolution, global economic competition, the growing power of finance relative to production, and increasing migrations from developing countries to New York City have all weighed heavily against the improved life chances of poor Puerto Rican women and their families. According to Roger Waldinger, "the shift toward corporate, nonprofit, and public services produced important changes in the occupational mix and the nature of the city's labor market at a time when racial succession and immigration were simultaneously reshaping the city's population and labor force. These demographic shifts intersected with economic change to produce a new racial/ethnic/gender division of labor and, as wealth and poverty both grew, new forms of inequality" (Mollenkopf and Castells 1991: n. 20).

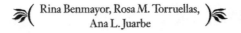

In *The Dual City*, John Mollenkopf and Manuel Castells (1991) report that from 1977 to 1987, poverty in New York City increased from 15 to 23 percent, with more than one million people with incomes of less than 75 percent of the official poverty level. The number of female-headed households with children grew 15 percent while the labor force participation of blacks and Latinos declined for women along with the real value of the basic welfare grant. During these ten years, they note, Latino families fared worse than other groups and became a larger proportion of the city's population.

> Latinos, particularly Puerto Ricans, lagged behind whites and blacks. Puerto Rican median real income fell fully one-fifth relative to whites over the decade, despite falling unemployment rates for Latinos. . . . Blacks were able to expand their access to jobs in government, social services, and a few corporate services, expanding the black middle class. Public service in particular provided a path for upward mobility in income and occupation. Latinos, by contrast, were concentrated in sectors like durable manufacturing that have declined most rapidly in recent decades. (Mollenkopf and Castells 1991: 15)

The impact of this downward trend on space and place has translated into massive decay of poor neighborhoods and public facilities. Roughly half of the women in our study lived in public housing projects in El Barrio (East Harlem). Others resided in the Bronx, the Lower East Side, and different neighborhoods in Queens. These neighborhoods have a marked Puerto Rican and Latino character. As Mrs. Tavárez suggests, they project the feeling of *pueblo*:

Ya son muchos años los que he vivido en el Barrio, y la vida se le hace a uno más fácil aquí. . . . Aquí uno tiene todo a la mano. No es como uno ir a otro sitio, que no conoce a nadie. Y además, cuando uno está criando hijos y los tiene en la escuela . . . mientras pueda, yo me quedo aquí. (Aprender a luchar 1988: 20)

I've lived in El Barrio for many years now, and life here is easier. . . . Here you have everything within reach. It's not like going to another place where you don't know anybody. And besides, when you are raising children and you have them in school . . . as long as I can, I will stay right here.

The institutional, organizational, and political entities in the barrios are connected to the identity of the community. Cultural practices embodied in lifestyles, values, and perspectives, all lived within the social interaction of neighbors, family, friends, and strangers, contribute to this feeling. In addition, commercial establishments cater to Latinos in language, custom, and taste (Benmayor et al. 1992: 7). This familiar milieu offers residents some feeling of control over the urban social landscape. At the same time, "The 'barrios' are among the poorest sectors of New York City. City service agencies blatantly ignore their environmental and economic needs. They tend to be dirty, polluted neighborhoods in which drug dealing, substance abuse, and hard-core crime abound. The unavailability of jobs is one of the most significant defining features of the present difficult situation, unrelieved since the late sixties in intensity. All these factors convert daily existence into a constant struggle for survival" (Benmayor et al. 1992: 7).

Esther Huertas's essay for class effectively captured the stressful circumstances in which many poor Latinos are forced to live:

Hoy por la mañana yo fui al 'cashiar' [sic] *a sacar mi dinero para pagar mi renta y cuando me metí al elevador, en el cuarto piso se metieron dos personas. El hombre me puso un cuchillo en la espalda y la mujer me quitó todo lo que yo tenía. . . . ¡Qué susto he pasado! Y ahora ¿qué voy a hacer para pagar mi renta y el teléfono y para la comida de los nenes? Tendré que coger prestado hasta que me toque el otro cheque. Como no soy mala paga, me los prestan. Son tantas cosas que me están pasando que una más no importa. . . . ¿Por qué me pasan a mí las cosas en esta vida? (Buscando un futuro mejor* 1988: 111)

> This morning I went to take out money to pay my rent and when I got into the elevator, on the fourth floor two people got on. The man pressed a knife to my back and the woman took all that I had. . . . I was so scared! And now, what am I going to do to pay the rent and the telephone and to feed my kids? I'll have to borrow money until my next check comes. Someone will lend me the money because they know I will pay them back. I have so many problems to deal with that one more doesn't make a difference. . . . Why do these things happen to me?

What Mollenkopf and Castells call the paradoxical mix of splendor and decay has been visible in New York City for several decades now. It is a dramatic illustration of disinvestment, not only in certain employment sectors that supported the city's poor, but also in their home environments, that has intensified racial and economic segregation, crime, and environmental racism. Individuals not only feel unprotected, they *are* unprotected, unsupported, and keenly aware of the myriad ways in which the system ambushes them at every corner.

We consciously chose *not* to circumscribe our study within the terms of the current debate on the "underclass."[9] Instead, we wanted to examine the premises of that debate from another perspective. We propose that many of the responses to conditions of poverty and exclusion that emerge from within subordinate communities are affirmations of cultural citizenship. This theoretical framework helps us look at cultural practices in the light of collective resources and social equity rather than deviance. Our focus has been to understand the ways in which poor Puerto Rican women actually negotiated their circumstances, perceived their options, and defined their goals through community self-definition and cultural practices.

When the cultural and historical meanings of work are brought into the analysis, the gender, racial, and class biases of the "welfare dependency as deviant behavior" argument so popular today become clearer. The life histories of these women show that the issues of work and welfare are more complex than simple participation in wage labor. We saw in our sample that, since childhood, these women were socialized into what could generally be called "women's work," which included domestic care, child care, sewing, and other forms of manual labor. At particular points in their lives, they might have engaged in paid and unpaid home work or in formal employment outside the home. For poor and working-class women, defining as "work" only that which is paid labor is artificial, since the jobs performed for wages are usually an extension of the work performed at home. Regardless of the context, the women saw themselves as fulfilling their productive obligations in society, performing the type of work that they as women were entrusted to carry out. Consequently, even when becoming welfare recipients may have represented a last choice, the women did not see this as a strategy for cheating the state but as one that enabled them to continue to exercise their reproductive and social responsibilities.

Mrs. Jovellanos's life story exemplified ways in which women actively resist the terms upon which the system defines their entitlement. On the surface, Mrs. Jovellanos fit the stereotype of the long-term welfare dependent. Once on the welfare rolls, she did not pursue reentry into the labor force, even though she had some elementary education and a substantial employment history. Her desire to raise her six children herself influenced her decision to stay home. As Luis Duany's 1991 study of Puerto Rican welfare recipients in New York City points out, many Puerto Rican and Latina women fear low-quality care of their children if entrusted to somebody else. From Mrs. Jovellanos's perspective, hers was not a story of social deviance. On the contrary, the following account of conflict with the welfare office poses the problem in very different terms. The story illustrates a claim for cultural and reproductive rights.

One month, upon failing to receive her welfare check, Mrs. Jovellanos immediately went to see her local caseworker, with her children in tow. She recounted that she arrived at the welfare office at nine in the morning. She was kept waiting until noon, at which time she decided to rebel:

Entonces yo voy y le digo a la investigadora: "Hey, listen. I stay there [waiting] desde nine o'clock in the morning. Look at my kids! I no eat breakfast, I no eat lunch, I

> *no eat nothing. What happen? What happen?" Ella me dice: "Never mind, no is my family." Yo digo, "What?" . . . Porque ella dijo ¡que los hijos míos no eran familia suya!*
>
> So, I went up to the investigator and said to her: "Hey, listen. I stay there [waiting] since nine o'clock in the morning. Look at my kids! I no eat breakfast, I no eat lunch, I no eat nothing. What happen? What happen?" And she replied, "Never mind, no is my family." And I said, "What!" . . . Because she was telling me that my children were not her concern! (Benmayor et al. 1992: 28, App. 22)

Finally, a supervisor intervened and explained to the caseworker that:

> *"Está supuesta a atenderla porque esos son nenes chiquitos los que hay aquí. Los que ella tiene son babies, no son teenagers . . . y los babies no saben de 'no hay' cuando tienen hambre."*
>
> "You are supposed to attend to her because those are little children. Her children are babies, they aren't teenagers . . . and babies don't know the meaning of 'We don't have any food' when they are hungry." (Benmayor et al. 1992: 28, App. 23)

Through her story, Mrs. Jovellanos was not only affirming her prerogative to have children and to ensure their survival, in this case by demanding that she receive what she was entitled to by law, she was also demanding to be treated with respect and dignity as a Puerto Rican and as a mother. Her account presented the incident in terms of a Puerto Rican woman's right to fulfill the gender responsibilities society had entrusted to her. Although she was seeking justice for herself, Mrs. Jovellanos's claim was informed by her membership in a gender and national community that commonly suffered the same ill treatment from the welfare bureaucracy. Beneath her feelings of personal indignation was a larger sense of the rights of Puerto Rican women as a community. This is a good case example of how a gendered claim for cultural respect, although posed as an individual demand, is informed and supported by a community of meaning, by a cultural understanding of citizenship.

Enrolling in school was the one productive alternative offered by the same welfare system that had restricted these women's options for years.[10] It was an attractive alternative for many reasons. In the first instance, compared to the job market, school was not an alienating situation but one that signified internal growth and expansion. Second, it did not threaten to disrupt family unity. The El Barrio Program allowed the women to continue to exercise their responsibilities and central role within the home. Their school hours coincided with those of their children or grandchildren. In addition, going to school did not violate a prescribed social norm, since in Puerto Rico education was an arena in which women participated, in spite of the economic circumstances that prevented many from doing so.

Moreover, the educational alternative brought these women important and unexpected rewards. It brought them into a collective environment that was, in our analysis, one of the reasons why the El Barrio Popular Education Program became so meaningful in their lives. The following two sections examine how these women struggled for personal empowerment through education, to create a context in which they could affirm community resources and values, validate a shared sense of cultural rights and entitlement, and act as a group to claim cultural citizenship.

Personal Transformation, Collective Meanings

Ha llegado ya la hora
del estudio de los problemas
de problemas personales y de la comunidad.

. . . En la clase de problemas
todo el mundo ya pensamos progresar
y seguimos adelante
para el progreso y bien de toda la comunidad
para dar la enseñanza a todo el que quiera luchar.

The time has come
to study the problems,
our personal and community problems.

. . . In our class
everyone is progressing
and we move forward
for the progress and good of all the community
to bring education to everyone who wants to struggle.

POEM BY MRS. LUZ DE JESÚS,
ADOPTED AS THE PROGRAM'S CREDO,
Paso a paso 1989: 74

Classroom observations and life histories confirmed that this community of Puerto Rican women, born into rural or semi-urban poverty on the island, placed an enormous value on education. The words of one participant, Mrs. Carmen Ayala, illustrate the importance of acquiring knowledge, intertwined with the significance of respectful behavior and extended familial relationships:

> *[Nuestros padres] nos enseñaron las cosas más hermosas de la vida. Nos enseñaron el entusiasmo, el amor y el respeto a nuestra escuela al igual que a nuestros maestros, pues siempre me decían en mi casa que los maestros son nuestros segundos padres. (Buscando un futuro mejor*, 1988: 147)

> [Our parents] taught us the most beautiful things in life. They taught us to be enthusiastic, to love and respect our school and our teachers. In my house, they always taught me that our teachers were our second parents.

While many women arrived at the Program through welfare referral, they had much deeper reasons for returning every day. The opportunity to finally fulfill a long-deferred dream was at the heart of their commitment. Similarly, the Program's objectives were not simply to teach literacy or to equip the participants with greater skills to compete in the service economy, but to empower the community in culturally affirming ways. The educational environment participants encountered and the cultural space they created stimulated a process of personal transformation based on collective cultural meanings. As Alessandro Portelli states, "There is perhaps no 'individual' text without communal meaning. On the other hand, all 'communal' texts are filtered by individual consciousness" (1991: 74).

FULFILLING A LONG-DEFERRED DREAM

Enrolling in the El Barrio Program was a life-changing move. Every one of the women in our sample was profoundly transformed by this experience and openly said so. The images they used to describe these changes were drawn from a vernacular poetics in which coming to consciousness is likened to an awakening, an awareness of one's place and space in the world, and an expanded sense of possibilities. As is often found in the poetics of rural experience, acting in the physical world serves as a metaphor for self-knowledge, consciousness, and change. The Program, they said, helped them: "*abrir la mente*" (to open the mind), "*tener la mente más clara*" (to think more clearly), "*uno mismo ver dónde está parado*" (to see yourself and where you stand), "*despertar*" (to awaken), "*tener alas para volar*" (to have wings to fly). As Mrs. Cossio explained: "*Una persona no se conoce ella misma hasta que no sabe leer y escribir*" (A person does not know herself until she learns how to read and write).

Lack of education was a liability that most of the women experienced from an early age and which they were now overcoming. Every life history we collected introduced education as a fundamental theme. The decision to go to school meant more than just choosing the best option the welfare system had to offer. The women recognized going to school as a chance to fulfill a long-deferred dream.[11]

In their accounts, for example, being pulled out of school figured as a prominent theme. Mrs. González's story highlighted the lack of social supports the women found for pursuing an education, as well as the pressures exerted by poverty on parents and children alike:

> *Yo recuerdo cuando ya estaba en tercer grado, que en las tardes cuando yo salía de la escuela yo tenía que ir en casa de una señora a ayudarle en la casa. . . . Entonces me*

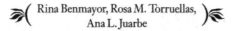

acuerdo cuando la señora mandó a llamar a mi mamá y le anunció que me tenía que sacar de la escuela porque no me daba tiempo de hacerle las cosas. . . . Yo me quedé mirando a mi mamá como suplicándole, "No me saques de la escuela." Pero como estaba tan dura la situación, mi mamá lo primero que pensó, "Sin la ayuda de ella . . ." Mi mamá no puso reparos. . . . Dijo, "Pues está bien, Lula, yo la saco de la escuela." . . . Esa noche yo me la pasé llorando.

I remember when I was in third grade, I had to go to work at a lady's house after school. . . . I remember when the lady sent for my mother and announced to her that she had to pull me out of school because I didn't have time to do my work well. . . . I looked at my mother like begging, "Don't pull me out of school." But since the situation was so difficult, the first thing my mother thought was, "Without her help . . ." My mother did not raise any objections. . . . She said, "All right, Lula, I'll pull her out of school." . . . I spent that night crying. (Benmayor et al. 1992: 43, App. 35)

Mrs. Romero's poignant story was a particularly vivid testimony of a young girl's attempt to claim for herself an opportunity she was being denied. As she said:

Nunca se me olvida aquello, después de tantos años. Yo luché una vez porque la gente del mismo pueblo me decía, "¿Por qué tú no te vas a la escuela? ¿Por qué tú no estudias? Tú eres una muchacha chiquita, joven, que todavía puedes."

Y un día, pues yo cogí y me fuí a apuntarme. Ya yo tenía como ocho años. Ya era grandecita. ¡Ay, Dios mío! ¡Lo que me pasó!

Me voy a mi casa y fuí y preparé una faldita y una chaquetita. Era una faldita negra y una chaquetita blanca. Y la lavé, la planché, la puse así [como extender la ropa]. ¡No quiero ni acordarme de aquéllo porque en seguida me pone mal!

Resulta que no tuve inteligencia y la puse encima de la cama donde mi mamá dormía. La enganché en un gancho. Bueno. Y yo estaba loca de contenta que llegara el otro día pa' yo irme pa' la escuela. Y, voy, me levanto muy temprano. . . . ¡Ay, Dios mío! Cuando yo iba a coger mi ropa, no me dejan cogerla. Porque no me dejaron entrar al cuarto. Porque estaban durmiendo todavía. Entonces yo cojo y me fuí y me dio como un sentimiento bien grande al no poder coger mi ropa. Y me fuí pa' la calle. Y fuí y me senté por allá, en una esquina a pensar y pensar y pensar. Y como no pude ir ese día, pues yo dije, "No voy." Yo no fuí. Entonces después, pasaron los tiempos, los tiempos y los tiempos, y no volví. Pero me quedé como con esa cosa.

> I'll never forget that, after so many years. I fought once, because the people in the town asked me, "Why don't you go to school? Why don't you study? You are a young girl and you still can do it."
>
> So one day I went to sign myself up. I was already about eight years old. I went to sign up. But, oh God! What happened to me!
>
> I returned home to prepare a skirt and a blouse. It was a black skirt and a white jacket. I washed and ironed them and hung them up. Oh, I don't even want to think about it because I get sick!
>
> It turns out that I was not very smart and I hung them over my mother's bed, on a hanger. Well, I was really excited, waiting for the next morning so that I could go to school. And I got up very early. . . . Oh, God! When I went to get my clothes I couldn't! They wouldn't let me into the room. They were still sleeping, so I couldn't get my clothes. So I left feeling tremendously disappointed that I couldn't get to my clothes. And I left. And I went out to the street and sat down at the corner to think and think and think. And since I couldn't go that day, I said to myself, "I'm not going." So time passed, and passed, and passed, and I never went back. But that feeling stuck with me. (Benmayor et al. 1992: 43–44, App. 36)

Mrs. Romero ended her story on a passive note. She lamented her failed attempt to go to school but settled for the outcome. Nonetheless, she constructed the narrative with an unresolved ending: "That feeling stuck with me." The account was enabled by her current efforts to attain an education. For her, as for all the other women, coming to the El Barrio Program was a first step in a process of self-assertion.

Making an active claim for oneself also involved issues of self-esteem. As we noted earlier, some women linked their lack of formal education to limited supports within the family. Mrs. Romero stated: "*Yo no tenía interés (en estudiar) porque no tenía apoyo, no tenía quién me ayudara en nada*" (I had no incentive to study because I had no support, I had nobody to help me). Looking back, some attributed responsibility more to harsh socioeconomic conditions that placed their parents under severe stress. Mrs. González said: "*La situación estaba difícil, esa es la palabra. Eramos muchos. . . . Era una pobreza terrible*" (Times were very rough, that's the truth. We were a large family. . . . And the poverty was terrible). *Apoyo* (support) became the symbolic term that connected the present with the memory of the past. Because the Program stressed the importance of collective support and encouragement, many participants were reminded of how their own families were unable to fulfill that important supportive role.

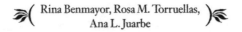

To a large extent, childhood experiences of class and gender exploitation had important bearings on the women's vision of their capabilities and potential in the present. Internalized colonial, class, and gender oppressions translated into feelings of personal incapacity or low self-esteem and held many of the participants back. For years, Mrs. Velázquez resisted moving on to take high school equivalency classes. While she was capable of handling the intellectual level of the material, she did not take up the challenge, invoking lack of self-confidence as a shield. The addition of a GED (high school equivalency) class within the Program, however, was a turning point. Feeling encouraged by the supportive cultural and educational environment, Mrs. Velázquez began to move toward acquiring her diploma, finally enrolling in the GED class.

The empowering changes the women experienced revolved around shared understandings of key cultural values that permeated the educational environment: *respeto* (respect), *cariño* (caring and affection), *apoyo* (mutual aid and support), and *cooperación* (cooperation and sharing). And, while the Program sought to emphasize *colectivismo*, underscoring the belief in working together toward a common goal, it also placed equal importance on developing each individual's unique capacity to contribute. As the women themselves said, reflecting individual humility as well as individual contributions in forging the whole: "*Cada persona es un mundo*" (Each person is a world unto herself), but "*Cada uno pone su granito de arena*" (Each one contributes her little grain of sand).

The process of finding one's place in the educational environment began as soon as the participants enrolled in the Program. First, they were encouraged to express out loud their educational goals. On this basis, each would embark upon the "program of study" with a clearer definition of personal objectives and steps required to achieve them. Sitting in a circle, students were asked to articulate their goals and their ideas of how to achieve them. As one of the older participants told an incoming group during an orientation session: "*Aquí no hay tal cosa como 'Yo no puedo' o 'Yo no sé'*" (Here there is no such thing as 'I can't' or 'I don't know'). High learning and leadership expectations were conveyed by peers and staff from the very first day.

The staff believed in each person's ability to learn, to reach beyond their initial expectations, and to redefine their goals. The attitude of respect and importance with which their aspirations were regarded conferred upon participants a feeling of confidence. For example, many women were encouraged because the Program acknowledged the effort involved in pursuing education at a later stage in life, which added a new set of daily responsibilities and obligations to those already shouldered by poor women. As Cecilia Santos wrote:

> *Me siento muy bien en Casita María [El Programa de Educación Popular de El Barrio] aprendiendo después de los 30, lo que no pude aprender antes de los 20. Yo estoy en el grupo de los que dicen que para aprender no importa la edad y menos si es en Casita María. Aquí se siente uno como si fuera su propia casa.* (*Buscando un futuro mejor* 1988: 127)
>
> I feel so good at Casita María [in the El Barrio Program], learning in my thirties what I couldn't learn before my twenties. I'm in the group that says that age is not important when it comes to learning and that is even more true at Casita María. Here we feel that we are in our own home.

Perhaps most immediately significant to incoming learners was the understanding that each would receive the necessary collective support and understanding to realize their goals. Participants acquired faith in their ability to face obstacles and work out problems in an atmosphere of positive understanding and collaboration. Expressions of concern for the individual student often included phone calls about absences from class. Within the cultural environment of *cariño* (caring, affection) and *confianza* (shared trust), such inquiries were understood not as an invasion of privacy or as an enforcement of bureaucratic rules but as a genuine interest in one's well-being and need for support. Demonstrations of *cariño* invited trust, expressed a sense of cultural connection and encouragement, and were what the women considered necessary and appropriate conditions for approaching problems. Rather than stressing violations of rules, delinquency, or deficiencies, *cariño* and *confianza* expressed positive belief in people's capabilities. As Bethzaida Ortiz wrote in a letter, alluding to competing demands from family:

> *Quiero agradecer a los que colaboran día a día con nuestra educación y nos brindan el cariño y la comprención* [sic] *que muchos de nosotros no tenemos en nuestros hogares.* (*¡Progresando en español!* 1990: 8)
>
> I would like to thank those who contribute day by day to our education and give us the affection and understanding that many of us do not get in our homes.

The women often made it known that such expressions of concern encouraged them to return to school and stay on course.

The El Barrio Program was established as one of the few Spanish literacy programs in the country to espouse a culturally relevant, progressive approach to learning. The Program was guided by the Freirian philosophy of *concientización* (conscientization), of empowering people through activation of their own cultural values, practices, language, and experiential knowledge. Pedagogically, the curriculum validated and built on the class, gender, and national cultural resources of the participants (Freire 1972; Freire and Macedo 1987). In the classroom, teachers often constructed lesson content around the women's vernacular language, expressions, folk sayings, Spanish neologisms based on English words, popular medicinal practices, religious beliefs, life in the barrio, and national histories.[12] This process strengthened a sense of cultural pride, entitlement, and citizenship, as participants collectively recognized the importance and value of their native "funds of knowledge" (Vélez Ibáñez 1996). This empowering process helped women not only to find their place in the Program, but also to find their voice. Lucía Plácido wrote:

> . . . *una persona que no conoce la historia de su tierra, es como si no tuviera memoria y eso era yo cuando no sabía escribir.* (*Paso a paso* 1989: 57)
>
> . . . a person who does not know the history of her country, in a way, is a person without memory and that is how I was before I learned how to write.

This approach stimulated the women to think of themselves in terms of expanded capacities. Their cultural knowledge was validated and respected in the classroom and helped strengthen positive self-images. This was a fundamental step in the affirmation of cultural citizenship, particularly for women who have suffered the historical effects of colonization, migration from their native land, poverty, and second-class citizenship.

As researchers, we became witnesses to as well as co-constructors of learning that encouraged women to take control of their lives in new ways. In the following statement, Mrs. González gave us a measure of how participation in an empowering educational dynamic affirmed cultural citizenship by transforming participants' self-confidence in acting on behalf of their community:

> *Aprendí a desenvolverme, a estar con otras personas, porque antes yo no le hablaba en la cara a nadie . . . que ya si tengo que ir a hablar hasta con el gobernador en la cara voy y hablo con él. He aprendido algo de liderazgo. . . . Aquí desarrollé muchas destrezas, como por ejemplo cómo pararme al frente de un grupo de gente, explicarles las cosas de aquí . . . y sí, me siento segura que yo puedo ayudar a otras personas.*
>
> I have learned to feel at ease with other people, because before I would not talk and look at people in the face . . . and now if I had to go to the governor and speak to him, I would. I have learned some leadership skills. . . . Here I have developed many skills, like for example, how to stand in front of a group of people, explain to them how things work here . . . and yes, I feel confident I can help other people. (Benmayor et al. 1992: 47–48, App. 40)

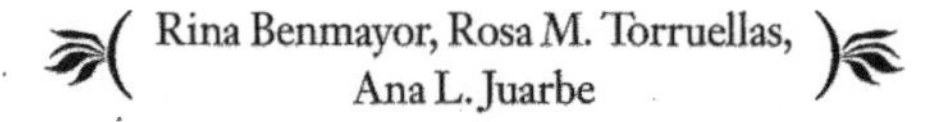

SHIFTING PRIORITIES AND NEW GOALS

In order to get this education, the women had to struggle against structural constraints and change daily life practices. In their relationship with the state, this meant asserting their legal choice for education over workfare; in their relationship with the family, they had to insist on the space for their education within the daily agenda; and in the personal realm, they had to reorganize their own priorities and time to be able to meet the demands on them as homemakers, mothers, and students. Mrs. Cossío told how she reorganized her day to include school and domestic work:

> *Yo me levanto a las 6 de la mañana. Hago el desayuno. De ahí, cojo, pongo el grano, lo dejo puesto . . . saco la carne si es que la tengo que sacar para dejarla afuera . . . me meto al baño, me cambio de ropa y para la escuela que voy. De ahí salgo a las 11 . . . y vuelvo otra vez y pongo el grano si le falta . . . entonces pues . . . me voy para Casita María. De Casita María pues, vengo a cocinar. That's all!*

> I get up at 6 A.M. I prepare breakfast. Then, I put the beans to soak . . . and I take the meat out to defrost if I need to . . . I bathe, I change clothes, and off I go to school. Then, I get out at 11 . . . and I come home to check on the beans . . . and then . . . I go off to Casita María [to the El Barrio Program]. From Casita María, I come home to cook. That's all! (Benmayor et al. 1992: 48, App. 41)

Prioritizing education was not always consistent. For some of the women in the Program, schooling competed with the grandparenting phase in their life cycle. Many were called upon to play a supportive role within their extended family. For example, Mrs. Quiroz dropped out of the Program after three years, explaining that she had to take care of an infant granddaughter and that she was about to remarry. By contrast, Mrs. Romero decided to stay in school over the objections of her daughter, who was reluctant to do without her mother's support in raising the grandchildren. Having fulfilled what she saw as her primary gender obligations, Mrs. Romero asserted her own aspirations over her daughter's wishes. Like Mrs. Romero, many of the women felt they were now entitled to prioritize their own needs, to "raise" and nurture themselves: "*Ya yo crié mis hijos, ahora me toca a mí*" (I raised my children, now it's my turn).

These two examples highlight the contradiction embodied in their commitment to family. On the one hand, the assertion of family values and gender roles was a source of strength; on the other hand, these roles held women back. At the same time that the women were struggling for change, they were fighting to recreate cultural structures of support. Consequently, working from within the parameters of the culture could be both empowering and restrictive. This complexity is also evident in the concrete collective efforts addressed later in this chapter.

Becoming part of an empowering educational process led many of the women to redefine their educational objectives. Initially, most came to the Program with very concrete and practical goals. Some could only sign their names with an X. This was a source of tremendous embarrassment and shame in a modern print-oriented world. The women spoke about the humiliation and dependence they felt at having to rely on someone else to read personal letters, for example, explaining that illiteracy robbed them of their right to privacy. They derived immense satisfaction from their newly developed ability to sign their names, fill out application forms, or read and write letters and greeting cards. Natalia Guerrero, a Central American woman, described her feelings upon receiving a letter from home:

> *Cuando yo abrí el buzón y vi que decía "Natalia Guerrero" yo entré ligerito al cuarto y la abrí y entonces a leer y a leer, verdad. Pero me daba, cómo se llama, no la podía leer en ese momento. Porque [estaba] llorando y llorando de la alegría de ver que me habían mandado y todo eso.*
>
> When I opened the mailbox and saw that it said "Natalia Guerrero" I hurried to the room and opened it and began to read and read. But I wasn't able to read it right away, because I was crying and crying with happiness to see that they had written to me and all. (Benmayor et al. 1992: 49, App. 42)

Mrs. Cossío remembered how illiteracy made it difficult for her to work in New York. She had to quit her first and only formal job after three months:

> *Lo tuve que dejar ¿sabes por qué? Por no saber caminar; por no saber leer ni escribir. Porque yo iba con 2 o 3 amigas y si ellas no iban a trabajar, yo no podía . . . porque yo no sabía caminar para allá.*
>
> Do you know why I had to quit? Because I didn't know how to travel there, because I didn't know how to read or write. I used to go with 2 or 3 friends, but if they didn't go to work, I couldn't . . . because I didn't know how to get around by myself. (Benmayor et al. 1992: 50, App. 43)

By contrast, she recalled the thrill of being able to read the letters on a bottle of seasoning that she always had in her kitchen:

> *Pues un día vengo y cojo un potecito de adobo para la carne y yo vengo y lo leo. Cuando yo leí ADOBO, esa alegría que recibí. Como que con eso . . . como que desperté, y como que uno va despertando de ese sueño. ¿Qué más yo te puedo explicar?*
>
> One day I took a bottle of meat seasoning and I read it. When I read ADOBO I felt such happiness. That experience . . . kind of woke me up, like I started waking up from a dream. What else can I tell you? (Benmayor et al. 1992: 50, App. 44)

Some of the younger women recognized the need to participate more in their children's schooling process. In her life history, Mrs. Huertas commented on the difficulty of assisting children when one lacked the necessary skills:

> *Yo les iba diciendo las letras, aunque yo no sabía si las ponían bien o no.* (Torruellas et al. 1991: 19)
>
> I would dictate the letters [to them] even though I didn't know if they were writing them down correctly.

Many women saw the Program as a chance to complete their own interrupted elementary or secondary education and get a high school equivalency diploma. Those still of working age saw it as a chance to get a different foothold on the future. Attracted to the idea of gaining computer literacy, some hoped the Program would be a ticket from a factory to an office job, or at least "*a un trabajo más limpio*" (to a cleaner job).

While education was considered a means to a better job, some women developed a new vision in this process. In a major shift in thinking, they began entertaining the notion of going to college. Mrs. Resto led the way when, after two years in the Program, she passed her high school equivalency exam and enrolled in community college. She graduated with an Associate of Arts degree and is close to finishing her elementary teacher training program. Other women began to imagine careers for themselves, in teaching, counseling, or nursing. These were traditional female occupations in Puerto Rico as well as in the United States. But, as we have stated, "Although typically female careers, these are not mere jobs, but the type of work *they* want and are learning how to define" (Torruellas et al. 1991: 58). This move represented a qualitative leap based on a newly acquired sense of self-capacity. Other studies confirm the importance of enrolling in college as a decisive step in welfare recipients' confidence in themselves and in their objective abilities to become self-sufficient (Gittell et al. 1990).

Overall, one of the fundamental achievements of the El Barrio Program was to enable its participants to experience education not simply as training for the future but also as a process of self-fulfillment and collective advancement. This was especially true for the older women, for whom schooling was no longer linked to opportunities in the job market. Some said they wanted to "*aprender a hablar bien*," to learn to discourse in the manner of educated people. This meant both being able to express their ideas more precisely and being perceived as educated. Communication and knowledge were valued as social assets because they command respect and consideration. For the women, class status was not abstract but directly related to the form of treatment one receives. As Mrs. Jovellanos said:

> *Si yo voy a hablar un lenguaje que no es adecuado, ¿qué impresión va a tener ese personaje de mí? Va a decir, "Caramba, esta señora no es educada. Esta señora parece que no ha ido a la escuela."*

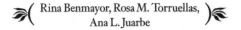

> If I am going to use inadequate language, what impression will the other person have of me? That person will say, "Gee, this woman is uneducated. It seems that she has never gone to school." (Benmayor et al. 1992: 51, App. 46)

Many who came for the purpose of learning to read and write began to contemplate the possibility of completing a high school diploma. They did not necessarily view this move as a way of entering the labor market, but as a personal accomplishment of which they and their families could be proud. Mrs. Huertas related her son's response of personal pride in his mother's accomplishment. Her achievement, however, marks more than a story of individual triumph. Its meaning lies in the impact of the individual on family and community:

> *Mi nene me dice que quiere que yo escriba el libro y tenga mi foto al frente. Entonces, cuando él se case y tenga hijos se lo enseñará.* (Torruellas et al. 1991: 21)

> My son tells me that he wants me to write my book and that it should have my picture at the front. Then, when he gets married and has children, he will show it to them.

Knowing that she was "progressing" was a tremendous source of motivation for each woman. A telling measure of the determination to *superarse*, to get ahead, was the consistent effort most of the women made to continue their education. In the six-year period, about 75 percent of the participants returned, year after year, to further their studies. Some later transferred to other literacy programs that followed more traditional pedagogical methods, but very few abandoned the effort altogether. This constancy was remarkable given the overwhelming obstacles they faced in their daily lives. Family responsibilities, housing problems, welfare appointments, and health problems often intruded on attendance rates. Their perseverance alone signaled a proactive move rather than a reactive one. Making education a priority was a step beyond resistance or strategic manipulation of the system, a move toward self-definition and affirmation on one's own terms.

As the women moved toward fulfilling their personal goals, they also articulated a clear sense of their connection to each other and to a larger Puerto Rican or other Latino community of people. In this way, individual goals became collective goals. In her life history, Mrs. Resto situated her progress toward a career in light of collective responsibility more than individual achievement:

> *Yo pienso que si yo logro esto [ser maestra] pues de una forma o* [sic] *otra yo puedo ayudar más a la comunidad porque . . . no es llegar a ser maestra, sino saber ser maestra, tú entiendes.* (Torruellas et al. 1991: 39)

> I think if I achieve this [goal of becoming a teacher], in some way or another I can help my community. [The idea] is not merely to become a teacher, but to know *how* to teach, you know?

Her motivation became not simply to get a better position in the job market but also to contribute to the community's advancement. Through their speech and their writings, the women expressed an understanding that they were participating in and contributing to a larger enterprise of building the strength and educational resources of the entire community.

As we noted elsewhere, literary critics have pointed out the particular relationship of Latin American women to community, in theory and in practice (Benmayor 1991: 169). Doris Sommer argues that in Latin American women's *testimonios* "singularity achieves its identity as an extension of the collective" (Sommer 1988: 108) This, she states, "is consistent with existing cultural assumptions about the community being the fundamental social unit. . . . When the narrator talks about herself to you, she implies both the existing relationship to other representative selves in the community and potential relationships that extend her community through the texts" (ibid.: 118). Mrs. Rolón's words corroborate this understanding directly:

> *Yo digo que éste es un programa . . . para nosotros mismos, para la raza hispana. Es un programa de nosotros . . . que necesita el apoyo de nosotros para que crezca y para que así otros, por medio de nosotros, tengan la oportunidad de hacer lo que nosotros estamos haciendo ahora y llegar a lo que sea.*

This is a program . . . for us, for the Hispanic people. It is our program. . . . It needs our support so that it can grow and so that in this way others, through our example, can have an opportunity to do what we are doing now, and to achieve any goal. (Benmayor et al. 1992: 53, App. 50)

Collective Identity and Building Community

Every member participated in building the "community" of the Program. The process ranged from reinforcing collective identities and memory, expressing mutual support, to engaging in group mobilization. In contrast to other times in their lives when they fought individually and essentially alone around gender or educational issues, the Program stimulated the women to conceptualize and make *group* claims. Participation in the Program activated collective and community frames of reference and forms of action that expressed and affirmed cultural citizenship.

RECREATING FAMILIA

Many times the women referred to the Program as their *segunda familia* (second family), a common metaphor in Puerto Rican Spanish, especially in the context of the Puerto Rican migration and presence in the United States. *Familia* described both the depth of interaction and the sense of mutual responsibility the women felt toward the Program as a whole. It also invoked the importance these women ascribed to membership in a family and a national community. Their memories of Puerto Rico were grounded in rural and small-town life where extended families were the primary networks of solidarity and support. In New York, these networks spanned blocks, barrios, boroughs, and the ocean, and neighbors often assumed the roles and affective relationships of kin.

Understood from this vantage point, the Program was not simply a school. It was a place where the women shared their lives, where they learned and celebrated together, and a place in which they felt "safe" and among peers. They brought their referent of *familia*, with its social class and gendered implications, to bear in shaping their educational environment. Being able to rely on shared familial values of mutual support, trust, and accountability stimulated a process of building community in the Program. It enabled the women to use their cultural values as positive resources in working toward common goals.

Familia expressed itself in many ways, including the various Program celebrations and festivities as well as the interactive practices of the women in the classroom setting. Program parties at Christmas time, at graduation, and for special events (Mother's Day, a baby shower, Valentine's Day) were occasions in which the women recreated the ambience and forms of interaction that characterize a family fiesta. They activated cultural resources of female cooperation. They collectively planned menus and entertainment, decorated the room, and cleaned up. Essentially, they took total charge of cultural events. Puerto Rican and Latin dance music and live entertainment, including poetry and song performances, were integral to these events. Along with their culinary skills, the women often displayed their declamatory and musical talents, giving speeches, reciting original verses, and singing favorite songs. They also organized choral singing, group skits, and other forms of group entertainment.

Like the family fiesta, which is always, in essence, a community fiesta, the Program celebrations were more than folkloric expressions of Puerto Rican or Latino "heritage." Much like summer parties at the *casitas* in New York barrios,[13] they were highly symbolic practices in which the women felt free to affirm and recreate their national culture. For example, the *bomba y plena*, a form of Puerto Rican music and dance, was a requisite, regardless of the event. One year a conflict occurred over the entertainment for a Christmas party. One of the classes had spent several weeks writing and performing a play around the war in El Salvador. When it was suggested that the play be performed at the party, opposition was voiced by all. The women affirmed, instead, their preference for a more festive *asalto navideño*, a typical Puerto

Rican version of Christmas carolling, which more clearly expressed their cultural and national identification.

At the fiestas, the women typically engaged in other gendered cultural practices. They gave presents to the teachers and staff and organized raffles in which the prizes were homemade dolls and other handicrafts. Perhaps the most elaborate ritualized event to take place at the Program was a traditional baby shower, recreated by the women down to the most minute detail as they remembered it from Puerto Rico. Many of these practices seemed surprisingly archaic to island visitors who came to these parties on occasion. "*Ya ni en Puerto Rico se da este tipo de celebración* (You don't even see this in Puerto Rico anymore!), they would exclaim. These visitors witnessed the importance the first generation of migrant women contiued to give to their cultural identity in the "foreign" context that was often experienced as cold, hostile, and disempowering. Their national identity as Puerto Ricans maintained a vitality and a cultural primacy vis-à-vis their legal United States citizenship. The Program was seen by the women not just as a school, but as a vital space in which their gendered, class, and national forms of knowledge and identity could be recreated. The Program was a catalyst through which the women themselves built their *segunda familia*, asserting collective values, forms of cooperation, cultural memory and practices.

The feeling of family that permeated the Program also derived from the fact that regardless of nationality, as Latinos the participants recognized in one another a common set of qualities and experiences. Although most of the participants in the Program were Puerto Rican, all were Latinas or Latinos who shared a common language, often rural origins, and a class position both in their home countries and in the migration. They lived through very similar realities of oppression, even if they came from different countries or were of different age cohorts. And, as Latinas, the women shared many practices and positions with regard to negotiating daily life within capitalistic and highly patriarchal social structures. The Puerto Rican women also shared a culture and dialect of Spanish, geographical references, kinship networks, a specific history of colonialism, migration, and settlement in New York, and, for the most part, a common labor history.

As described earlier, the use of *testimonio* in the classroom contributed strongly to building recognition of shared experience and to bonding as a cultural community. Testimonies enabled the women to mutually identify and to construct a collective story. For many of the women, testimony was also practiced regularly in evangelical religious worship, so the practice was not alien to them. But the autobiographical process entailed self-revelation, which at first we observed that some women were too shy or reluctant to do. The following accounts from our field notes describe the women's interaction and engagement in the classroom:

> Haydée has written a very lyrical description of the countryside where she grew up. She follows it with a tearful recollection of how she would find refuge in nature during a very lonely childhood. Leticia, sitting next to her, strokes her back gently to comfort her.
>
> The teacher asks Ana whether she wants to read the first part of her autobiography. Ana says, "*No, lo que escribí no tiene importancia*" (No, what I wrote isn't important). With the encouragement of her classmates, she reads a descriptive account of her life in the countryside. When she finishes, everybody applauds. Félix, the teacher, tells her, "*Has escrito muy bien. Todo lo que has escrito son cosas a las que hay que darle valor*" (You've written very well. All that you have written about are things that we have to learn to value). Beatriz is crying. Félix asks her if she wants to read her story. She says no.
>
> Luisa is reading her autobiography. She says, and it's obvious, that she is nervous. She reads quickly. She takes a breath. . . . After she's done reading, she talks nonstop for twenty minutes about her life. Then, she says, "*Es bueno hablar lo que uno siente*" (It's good to say what you are feeling). Félix: "*Es bueno escribirlo también*" (It's also good to write about it).

Writing, reading aloud, and collectively discussing their life stories enabled the women to understand that they were not individually at fault for the difficulties they had encountered in life. In a conversation, Eladia Rodríguez remembered how she felt when she started going to the Program:

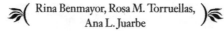

> *Yo pensaba que era la única que no sabía leer y escribir. Pero cuando vi que tantas otras muchachas sabían menos que yo y eran mucho más jóvenes que yo, cogí confianza y dije, "Yo puedo aprender." Y de allí p'alante seguí.*
>
> I thought I was the only one who didn't know how to read or write. But when I saw that so many other women knew even less than I did and they were much younger than me, I gained confidence and I said to myself, "I can learn." And I haven't stopped since. (Paraphrased conversation, March 11, 1992)

The recognition of mutual experiences strengthened the process of bonding. As Esther Martínez wrote:

> *He compartido en unión fraterna con todas las demás compañeras, y también he aprendido mucho de ellas. . . . Pues aquí me siento como en familia, aquí conversamos de nuestros problemas, de nuestras enfermedades y nos auto respetamos, o sea, esta escuela nos sirve hasta de terapia.*
>
> I have shared fraternally with all my companions, and I have learned a lot from them. . . . I feel like this is my family, we talk about our problems, our ailments, and we respect each other, in other words, this program is even therapy for us. (*Paso a paso* 1989: 59)

Recounting individual stories of childhood also reminded participants that they shared a common history of growing up in peasant and semi-rural cultures. These stories sometimes focused on fond memories of family and neighborhood networks, and of a sense of mutual responsibility. Mrs. Minerva Ríos remembered how, in her childhood, the neighbors cared for her and her siblings after school:

> *Allá no se quedaba nadie cuidando a nadie porque el vecino está allí con la puerta abierta. Vela, vela, tú sabes cómo es. Allá no es como aquí, digo en aquel tiempo. Los otros vecinos se velan por la cuestión que están las casas allí una con otra . . . de puerta con puerta, tú sabes.*

> Nobody had to be home to watch us because the neighbors were right there with their doors open. They'd keep a sharp eye on us, you know how it is! Things were different there, at least in those days. The neighbors looked out for one another since their houses were so close together . . . face to face, you know. (Benmayor et al. 1992: 59, App. 53)

In their memory, poverty, hardship, and the traumatic experiences they produced, were somehow tempered by the sense of connectedness to community and the human concerns that people demonstrated toward one another. As Mrs. Carmen Clemente wrote:

> *La persona humilde de mi patria era persona de buen corazón. Cuando ellas hacían el almuerzo, lo que se hacía era llamar a la vecina para darle un plato de comida. No le importaba que le vecina tenía también qué comer, pero eso era una costumbre que todo puertorriqueño de buen corazón y humilde tenía.* (*Nuestras vidas* 1987: 28)

> Poor people of my country were people of great heart. When they cooked a meal, they would always bring the neighbor a plate of food. It didn't matter that the neighbor already had something to eat, but this was the custom among all humble and good-hearted Puerto Ricans.

Bringing these memories into the classroom recaptured a sense of community, of relationship and belonging that the women associated with their lives in Puerto Rico. The quality of interaction and mutual support they spoke about represented an extension of *valores de familia* (family values) to neighborhood and community. They also situated women at the center of this network of relations. In writing about her concept of family, Mrs. Rosario Collazo said:

> *Por familia yo entiendo desde mis abuelos hasta mis bisnietos. . . . Cuando hay problemas en la familia, la persona que más lo sufre es la madre; por lo menos es quien más lo demuestra. Los problemas de una madre empiezan cuando tiene un mes de embarazo y terminan cuando muere ella. Aparte del problema de la crianza, la madre sufre los problemas de la escuela, la vivienda, las drogas, las gangas, las rentas, la falta de trabajo, la guerra. Y sufre los problemas hasta de los buenos vecinos.* (*¡Progresando en español!* 1991: 42)

> For me, family means from my grandparents to my great-grandchildren. . . . When the family has problems, the mother is the one who suffers the most; or at least she is the one who shows it the most. A mother's concerns start with one month of pregnancy and end when she dies. Besides childrearing, a mother has to deal with education, housing, drugs, gangs, rents, lack of jobs, war. And she has to deal with the problems of the good neighbors, too.

The context of the Program provided an opportunity to recreate those cultural and gendered values of reciprocity and to affirm a shared commitment to them in the new setting.

Familial, female strategies of *ayuda mutua*, mutual support, were reinforced through collective practices in the classroom. For example, one year a group of women expressed great anxiety over the kinds of intellectual demands that would be made on them once they graduated to the advanced level class. On the suggestion of the teacher and two of the researchers, it was agreed that a good way to approach this concern would be to do investigative research. Questions were formulated and then posed to two former classmates who had moved to the advanced level. Collective confrontation of this issue turned out to be a very effective means to overcome individual fears associated with intellectual advancement. Once in their new class, these women sat together, helped one another with in-class assignments, and gained strength and a sense of safety.

The Program became a key cultural network in the participants' lives. From the life histories, we found that generally working-class Puerto Rican women did not belong to many formal groupings or organizations. Religious congregations have been central institutions in their lives, reinforcing communal values. The majority of the women in our study were profoundly religious. Some were extremely involved in their congregations and actively participated in community service. Those who did not might have expressed dissatisfaction with the impersonal nature of their church, wishing that it would foster close relationships among parishioners.[14] However, beyond church, there were few organized and safe public centers in El Barrio where women could come together on an organized and sustained basis.

Most socializing took place while carrying out daily responsibilities such as doing the laundry, shopping, or child care. While the laundromat or the bodega were important networking spaces, the Program became another kind of arena, of which there were few. It was a safe and transformative space, where women forged friendships and collective solidarity. Unlike church, in the Program the women took charge, collectively prioritizing their cultural, social, and educational needs.

The previous examples point to the prominent role played by cultural values and memories of community in the way these women organized their interactions and affirmed cultural identity. The Program recognized these values and memories as important resources and provided a comfortable social space in which to put them to work. Extending the notion of *familia* to the Program meant activating practices of mutual support in the process of building a collective environment. Setting the parameters of action within a familiar, safe arena allowed this community of women to define their own forms of interaction. The women became invested in this new *familia* and mobilized to defend its continued existence as a culturally meaningful educational institution for the Puerto Rican community. The Program thus became a primary site of cultural citizenship.

A SITE FOR CLAIMING CULTURAL CITIZENSHIP

When we began our investigation, one of our assumptions was that the process of educational empowerment would enable participants to become more active in community mobilization around pressing problems and issues. This did not happen. The women in the Program did not become neighborhood organizers or leaders of political protest, as happened to the striking cannery workers in Watsonville described next in this volume. The women in the Program were, however, deeply engaged in another type of action. Instead of seeing the El Barrio Program as a catalyst for political activity on a mass scale, we came to realize that the Program had become the primary arena for social action. Smaller in scope, the struggle for education reflected the women's definition of their own needs, issues, and concepts of social change. This suggested that resistance, opposition, and claims to rights frequently occur within the framework of daily life activities. Thus, traditional models of mass political action did not necessarily encompass the range of oppositional sites, strategies, and practices existing in subordinated immigrant communities.

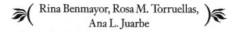

We observed several instances in which the women engaged in efforts to voice demands around issues of educational and cultural rights. As they themselves began defining their priorities and goals and the place of education in their lives, they began to confront state control. For example, early on in the Program, participants began incurring absences because of required periodic appointments at the welfare office—the "face-to-face" interview with the caseworker. During a welcoming orientation meeting in the second year, student representatives proposed that there be a limit to the number of absences allowed. They suggested that participants no longer allow the serious business of their "face-to-faces" to be scheduled on days when classes were in session. Participants began insisting that these meetings fit into their own rather than the caseworkers' schedules. Despite the fear of bringing up the issue with caseworkers, the participants confronted the problem successfully and the number of absences declined. Having done so, they then decided to tackle another problem, this time collectively. A group of participants who lived in the Bronx and traveled to and from East Harlem every day decided to become proactive about their workfare entitlement to travel and lunch monies. Although they had repeatedly made this request as individuals, these requests had been repeatedly denied. They then turned to a collective strategy of action. Motivated once more by a strong commitment to pursue their educational goals, this group of participants from the Bronx decided to go as a group to their local welfare office and demand that their stipends be honored. They were successful in getting their stipends. But more important, they became sharply aware of their power to negotiate as a group, to affirm not only their legal entitlement but their cultural rights as well. Their claims were based on their negative experiences with the public assistance system, which, as we saw in Mrs. Hernández's declaration at the beginning of this chapter, they readily attributed to being Latino and poor. Their claims were also based on the fact that this was an educational program in Spanish providing an important opportunity for poor Latinos to which they were entitled. Posed in this way, these participants were affirming rights to education as Latinos, affirming a citizenship based both on legal and cultural grounds. In other instances, participants constructed entitlement and rights on cultural grounds. Over the course of six years, from 1987 to 1991, Program participants engaged in a number of collective actions. Each expressed an affirmation of rights, entitlement, and the practice of cultural citizenship.

In 1987, a large group prepared picket signs and banners and went to City Hall to take part in a city-wide demonstration calling for Latino representation on the New York Board of Education. Although the Program staff were the prime movers in this action, those who participated recognized the value and importance of becoming visible and vocal about Latino participation in government. Two years later, during a student strike at Hunter College to protest tuition increases, the women became active supporters of students who had occupied a college building. The students formed a multi-ethnic, multi-racial, and multi-gendered coalition in which Latino students were in the leadership. Hearing that the students were spending day and night in the administration building, the women decided to send food to them. They bought ingredients and cooked large pots of rice and beans, which they then took down to the college and delivered to the strikers. While obviously expressing cultural solidarity and maternal concern, the women also understood the student struggle in class and national terms. These students could be their own children or grandchildren, for they represented the generations that these women had worked so hard to put through school. They were also the generation that embodied the collective hope for improved life chances in the Puerto Rican and Latino communities. Referring to this, Mirtha Vélez wrote:

Me acuerdo cuando mi hijo fue a Hunter College el año pasado, lo difícil que se le hizo estudiar, pues él quería ser médico y no pudo seguir estudiando por lo caro que era esa carrera. Imagínense si aumentan la cuota de los estudiantes, los pobres no podrán seguir estudiando. (*Paso a paso* 1989: 1)

I remember when my son was attending Hunter College last year, he found it very difficult to pursue his education. He wanted to study medicine but he couldn't continue because it required a lot of money. Imagine, if they raise the tuition, the poor will not be able to pursue an education.

Supporting the CUNY students was a familial, cultural, and gendered response of class and ethnic/racial solidarity.

In 1990, women registered angry protests in class about racist and sexist remarks about Puerto Rican women and welfare broadcast by a Cuban male journalist on one of the Spanish-language television channels. In his remarks, the journalist had stated:

. . . there is a serious family problem in the Puerto Rican ghettoes in the United States, where there are thousands of single mothers who are very young, who try to escape poverty through welfare or by acquiring new [male] companions who later leave [them] and leave other [new] children to aggravate the problem. With these conditions, it is impossible to correctly raise and educate children to later triumph in life. In conclusion . . . what is missing among Puerto Ricans in the ghettoes in the United States are families, and that is the problem.[15]

In their letters, the women demanded that the journalist be fired. Writing to express outrage and to demand redressive action was a new form of political action for most of the women. Letter writing was both an act of political protest and an act of literacy, coherent with their educational efforts. More important, their act was motivated by what they felt to be a direct attack on their identity, character, and social contribution as Puerto Ricans, as women, as urban poor, and as mothers. They were being accused of dysfunction in the very realm to which they were most deeply committed: that of reproducing *familia*.

Two months later, a contingent of Program participants assembled in front of City Hall with thousands of teachers, students, and staff from the public schools, adult education programs, and the university. They came out to protest cutbacks in education that threatened to eliminate public funding for adult literacy programs, including the Barrio Program. Faced with severe budget cuts and the lack of policy commitments to alternative, native-language literacy and adult education programs, the Barrio Program became almost entirely dependent on short-term grants. The women became engaged in the defense of their Program's right to exist and to grow. Protests were both spontaneous and organized.

Fearing the loss of their Program, the women immediately suggested mounting another letter-writing campaign, this time to public officials and the press. The staff then escalated this action by organizing group visits to local legislators and bringing newspaper reporters to the Program to interview the women on site. An article in a Spanish-language newspaper about the precarious status of the Program and of Spanish literacy education for adults included the following quote from the many offered by the women:

> *Este programa ha sido muy importante en mi vida. Aquí he aprendido a leer y escribir y así se me ha hecho más fácil aprender el inglés. Antes de venir a este programa yo no sabía que podía progresar. Si por culpa de los cortes este programa desaparece, sería muy triste para nosotros, porque nos quedaríamos brutos.* (Ochoa 1991: 10)
>
> This Program has been very important in my life. Here I have learned how to read and write, and that has made it easier for me to learn English. Before coming to this program, I did not know that I could get ahead. If the [budget] cuts cause this program to disappear, it will be very sad for us, because we will remain brutish [illiterate, uneducated].

Their claims were posed in terms of class, gender, and nationality. They understood the conflict as a class issue of the poor being deprived of their educational rights. The chosen title for the 1991 student yearbook, *Progresando en español porque es nuestro idioma* (Progressing in Spanish, Because It Is Our Language), was one of many examples of how educational demands and cultural rights were closely entwined. Education was an issue of cultural citizenship, of the right to have cultural rights and the right to contribute to society through cultural strength.

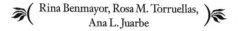

All of these group actions generated different degrees of enthusiasm and involvement. On the whole, these instances were experienced by the women as new and different processes of affirmation. Linking the CUNY student strike and the City Hall demonstration as a common struggle for public education, Carmen Ayala wrote:

> *Para mí fue una experiencia muy grande, pues yo nunca había estado en semejante cosa. Me sentí contenta y orgullosa de mí misma porque yo estaba ayudando a los estudiantes en su lucha.* (*Paso a paso* 1989: 3)

> This was an important experience for me because I had never participated in such an event. I felt happy and proud of myself because I was helping the students in their struggle.

By providing an organized social context for responding to social inequities, the El Barrio Program challenged the women to connect the very cultural space they had helped construct to larger political issues affecting Puerto Rican and all Latino communities. The attack on the Barrio Program was also an attack on *familia*, and in response the women asserted and affirmed cultural citizenship in visible and public ways.

Although these experiences introduced many of the participants to political mass action, often the organizing impetus did not come spontaneously from them. Teachers and staff frequently brought protest activities to the participants' attention and in many cases organized their involvement. This situation suggested several things: that the women did not immediately identify these problems as their own issues; that they did not regularly receive information about community mobilizations; thay they were not connected to formal political organizations; and that they felt disenfranchised and powerless, understanding that the voice of one individual was isolated and would not be heard: "*¿Qué yo voy a hacer como persona sola?*" (What can I possibly do as one person alone?). However, it is also true that women recognized the power of collective efforts in bringing about change. Equally common to their vernacular was the realization that "*Tenemos que unirnos*" (We have to unite), and they were more inclined to become actively involved once organized opportunities were created.

The very cultural values that promoted a process of collective awareness in the Program at some times were at other times a limiting factor. The women's ability to take part in mass demonstrations or other activities outside the Program depended, first and foremost, on their being able to cover home and child care obligations. Aside from the sheer logistics of managing the daily routine, "taking to the streets" was not part of the cultural practice of this particular group of women.[16] The often-used response to calls for participation in unfamiliar activities, "*Tengo que ir a cocinar*" (I have to go home and cook), not only implied the primacy of obligation to family and home responsibility. It also expressed a reluctance to venture into a larger and perhaps uncomfortable public sphere. When actions fell within an already established, everyday framework—the classroom or the home—the women more readily became organizers. When the sphere of action extended beyond the habitual context, however, participation became more difficult.

Other ideological tensions existed. The women sometimes invoked the lack of formal education as the reason they did not "get involved" in social action: "*Eso es para gente que sabe de letras*" (That is for people who are educated), a class of people to whom they did not belong. They might also rely on privatized notions of problem-solving, practices that contradicted the development of collective identities:[17]

> *Cuando uno tiene un problema, ¿cuál es el uso de que ese problema que tú tengas se lo vas a decir a to' el mundo si esa persona no te va a poder resolver tu problema?*
>
> If you have a problem, what's the point of telling the whole world about it if that person won't be able to solve your problem? (Benmayor et al. 1992: 63, App. 58)

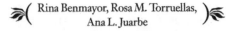

These examples suggest that the women in the El Barrio Program were not embarked on a straight path to greater social enfranchisement. Rather, their efforts were lodged in an affirmative process of *superación*, of advancement that was uneven. This struggle entailed continual negotiation between practices that reinforced self-generated solutions and those that grew out of an empowering group process with communal referents.

This discussion about building community and engaging in collective actions—that is, affirming cultural citizenship—on the part of the women in the El Barrio Program has important implications for organizing efforts. The analysis implies that it is essential to provide physical and discursive spaces through which people can engage in public dialogue and actions. These women represented a sector of the Puerto Rican community that is largely divorced from the more traditional contexts for expressing collective demands, such as the workplace. The need for spaces where the expression of collective claims can be organized becomes more urgent. The El Barrio Program provided a forum for the women's participation in activities outside their normal, daily sphere and familiar roles. These experiences expanded their frames of political reference. And yet, typical forms of mass dissent, such as pickets or demonstrations, were not by themselves sufficient to engage members of the community in direct redressive actions. We learned how essential it was that people themselves define their issues in accordance with their own analysis of needs; that in doing so, people are exercising their own sense of membership and rights, their cultural citizenship; and that these identified issues have to be addressed through culturally rooted practices.

COLLECTIVE IDENTITY AND GROUP RIGHTS

Participation in forms of mass political action contributed to building the "community" of the Program. In these mobilizations, none of the women acted alone. The group dynamic catalyzed changes in their social consciousness, which contributed to their *concientización* (conscientization). Doing so brought a vernacular sense of human and cultural rights to the fore. The very fact that the women were surrounded by others like themselves—who had similar histories, who faced the same social struggles, and who were engaged in an effort of advancement—produced notable changes. Among these, a shift in discourse around questions of rights and entitlements occurred.

In the previous section on the educational process of the Program, we noted how many women were affirming the position that, after much deferral and sacrifice, it was their turn to go to school: "*Ahora me toca a mí*" (It's my turn now). Where once education had been considered a privilege, it was now seen as a right and an opportunity to be seized. At the same time, the experience of the Program expanded the frame of reference to encompass dimensions of social responsibility. As the women began to think in collective terms, the obligations of society and government came more sharply into focus. In a conversation about the ability of the Program to survive impending budgetary cuts, Mrs. Romero and Mrs. Cossío remarked:

> *Sra. C: Tengo tristeza para el próximo año porque no sé qué va a pasar.*
>
> *Sra. R: Que no es justo, porque si el gobierno ve que la persona está adelantando, está ayudándose, es que no puede mandar a sacar a uno, porque uno lo que quiere es aprender.*
>
> Mrs. C: I'm afraid. Because I don't know what will happen next year [with the Program].
>
> Mrs. R: It's not fair. Because if the government sees that a person is moving forward, helping herself, it can't just order us to leave [the Program], because we *want* to learn. (Benmayor et al. 1992: 65, App. 59)

This type of vernacular phrasing, suggesting that these women now viewed education as their right, was common. They drew the connections between their responsibility to themselves and the responsibility of society to its members. They were fulfilling their part of the bargain with themselves, but the society (government) was not honoring its contract with its members. Some women used more explicit language, as in Mrs. González's comment:

Uno no tiene que dar su brazo a torcer. Porque para eso tenemos nuestros derechos. Y aunque tengamos que luchar pelo a pelo, siempre uno [debe] pelear y luchar por sus derechos.

You can't let yourself be swayed. That's why we have rights. And if we have to fight tooth and nail, we always should fight for our rights. (Benmayor et al. 1992: 66, App. 60)

These statements illustrate Blanca Silvestrini's argument in this volume for cultural citizenship as the expression of Latinos trying to connect with their cultural community within a framework of a larger society that excludes. Individual claims became shared claims in the context of the Program, commonly expressed through the plural subject: "*Queremos aprender*" (*We want* to learn), they would say. "*Tenemos derecho*" (*We have* the right). Collectively, they were able to make claims for cultural citizenship and articulate more strongly their awareness of the rights they had historically been denied. Their support of the striking students at CUNY and their protests over budget cuts, for example, were framed in terms of how they saw themselves, as the "poor" being deprived of their education. Their response to the television interview attacking Puerto Rican women on welfare represented an affirmation of their right to bear children and to provide for them. It also represented a collective defense of their identity as Puerto Rican women, a kind of "class action" protest to a nefarious stereotype.

The process of affirmation that was activated by an empowering educational environment provides a good example of "the right to culture" (Silvestrini herein). The new understanding of rights expressed by the women emerged from the group interaction and from the collective identities that the women forged. "*Nosotros los pobres*" (We the poor), and "*nosotros los puertorriqueños/los hispanos*" (we Puerto Ricans/Hispanics) verbalized their sense of community. The process of bonding enabled them to articulate more clearly the ways in which ethnic and economic disenfranchisement violated their collective rights. Rather than seeing their circumstances as a result of their own personal insufficiency, they started seeing their claims as related to their cultural, national, and gender identities as *puertorriqueñas*.

Identifying as a group strengthened the women's belief in themselves and in their values. As poor Puerto Rican women struggling to get ahead, they were making a claim not just to get an education but to recreate their culture. What was at stake was not only the survival of their Program. In more symbolic terms, the issue was the survival of their *familia*, of their forms of cooperation and mutual support, of their right to study in their own language, and to affirm their culture as a resource and as a right. Connecting language and education, Ana Ríos wrote:

> *Aunque nosotras estamos en los Estados Unidos, no se nos puede quitar la oportunidad de aprender y tener una educación en español, nuestra lengua natal. . . . Con el español hay contacto con nuestras raíces, cultura y nuestra identidad hispana.* (*¡Progresando en español!* 1991: iv)

> Although we are in the United States, they can't take away from us the chance to learn and get an education in Spanish, our native language. . . . Through Spanish, we touch our roots, our culture, and our Hispanic identity.

The women's practice in the El Barrio Program illustrated the importance of collective cultural values and frames of reference in their worldview. We argue that individual actions are not individual but are deeply informed by community frames of reference, and that the claim by any one individual is a claim by and for the community.

Recreating community values, forms of organization, and cooperative practices, then, represents an affirmative alternative to the individualistic terms of legal and social practice. The public institutions—housing, health, welfare, legal, educational—with which the women have had to negotiate on a regular basis do not validate collective approaches to problem solving. On the contrary, they tend to treat even highly generalized situations as particular "cases" to be attended to on an individual basis. People are required to negotiate for themselves and their immediate family problems as individuals, isolated from their cultural communities. In so doing, Silvestrini points out, people's claims are weakened, since they are estranged from their shared, communal source. Thus, people are discouraged from developing joint strategies.

We may ask, then, if they have to confront problems in the larger society on their own, what did this community of women gain from activating values of reciprocity and collaboration in their Program practices? Greater awareness of their human and legal rights to an education, to decent housing and health care, or to have children and provide for them, infuses new strength into their claims. It produces a greater ability to fight back and demand recognition of the cultural dimensions of citizenship. Mrs. Hernández's account of how she dealt with a problem at a public hospital suggested a strengthened sense of entitlement and understanding of the importance of solidarity. During a classroom discussion, she told her peers that when she approached a receptionist for help in understanding a hospitalization record, the woman responded that she was not there to serve as her interpreter. Mrs. Hernández said that she became incensed, took the record away and told the receptionist: "*Tú eres puertorriqueña como yo ¿y no puedes ayudarme? O.K., dame acá*" (You are Puerto Rican like me and you can't help me? O.K. Give that back to me). She proceeded directly to the supervisor's office and reported the incident. The receptionist had violated cultural solidarity, what Mrs. Hernández experienced as the ultimate slap in the face.

Like Mrs. Jovellanos's confrontation at the welfare office cited earlier, Mrs. Hernández's story illustrates a recognition by the participants of the collective nature of apparently individual claims. This understanding may not necessarily result in the women becoming the organizers of wider mobilization efforts. There is, however, a greater possibility that they will connect with larger movements within the community, especially if these address their most pressing concerns and honor culturally based forms of action. Undoubtedly, the power of dominant ideology to privilege "individual efforts," together with traditional cultural values defining "home" as the only sphere of female activity, and the effect of a subordinate social position on self-image, will continue to set strong barriers for women's *and* men's involvement in collective redressive actions. However, new community voices, spaces, and struggles will continue to emerge, engendering new discourses and affirmations of cultural citizenship in oppressed communities.

Citizenship as Affirmation of Cultural Rights

Language, forms of work and cooperation, norms of interaction and social behavior, gendered commitments and class practices constituted the cultural terrains through which the Puerto Rican women in the Barrio Program contested the oppressions they have experienced. More concretely, in fighting for the right to become educated in their native language, to participate in shaping the terms of that experience, and to be encouraged and supported in that endeavor, these women were making a claim for cultural citizenship. The right to participate and contribute to the social good through cultural difference, then, became the basis for challenging structural poverty and racism. The Puerto Rican case especially illustrates the contradiction that legal citizenship does not in itself confer or imply that people enjoy full and equal rights in the United States. Rather than accepting the marginal position to which they were assigned, rather than perceiving themselves as social dependents, deviants, or as an "underclass," the women of the El Barrio Program placed themselves at the center of action,[18] affirming as well as redefining their own cultural values, identity, and practices. From the perspective of their own cultural center, the women also challenged the assumption that assimilation leads to equality. First of all, they were well aware of the racial, class, and language prejudices that excluded them from entry into the mainstream. More important, from their own perspective, the move toward *superación* (advancement) was not an effort to become *americanas*. They did not contemplate the need to modify or even hyphenate their Puerto Rican identity. Mrs. González expressed a sense of pride common among the women:

> *Pues le doy gracias a Dios por haber side puertorriqueña, porque la verdad es que me siento muy muy orgullosa . . . que a esa gente que nos han señalado con esa imágen fea y bochinchosa de Puerto Rico, que fuera al revés, que dijeran "Puertorriqueño, eso es gente."*
>
> I thank God for having been born Puerto Rican, because the truth is that I feel very, very proud . . . and to those who paint an ugly and maligning image of Puerto Rico, [I would like] to hear them say instead, "Puerto Ricans, a fine people." (Benmayor et al. 1992: 73, App. 62)

For Puerto Ricans, colonial citizenship is a complex and thorny issue, the subject of intense political debate. Precisely because U.S. citizenship was an imposed legal and political status, culture has become the terrain of contestation. In Puerto Rico, the response to the English Only movement was to propose Spanish Only legislation. Repeated attempts throughout the century to mandate English as the language of instruction in public schools have failed. Historically, culture has been the site of strongest resistance and the indelible mark of nationhood. Cultural commitments become even stronger in the context of a migration that has been disenfranchising and has imposed de-facto second-class status on a colonial people. Thus, the claim to cultural citizenship is an affirmation of a historical identity, a claim for social dignity, and a challenge to the exclusionary practices upon which legal and political citizenship have so long been based.

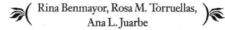

Significantly, we did not find among this group of women a discourse of national independence, colonialism, and Puerto Rican sovereignty. In fact, they had limited knowledge of contemporary political debates in Puerto Rico, including, for example, efforts to celebrate a plebiscite to define the political status of the island. Even though the women did not mobilize around the national question, they have always lived with the consequences of colonialism in their daily lives. Cultural pratices rooted in national identity were being asserted daily in the El Barrio Program in response to collective disenfranchisement. The women's discourse around their *puertorriqueñidad* (Puerto Ricanness) was eminently political. The discourse ranged from expressive language, "*¡Yo soy puertorriqueña!*" to visual symbols, such as wearing T-shirts with the Puerto Rican flag. The women spoke proudly of the ways they have transmitted their Puerto Rican heritage to their children. The entire fabric of their daily lives—from food to language, interpersonal relations, forms of recreation—embodied a Puerto Rican identity. National identity was most clearly manifested in the importance the women attached to the maintenance and usage of Spanish in the U.S. context. Their assertion of their right to receive an education in their mother tongue was an affirmation of membership in a linguistic and cultural community.

Our life histories, classroom ethnographies, and participant observations revealed how in the face of systemic power, the values and practices that the women held dear became meaningful vehicles for striking back. We heard them invoke a vernacular understanding of rights, based on cultural concepts of human entitlement: "We are poor, but we have our dignity." *Dignidad* and *respeto* (dignity and respect) were cornerstones of the women's shared cultural code.

Throughout this study, we marked instances in which the women articulated claims to rights. The ways they conceived of and expressed these claims were intimately linked to the multiplicity of identities they affirmed. The women's relationship to the state provided one of the clearest examples of how gender, class, and national identification formed the basis for their sense of rights. They expressed indignation over the discrimination they encountered in receiving welfare entitlements. This ranged from being treated poorly because they spoke Spanish, having to wait endless hours to see a caseworker, having to "plead" for the monthly check when it didn't come, to being assigned demeaning workfare assignments instead of more dignified jobs that they were qualified to hold. Faced with a constricted labor market and their inability to obtain good paying work, they nevertheless felt entitled to an income. They perceived this as a basic human right. Moreover, this sense of economic entitlement was more specifically linked to their widespread commitment to motherhood and family values, to provide for and raise their children. Thus, in their relationship with the state, the women came to assert economic, reproductive, and human rights all at once.

The frustration that the women experienced in their dealings with the state was due in part to the fact that they generally faced these conflicts alone. They were aware that the problems each of them confronted were also shared by many others in the community. In this respect, their claims had a collective class, gender, and national base. However, the state required them to make their claims as individuals, which enhanced a sense of isolation.

In many ways, the Barrio Program created a space where the women could articulate what Evelina Dagnino calls "the right to have rights" (Dagnino 1994: 75). The women came to the Program with an essential ingredient for change already firmly in hand: the recognition that they were systematically excluded from the economic and social opportunities for which they had come to the United States. The Program's particular contribution was to move the perception and the discourse forward, acknowledging the collective dimensions of their experience. Because the Program validated and strengthened their culturally derived vernacular conceptions of entitlement, the women could speak more forcefully of education as a right.

As other of our writings show (Torruellas et al. 1996), the women's educational claims sharpened their awareness of gender rights as well—of the right of women to an education, regardless of the constraints of poverty or parenting. The fact that most of the Program participants were female was a vivid reminder of the role gender played in being denied an education in the first place. The many ways the women had to assert their choice to go to school profoundly redefined the way they saw themselves.

We are hearing new voices and arenas of contestation emerging from communities that identify as "different." One of the important points that the concept of cultural citizenship makes is that affirmation of belonging to a cultural community does not in any way negate the desire and claim to be a full member of society. The women we worked with did not see a contradiction between maintaining their national identity and being U.S. citizens. They did not see their affirmation of cultural rights to be in conflict with their rights as members of U.S. society. "The term cultural citizenship reflects this dilemma. On the one hand, subordinate racial and ethnic groups such as Latinos seek cultural rights. On the other hand, they seek to be accepted as equal participants in society, as full citizens" (IUP Concept Paper No. 3, 1989).

That the mainstream is unable to recognize and validate a range of resources and positive contributions different peoples can make to the common good is a statement about its own racism and myopia. The women in the Program rightfully questioned why the opportunity to become educated in their own language was not adequately funded at the same time that the private sector, the government, and the press were giving widespread recognition to the serious future consequences of illiteracy for the country. Why was becoming educated in Spanish seen as a liability and an unnecessary expense rather than a resource to be cultivated and harnessed to the development of the Latino community?

These issues raise the larger political question of the kind of society we envision for our future. Continuing to characterize people in terms of deficits does not promise to yield any more equitable arrangement than that which prevails today. Conversely, acknowledging diversity as an asset opens the way to discovering the resources different cultural communities have to offer. Recognizing respect for difference as the basis for social unity expands the meaning of democracy and citizenship. So, like Dagnino (1991a), we can ask: "How will the 'new world order' respond to this dual sense of belonging, and to the claim to culture as a contribution and a right?"

POSTSCRIPT

Our research in the El Barrio Popular Education Program allowed us to identify strategies that empowered participants to shape their educational experience: a collective approach to learning; a culturally and socially relevant curriculum that drew on lived experience, native language, and culture; a mutual identification through shared life stories; and, importantly, an expression of cultural practices, family values, and women's forms of interaction in the educational context. We also learned that claims for cultural citizenship are not merely claims for empowering pedagogies but also for environments that privilege and value people's values and cultural frames of reference. Counseling, leadership development, and peer discussion were critical components in the process of *superación*. These women defended their own collective efforts at self-definition and the space where people could freely enter, feel as equals, and have their contributions validated. These practices set the stage for a truly participatory process. In this context people could imagine wider horizons and move toward new goals.

The women in the Program were not the only ones who were changed as a result of this experience. As researchers, we too were moved. We learned much about investigative practice in subordinated communities. We became more aware that ethnographic inquiry that sets people's views and understandings at the center is necessary in order to propose new strategies for community development. This requires a research practice that is more participatory and processual: a practice where lines between researcher and researched are crossed, where participants become researchers, and where researchers take on responsibilities of community service and become facilitators as well as advocates. In order to get at a more informed understanding, researchers need to predicate investigation on respect and mutual trust. A step beyond this would be a process where people themselves engage in analysis of their own reality as part of defining solutions that work for them.

To the extent that Latina/Latino scholars are increasingly involved in their communities, we can expect new perspectives and questions to emerge. The object of inquiry will be not only acquiring keener insights into structures of inequality, but also linking this knowledge to strategies for social change. This implies substituting neo-positivist approaches with more dialectical and engaged ways of conducting, interpreting, and using research to benefit Latino communities. From these critical perspectives, we can also expect new conceptual models for cultural analysis to be forged. Cultural citizenship is one such example. In a paper published posthumously, Rosa Torruellas wrote about socially responsible research as follows:

> In trying to understand all of the elements that enter into the configuration of a Puerto Rican identity in the United States it is important to examine not only the affirmative cultural practices that give strength, but also those negative messages that have an impact on self-worth and contribute to oppression. The construction of identity rests upon the negotiation of these two opposed referents. . . . The portrayals of people of color on television, the most powerful medium for the dissemination of ideology at the popular level, reinforce the "otherness" and "dysfunctionality" of poor minority communities: rioting in Washington Heights, looting in L.A., mass murdering of children in the Bronx. . . .
>
> I would like to end by posing three basic questions that have guided the Centro's work in the Puerto Rican community for almost two decades, and that, in a sense, pertain to all of us who aim to carry out socially responsible research: What type of research initiatives do we develop to provide truly alternative understandings of poverty and oppression? How can we use this knowledge to influence effective policy making that capitalizes on the community's resources instead of focusing on its deficits? And, finally, how do we turn our findings into self-empowerment tools that the community itself can utilize in their struggle to build a more equitable society? (Torruellas 1995: 184–85)

Increasingly, the challenges from disenfranchised communities to economic and social inequity will be expressed in cultural terms. Current deficit approaches and the piecemeal reforms that accompany them do not comprehend the new and diverse claims for rights and social participation being voiced. They fail to understand in a more profound way the broad demands that are being posed. Challenges such as those expressed by the women in the Barrio Program are not isolated instances. They are part of a growing phenomenon of social movements. Many of these responses are small, local, and relatively invisible. Sometimes they cross national borders and the north/south divide of the Rio Grande. Just as the Black Power movement in the United States has influenced the Afro-Brazilian struggle for identity, Paulo Freire's work continues to resonate in the barrios of the United States. There also seems to be a growing convergence in analysis. Our cultural citizenship formulation is echoed by new discourses about rights and citizenship in Latin America (Dagnino 1991b, 1994; Durham 1984; Jelin 1990). Dagnino writes: "The struggle for rights and for . . . the right to have rights, becomes the basis for the emergence of a new notion of citizenship. This new notion transcends the liberal framework of the original idea of citizenship, for it implies the creation of new rights. . . . It also implies the right to be different and the idea that difference shall not constitute a basis for inequality" (1991b:15).

These new, culturally constructed assertions of rights and citizenship imply expanding the concept and practice of democracy beyond liberalism. These challenges, presented by Latino and other communities, are spurred by changing demographics, by exacerbated economic marginalization, by the current English Only debates, multiculturalism, and the curriculum of inclusion.

The demands around the right to culture, equity, and citizenship challenge us to move beyond a purely pragmatic approach to social problems and to look within communities for creative joint ventures. More than that, as Benedict Anderson (1983) suggests, people are imagining communities differently, and are willing and able to put their cultural assets to work for social change. In conclusion, we can say that, regardless of their continued participation in the El Barrio Popular Education Program or of its future, the women who composed it embarked on a process of affirmation that, in the long run, matters more. In Mrs. Jovellanos's words:

> *Qué pocas oportunidades tenemos de contarle a alguien, "Esta fue mi vida, esta fui yo." Qué pocas oportunidades tenemos de decir, "Mira, si esto puede ayudar a un futuro, a la comunidad mía, úsenlo, ahí está pa'l record." El que lea estas historias va a decir, "Contra, esta gente fueron gente luchadora. Esta gente, fíjate to' lo que pasaron y siguieron adelante. Pues nosotros vamos a tomar el ejemplo, vamos a hacer lo mismo." Aunque nosotros no estemos, siempre nos van a recordar.*

What few opportunities we have to tell our story, to say, "This was my life, this is who I am." What few opportunities we have to say, "Look, if this can contribute to the future, to my community, use it, here it is, for the record." When people read these histories they will say, "These people were fighters. Look at all they had to go through and they still forged ahead. We're going to take their example and do the same." And even if we are no longer here, we will always be remembered. (Benmayor et al. 1992: 95, App. 64)

SEVEN

Mujeres en Huelga: Cultural Citizenship and Gender Empowerment in a Cannery Strike

William V. Flores

POLITICAL UPHEAVAL AND sustained mobilization can greatly transform the social and political culture of a people (Fagen 1973). This study centers on the experiences of Mexicana and Chicana[1] cannery workers in Watsonville, California, during a strike that lasted from September 1985 to March 1987. It examines how the women and their families became political subjects, and thus transformed their lives, their relationships with others, and the politics of the town.

This chapter illustrates cultural citizenship, that is, how groups form, define themselves, claim rights, and change society (IUP 1988). Cultural citizenship consists of everyday life activities that, as they are played out, create a sense of belonging to distinct social groups and set a basis for claiming rights in the larger society. Through their daily life activities these women carved out a space for social activism. Utilizing work and family networks and other cultural forms of organization, the strikers forged a strong political community that not only won their strike, but subsequently elected a Latino as mayor. Their victories, all the more remarkable given the class and racial segmentation that divide Watsonville, moved Mexicans from the margins to positions of power within the city.

Significance of the Strike

Labor struggles of Chicano and Mexican workers often have been supported by Chicano activists and have shaped both Chicano nationalist ideology and Chicana feminist ideology. For example, the United Farmworkers Union's boycott of grapes and lettuce inspired Chicano activists and corresponded with the Chicano movement's call for *tierra* (land) and self-determination (W. Flores 1987c; Acuña 1988). Leaders of the United Farmworkers, particularly César Chávez and Dolores Huerta, have served as icons for the Chicano movement.[2] Similarly, in the early 1970s, La Raza Unida Party built up networks of support, established labor committees to support the Farah strikers in El Paso, and built connections with labor and leftwing groups in Mexico (W. Flores 1973). *Salt of the Earth*, the film that portrayed women as key to the victory of Chicano mine workers in the 1950s, was recovered by the Chicano movement and shown extensively in celebrations of International Workers Day and International Women's Day in the 1970s.[3] The Farah strike and the La Tolteca tortilla workers' strike in the city of Richmond in northern California coincided with the rise of Chicana feminism. Both strikes were supported by Chicana activists and Chicana feminist organizations (see Mora and del Castillo 1980; Mora 1981; Cohen et al. 1980). Several Latinas have played important roles in labor history, including Lucy Gonzáles Parsons, who fought for the eight-hour working day in the early 1900s; Emma Tennayuca, who led a strike of pecan shellers in San Antonio in the 1930s; and Luisa Moreno, who served as vice-president of the United Cannery Agricultural Packers and Allied Workers of America (UCAPAWA) and was responsible for organizing food-processing plants throughout southern California in the early 1940s (Ruiz 1990). Documenting the labor struggles of Mexican and Latina women not only fills the gaps of a male-dominated history, but demonstrates agency and provides insight into how women organize, how they utilize networks, and how they transform their lives.

Recent work by Latina scholars has greatly contributed to our knowledge of the role that Chicanas and other Latinas have played in labor organizing and of the distinctive methods that Latinas have used to build labor and community empowerment efforts (Melville 1988; Mora and del Castillo 1980; Ruiz 1987; Ruiz and Tiano 1987; Zavella 1987, 1988). In an effort to understand how women adjust their lives to capitalism, Tilly (1978: 3) used the concept of "family strategies" to move away from "implicit acceptance of the powerlessness of people caught up in a process of large scale structural change." Several studies have found that women utilize extended family and work-based networks as "survival strategies" to respond to oppression and transform their lives (Leghorn and Parker 1981: 255–63; Zavella 1988). Networks have "provided a significant basis of support for sustained workplace resistance" (Sacks 1984: 30) and community empowerment efforts (Zavella 1988: 205).

Similarly, Caulfield (1974) has argued that in the Third World, among U.S. minorities, and in Appalachia, families, households, and communities represent "cultures of resistance."[4] Several authors provide examples of how Latino families serve as sources of cultural maintenance, production, and resistance.[5] Segura and Pierce (1993), for example, argue that *familia* (family) intertwines and overlaps with *comunidad* (community). *Familia* has been a powerful symbol in the Chicano movement as a source of unity and cultural resistance (Mirandé 1985; Muñóz 1988). However, nationalist calls for *carnalismo* and *hermandad* (brotherhood), while serving to reconstruct family through the social movement, have often attempted to reimpose images of machismo and male-dominated organizational structures. As a result, Chicanas have struggled against male chauvinism within these organizations, while also establishing their own separate organizations to "address the struggles of Chicanas as members of an ethnic minority and as women"

(A. García 1990: 428; see also Zavella 1989).[6] Still, the Chicano and Mexican extended family and household networks serve as sources of support for Chicanos during times of economic and personal hardship (Vélez-Ibáñez 1993). The family also links young and old and serves as a vehicle to remember the past, to develop collective identity through shared experience, and to consider the future (W. Flores 1993). Parents sacrifice for their children and struggle against discrimination and prejudice to make a better world for their children. Pardo (1990) suggests that the desire of Chicana mothers to create a better life for their children fuels their political and community activism.

This chapter examines how the Chicana and Mexican immigrant women of Watsonville viewed their roles in society and how those roles changed as a result of their participation in a cannery strike. Families became sites of conflict and contestation as well as resistance and proved to be powerful instruments for community and class organization. My study is based on field notes, observations, and interviews during and after the strike.

The Watsonville canning strike lasted eighteen months, from September 1985 to March 1987, and at its height involved 1,700 strikers. I first learned of the barely one-month-old strike when one of my students at Santa Clara University asked if she could write a report on the Watsonville strike as her mother was involved in it. Their home was adjacent to the cannery and picketers often rested there. We organized a food drive to assist the strikers and in October 1985 visited Watsonville. We arrived in the heat of a rank-and-file upsurge, just after the strikers had elected a Strike Committee (*Comité de Huelga*) to direct the strike.

I subsequently joined the Northern California Watsonville Strike Support Committee and made several visits to the town during the strike. Over time, I established rapport with several of the strikers and members of the community. Recognizing me as a supporter of the strike, they felt more comfortable in discussing their role in the strike, their feelings toward the union, problems that occurred in their personal lives, even conflicts that occurred within the Strike Committee. Formal interviews took place in 1988, 1989, 1991, and 1992.[7] In addition, I had worked in a dried fruit packing house and in a cannery in San Jose, California, in the early 1970s. This direct experience in cannery life and culture provided me with a better understanding of the conditions that the workers faced.

Watsonville: "Frozen Food Capital of the World"

Like most of California, the Pajaro Valley and nearby Santa Cruz were once part of Mexico. Spanish settlers established a mission system and compelled the Indian population to work on the missions and surrounding farms and ranches. In the 1850s, there were 650 inhabitants of the Santa Cruz mission, predominantly Indians and mestizos. After the U.S.-Mexican war and the Treaty of Guadalupe Hidalgo of 1848, all of California and most of today's Southwest were ceded to the United States. Anglos came to California during the Gold Rush and quickly displaced Mexicans as the majority population.

Founded in 1867, Watsonville remained mostly Anglo for the next century. In 1900 Mexicans accounted for only 118 of the 3,528 inhabitants of the town (Cruz Takash 1990: 81). In the first three decades of this century, the Pajaro Valley, Salinas, Hollister, Castroville, and San Jose to the north became centers for agricultural production. During World War II, California agribusinesses imported Mexican workers through the bracero program. After the end of the bracero program, Mexicans and Chicanos continued as the main work force in agriculture—planting, tending and harvesting crops, and working in the canneries and packing houses.

Immigrants from Mexico joined Chicanos who had lived in the area for generations. They settled in the town and raised families or brought relatives from Mexico. The canneries provided more stability than the life of migrant farmworkers. Able to live in one town rather than following the crops from town to town, the Mexicano immigrants rented or bought homes and their children attended Watsonville schools. Each year, the size of the Chicano/Mexicano population grew.[8] The town has undergone what Paule Cruz Takash (1990) and others have referred to as "Latinization." It is also part of a larger process of reterritorialization, as Chicano and Mexicano populations expand, reclaiming much of the Southwest.[9]

After World War II, demand for vegetables increased throughout the United States and fostered the growth of a frozen food industry. From 1940 to 1954, frozen food consumption in the United States grew by 650 percent. By the late 1960s, the Pajaro Valley was a major producer of strawberries, broccoli, cauliflower, cut flowers, and other fruits and vegetables. Along with nearby Salinas Valley, the area supplied nearly 80 percent of the country's fresh vegetables and was the nation's largest supplier of frozen broccoli and cauliflower (Bardacke 1988: 150). With eight frozen food plants, Watsonville became known as "the Frozen Food Capital of the World."[10]

Like agribusiness as a whole, cannery and frozen food production is dominated by a handful of industry giants—including Green Giant, Bird's Eye, Pillsbury, Campbell's, and Simplot—that control the process from planting to packing and distribution. Pillsbury, which owns Green Giant, sold nearly $6 billion in products in 1987. Mid-size companies, such as Watsonville Canning and Crocetti (both subsequently purchased by NorCal) and United Foods in Salinas, sold from $50 to $100 million, while small companies such as Del Mar and New West produced less than $10 million in products (Segal 1988a: 3).

The Chicano/Mexican cannery workers, however, have not shared in the wealth produced by the canneries.[11] Concentrated in the older sections of town, in woodframe homes and crowded apartments, Mexican families were the hardest hit by the October 1989 Loma Prieta earthquake and remained homeless for longer periods than other ethnic groups (Phillips and Hutchins 1991). In 1993, one-third of Watsonville Latinos lived in poverty exacerbated by the earthquake and recent cannery plant closures.

Since the mid 1970s, the number of jobs in the canning industry in California has steadily declined as a result of the wholesale transfer of agricultural production to other states and to Mexico. Between 1980 and 1985 canned fruit consumption in the United States dropped by nearly half. California's share of the nation's broccoli crop dropped while imports of frozen broccoli from Mexico tripled.[12]

U.S. firms often bankrolled Mexican agricultural production and canning and ship frozen and canned fruits and vegetables to the United States. For example, U.S. firms finance strawberry plants in Zamora, Mexico, where workers are often paid less than $4.00 per day; their pay is based on piece-work rather than on hourly wages (Arizpe and Aranda, 1986). In Mexico, U.S. firms on the average pay $50 less per day in wages than in the United States. In 1993 a general laborer in rural areas of Mexico earned $3.88 per day, while truck drivers earned only $5.80 per day (DePalma 1993). By contrast, in 1987 California cannery workers earned $6–7 per hour and benefits packages that boosted the amount paid by the employer to as much as $13 per hour (Schilling 1987).

Enjoying substantially lower labor costs, multinational corporations have garnered huge profits in Mexico.[13] High rates of returns on investment fueled transfer of canning operations to Mexico. In 1967, Bird's Eye, a subsidiary of General Foods, opened a frozen food plant in Mexico. Since then, several U.S. firms have moved canning operations to Mexico. U.S. firms now account for 50 percent of Mexico's broccoli and cauliflower production (Schilling 1987). Between 1980 and 1986, California lost more than 30,000 harvest-time jobs. In the early 1980s half of the state's canneries closed or moved to Mexico, which left only thirty canneries in the state by 1986 (Lindsey 1986). Most recently, in 1991, Green Giant laid off 300 workers and shipped broccoli operations from Watsonville to Mexico. Organized labor strongly feared that this trend would accelerate with the adoption of the North American Free Trade Agreement (NAFTA) (De Palma 1993).

The transfer of capital and agricultural jobs to Mexico has coincided with increasing demands for Chicano/Mexican political and social empowerment in Watsonville. As their numbers have grown, Chicanos have challenged the old power relationships, demanding that local government provide more and better social services. In the late 1960s and early 1970s, discrimination against Mexicans living in the town was commonplace. In 1969, the Watsonville Service Center found several instances of housing discrimination after sending both a Latino couple and a white couple to rent the same homes and apartments. In the most severe cases, the Latino applicants were told directly, "We don't rent to you people" (Cruz Takash 1990: 137).

That same year, Chicano and Mexican students organized a walkout and boycott of classes in Watsonville High School to protest discrimination and to demand that the school hire Chicano teachers and administrators (ibid.: 173–77). Throughout the 1970s and 1980s, Chicano and Mexican students trailed Anglo students in test scores and few were able to go to college. Through parents' organizations and groups such as the League of United Latin American Citizens (LULAC), the Mexican American Political Association (MAPA), and a variety of nonprofit agencies, Chicanos have fought to improve the schools and to increase Chicano participation in decision-making.

Perhaps most frustrating, the Chicano/Mexican population lacked representation within city government. The predominantly Mexican and Chicano sections of the town were largely ignored by the city government. Until 1985 no Chicano or Mexican had served on the city council. Between 1971 and 1985, eight Chicano candidates ran for a seat on the Watsonville City Council, but none was elected despite the fact that each received over 90 percent of the vote from Chicano precincts (W. Flores 1992a). The city had an at-large election system, in which candidates were required to be elected city-wide. This system effectively diluted Latino voter strength. In 1985, a Chicano, Tony Campos, was elected to serve on the city council. He, however, was supported by the chamber of commerce and his candidacy was widely viewed by Chicano activists as an effort to undercut a suit filed by

MAPA against at-large elections (ibid.; Cruz Takash 1990). The landmark case was not resolved until after the Watsonville strike, when the city was forced to draw districts and hold district elections, which resulted in the election of a leader of the strike support committee, Oscar Ríos, to the city council and to his subsequent election as mayor (W. Flores 1992a).

Life in the Canneries

The canneries provided an opportunity for women to enter the world of work with all of its social relationships, but women also brought their own forms of family and friendship to work (Lamphere 1985). Work-based and family-based networks overlapped and interrelated, thus reflecting an essential part of women's work culture in the canneries (Zavella 1985). According to Ruiz, cannery culture is "a curious blend of Mexican extended families and a general women's work culture, nurtured by assembly line segregation and common interests" (1990: 266). The cannery networks include men who become part of the networks through familial and ethnic bonds (ibid.). Kathleen Canning argues that workers develop distinct work identities, which she explains as "the meanings workers derived from their waged work and the ways this work was embedded in family, neighborhood, and community" (1994: 384). As Ruiz explains, "a collective identity among food processing workers emerged as a result of family ties, job segregation by gender, and working conditions" (1990: 265).

Prior to the strike, it was common for several family members to work in the canneries, although sometimes on different shifts or in different canneries. One young woman told me that she worked the second shift (swing), while her mother worked the day shift in the same plant and her brother drove a forklift in another cannery. At work the women talked with each other on the line, exchanged pictures of their children during breaks, and established close friendships that continued outside of the plant. Courtship was common. As Ruiz notes, "Cannery romances and courtships provided fertile *chisme* [gossip] which traveled from one kin or peer network to the next" (1990: 266). Often women and men developed personal relationships in the canneries and sometimes married and raised families.[14] One Mexicana in her late fifties explained, "I liked working in the plant. Each year, I could hardly wait to see friends that would come back from Mexico or people that you don't see other times. One of my friends [from the cannery] is my *comadre*. My daughter and her daughter are best friends."

For many women, cannery work provided a meaningful aspect of their lives. A Chicana who worked in the canneries for twenty-five years explained that work in the canneries gave her a brief escape from the drudgery of housework and childcare.[15] She told me, "When I'm not working, I stay home and take care of my grandchildren. I love them, but I need time to myself. When I'm working, I'm happy. I see my friends. I have my own money."

Work in the canneries did not free the women from the "double day." When they finished working at the plant, the women returned to their job at home. Even though they had a job and contributed income to the family, they still had the main responsibilities for child-rearing, cooking, laundry, and housecleaning. According to one of the women, "The men don't do anything around the house. You come home and you're so tired and they want you to get them a beer. Or they get upset because their dinner isn't ready when they get home."

Traditional Mexican family roles limited women's activism. As one woman explained, "My husband would tell me, 'You work all day and weekends. Leave the union to others who don't have kids.'" Gender stratification and the union structure also severely restricted women's participation in the union. Unlike the women whose jobs tied them to the lines, the men worked as general laborers, forklift drivers, mechanics, and machine operators, and often had more freedom of movement than the women. This stratification insured that men were more likely than women to hold year-round positions within the plant. As a result, they were more likely to hold union office and serve as shop stewards and chairs of union committees.

"La unión era cinco personas"

The International Brotherhood of Teamsters (IBT) first came into the canneries at the end of World War II at the invitation of the industry. In the 1920s and 1930s militant unions such as UCAPAWA organized cannery workers throughout the Southwest. The growers attempted to crush the unions, even deporting union activists during the 1930s. In the mid 1940s, the Teamsters worked closely with the California Processors and Growers (CPG) to shut out the more militant Food, Tobacco, Agricultural and Allied Workers (FTA-CIO). The Teamsters were brought in by the owners over the opposition of rank-and-file cannery workers in Stockton, Sacramento, Modesto, and other cities (Ruiz 1987).

Watsonville's IBT Local 912 was formed in 1952 with the assistance of Watsonville Canning's owners, the Console family, and operated for all intents and purposes as a company union (Segal 1988b). The sweetheart contracts between the CPG and the IBT bought labor peace for the industry for three decades and earned the Teamsters a steady supply of dues under the check-off system (where dues are collected directly from payroll checks). Richard King, who served as secretary-treasurer for many years, was also the father-in-law of David Shaw, a general partner of Richard Shaw Canning. King placed his wife on the payroll and established a bar down the street where he spent much of his time. King "considered union meetings a waste of time and rarely attended them" (Bardacke 1988: 165). As Gloria Betancourt, a leader of the Watsonville strike, explained, "The 'man' passed his time drinking at the bar. And that is why we didn't have faith in the union" (Ríos 1987a: 14).

Mexicans did not feel welcome in the union hall or at union meetings, which were conducted in English. It was not unil 1968 that a Mexican, Sergio López, was appointed as a business agent. For seventeen years, he was the only Spanish-speaking Teamster official in the local. López assisted Mexican workers with grievances or if a worker was short-changed on a check. Still, the union refused to fight for grievances that affected whole groups of workers. As Frank Bardacke explains, "the bosses allowed the union officials a good deal of personal power, as long as they refrained from challenging the employer's prerogatives in production or encouraging workers to organize themselves" (1988: 166).

Prior to the strike, very few women attended union meetings. The union did not provide childcare at its meetings. Moreover, the bureaucratic structure of union meetings, with its formalism and parlimentarianism, alienated most of the workers, men as well as women. But it especially stifled women. As Gloria Betancourt told me, "A lot of the men knew the rules. What to say. How to make a motion. We [the women] didn't. We just knew that they [the union officials] didn't care about us or our issues. Besides, women were uncomfortable talking in large groups, especially in English."

Rank-and-file caucuses formed in the early 1970s to challenge the Teamster leadership in the canneries. A Latino caucus, composed of workers from throughout San Jose, Stockton, Modesto, Sacramento, Hayward, and Hollister filed suit against the industry for wage discrimination based on gender and race (Zavella 1987). In 1980, the Teamsters for a Democratic Union (TDU), a national rank-and-file caucus composed mainly of white, male truckers, formed a small chapter in Watsonville. Eventually, Mexican participation in TDU increased as the group actively fought INS raids in the small town and won the right to hold bilingual union meetings in 1982.[16] Nonetheless the Watsonville TDU chapter remained overwhelmingly white and male (Bardacke 1988).

As Vicki Ruiz (1987) and Patricia Zavella (1987) have documented, the cannery industry was segmented along racial and gender lines, a process partially institutionalized and supported by the International Teamsters hierarchy. For years, dual seniority lists blocked women and Chicano/Mexicano workers from entering the higher-paid, skilled jobs. Incumbency rules permitted low-seniority workers (usually white males) to move to a higher classification skilled-labor job the following season, if they had previously worked in a skilled position. Entry to such positions was restricted to "heavy" workers, that is, men. Meanwhile, Mexican women were routinely denied such opportunities.

As Zavella (1987) argues, the seasonal nature of cannery employment combined with off-season unemployment benefits dovetailed with patriarchal family structures and discouraged women from seeking full-time employment in other industries. Thus, married women cannery workers often viewed themselves principally as homemakers who worked part of the year. The women identified not as cannery workers, but as seasonal cannery workers. In addition, the men viewed the women as part-time workers. This attitude also discouraged their union activism.

Cannery production is seasonal, requiring more workers at peak season, while maintaining a small work force during the remainder of the year. Women make up the bulk of these seasonal workers, while men make up the majority of year-round workers. Line workers, overwhelmingly female, sort the fruit or vegetables by grade, remove rotten and spoiling produce, and prepare the food for packaging. The men stack the loaded cases on pallets, move the pallets, load trucks and rail boxes, work as machine operators, and serve as mechanics and engineers. Since the companies require maintenance and replacement of equipment during the off-season, the vast majority of year-round workers are men. The union contract institutionalized this gendered division of labor with categories such as "heavy" ("men's") work and "light" ("women's") work, and institutionalized lower pay for "women's work" (Brown 1981). The companies and the union rationalized the difference in pay by arguing that women's wages represented a "supplemental" income to the family. In 1973 the Chicano-Mexican caucus filed suit against the industry and forced the industry to institute affirmative action hiring, training, and promotion a few years later (Zavella 1988).

Although classified as "light labor," the "women's work" is extremely difficult, tedious, and demanding. Women cut, sort, and prepare the fruit or vegetables for canning and packing. Having worked in the canneries, I can attest to the difficulty of the job. New hires sometimes faint from the heat or become nauseated from the constant swaying motion of the conveyor belt. New hires learn their jobs from veteran workers. On the broccoli line, women must slice the broccoli before it is packaged. As one women explained, "They pushed you so hard. Your back would hurt. Your neck would get sore. Sometimes, we'd cut ourselves." Moreover, the contract set a number of hours that must be worked before new hires earned seniority or medical benefits. Since the majority of Mexican women were seasonal workers, they often had to work several seasons before they made seniority or earned benefits (Zavella 1987).

The Teamsters Union has had a notorious record for restricting rank-and-file participation. They did so by means of complex and carefully crafted rules that limit voting through violence and intimidation. Several such practices limited participation of Mexican workers, who represented the majority of seasonal workers. For example, union elections were routinely held during the winter, when most seasonal workers were laid off and after many had returned to Mexico already. Further limiting the participation of the overwhelmingly Spanish-speaking work force, union meetings were conducted in English until 1982, when TDU and rank-and-file pressure forced the local to have the meetings translated (Bardacke 1988). To qualify for union office, members were required to have attended at least half of the union meetings in the past year and to have paid dues for twenty-four consecutive months, limiting union election to "regular" (non-seasonal) workers.[17]

Prior to the strike most of the Watsonville Canning workers were either indifferent or hostile to the Teamster Local 912 leadership. For the average Mexican worker, membership in the union was simply a requisite of job security. After a person had worked long enough, she or he was automatically made a union member—and found one more pay-check deduction, a payment for union dues. Very few Mexican women had ever attended a union meeting. Those who had were frustrated by their past experiences with the union leadership, whom they saw as closer to management than to the rank-and-file. As one worker explained, "Before the strike we never thought of ourselves as part of the union. *La unión era solamente cinco personas, los oficiales* [The union was just five people, the officers]."

In 1973 the union had 7,000 members with peak season employment in the canneries reaching 10,000. Each year that number declined as production moved to Mexico and other U.S. states. By the mid 1980s, peak season employment had declined to just under 5,000 workers. Union dues fell accordingly. Local 912 officials feared that Watsonville Canning might close.

Three years before the strike, in 1982, Mort Console, then owner of Watsonville Canning, broke with the Master Agreement between the IBT and the CPG. He unilaterally lowered wages from the industry standard of $7.75 an hour to $6.66. Arguing that the company was on the verge of bankruptcy, Console promised the workers that he would raise wages if business improved. The new agreement gave Watsonville Canning a competitive edge over other canning companies, which prompted similar reductions by other local canneries, such as Richard Shaw and J. J. Crocetti.

In the summer of 1985, Watsonville Cannery sped up the lines by 30 percent from 14 pieces of broccoli a minute to 19 pieces per minute. On-the-job accidents increased. Older workers complained that they could not keep up with the new pace. Then, twenty-five cannery workers (mainly women) were fired, some of whom had worked in the plant for more than twenty years (Corwin 1986). One of the women explained, "After all these years, they fired me. I felt so ashamed. How was I going to tell my family?"

Anticipating a possible strike, Watsonville Canning and Richard Shaw stockpiled product. In midsummer, the companies imposed further cuts with a two-tier wage of $5.05 per hour for experienced workers and $4.05 per hour for new hires or those without seniority. The plan eliminated dental benefits, reduced medical benefits, and increased co-payment requirements. On September 6, the companies cut wages again to $4.65 per hour, representing a 25–45 percent reduction depending on classification.

The new wage structure left Watsonville workers far below the rest of the industry. Since 1982, Watsonville Canning workers had lost more than $3.00 per hour in wages, while production quotas had increased. Angie Elisalde, a single mother of four with sixteen years in the plant, described her feelings: "I could barely make it getting $6.66 an hour; how am I going to survive on $4.65?" (Corwin 1986). Feeling they had no other option, 1,750 workers walked out of the two plants. On September 9, 1985, the strike began.

A Brief Chronology of the Strike

Contract negotiations began several months before the strike. According to Local 912 Secretary-Treasurer Sergio López, who was business agent at the time, "the company put forward twenty-two different offers—all rollbacks, cuts in wages, sick leave, and vacation." The workers considered a walkout in early summer 1985, but decided to wait until peak season, "when we could hit the owners the hardest." Meanwhile, Mort Console also prepared for the strike. In addition to speeding up the line to stockpile product, he obtained an $18 million line of credit from Wells Fargo Bank (Ríos 1987a).

On October 6, 1985, a Solidarity Day rally was organized by the TDU.[18] Workers and supporters marched to the factory. The police lined the streets. As one worker remembers, "We were mad. Everyone was screaming at the cops and the company. We were afraid, but our numbers made us strong." A week later, on October 15, more than four hundred workers met to elect a *Comité de Huelga.* The Strike Committee consisted of representatives from both plants and included Gloria Betancourt and Chavelo Moreno, who was later elected business agent of the local. The Strike Committee functioned as the rank-and-file leadership of the strike, and was independent of both the union and the TDU. According to Betancourt, who emerged as a leader of the struggle, "We didn't trust the union officials anymore. We felt as workers we had to form our own Strike Committee."

Watsonville Canning and Richard Shaw hit the union with an injunction limiting picketing. Several workers were arrested when they picketed on the sidewalks or blocked the entrance to the bus carrying the scabs. As Chavelo Moreno explained, "Many people were from Mexico. There, if there's a strike, people put up a red flag and no one crosses. But here the police were helping the company. People got very angry." The strikers grew angry at union officials, who told the workers to comply with the court order. As Sergio López, the union business agent at the time, recalled, "I had to explain the court order to people. They could not understand why people would cross a picket line. I told them we couldn't block the sidewalk. People said, 'How can we win if we don't?' They blamed the union."

The rift between the strikers and the union officials intensified. Feeling the anger within the local, Richard King, then secretary-treasurer, opted not to seek reelection. The strikers formed a slate made up of strikers and activists. They added Sergio López. López won the secretary-treasurer position, and some other members of the slate won office. Gloria Betancourt, however, lost her bid for president.

Five months into the strike, on February 14, 1986, workers at Richard Shaw agreed to a contract that set the wages at $5.85 per hour. This was above the $5.05 wage rate offered five months earlier, but significantly below previous wages of $7.07 per hour. Worse, the contract included language that would renegotiate wages if Watsonville Canning settled their dispute at a lower wage rate (Ríos 1987b). Chavelo Moreno recalls, "They were setting a [wage] ceiling for the industry. It made it that much harder for us [the workers of Watsonville Canning] to fight for a higher [wage] rate."

Throughout the strike, the union paid the strikers $55 weekly as strike benefits, but required that the workers still pay monthly union dues (which were twice the workers' hourly rate). At first, the Joint Council 7 of the Teamsters offered little assistance. But under pressure from the strikers and after the Central Labor Council of Santa Clara started giving assistance, the Joint Council voted a special assessment to help Local 912. As Sergio López explained, "Money was not sent, but they did send people to help us. . . . Bill Walsh formed the Food Committee, they were a great help. We got donations from San Jose and from the AFL-CIO. . . . But toward the end of the strike we ended up buying the food ourselves; it was a big cost."

In May 1986, the Joint Council took the issue of strike support to the

Teamster International Convention, which voted to undertake economic sanctions against Watsonville Canning, but stopped short of calling for a boycott of products. This further strained relations between the Strike Committee and the International. Still, the Strike Committee had to work with the union leadership and rely on the International for support. Moreno explained, "They viewed us as a bunch of radicals and saw us as a threat. We represented the opposition in the union and they didn't like that. But we had to work with them and they had to work with us."

The workers built strong support within Watsonville and surrounding communities. Two support committees formed to assist the strikers within a few weeks of the beginning of the strike.[19] The workers also received donations and support from churches, several nonprofit organizations, and Chicano groups such as LULAC. Through the Northern California Watsonville Strike Support Committee, the strikers initiated contact with a statewide organization, the Latino Agenda Coalition, and addressed a conference of the coalition held in Los Angeles. At the time, I was vice-chair of the organization and arranged a meeting with Mario Obledo, then president of LULAC, Bea Molina, president of MAPA, and Jesse Jackson, who addressed the conference. Over the next few months, the strikers received strong support from each of those groups, including donations.

On June 29, 1986, a second mass rally, organized by the Strike Committee and the Northern California Watsonville Strike Support Committee, was held in Watsonville. The rally drew supporters from throughout Northern California, including a large contingent from the United Farmworkers Union (UFW), the Teamster Joint Council, strikers from J. J. Crocetti, students, and many Chicano organizations. More than four thousand strikers and supporters attended the rally, most notably Jesse Jackson, who was a candidate for the Democratic Party nomination for president.

The Teamsters International leadership resisted the idea of having Jackson address the rally. The Strike Committee held firm and Jackson spoke, drawing national media attention to the strike. He likened the strike to Selma, Alabama, stating that, "What Selma was in 1960s for social justice,

Watsonville is in the '80s for economic justice." A month later, UFW leader César Chávez visited the strike and urged strikers to organize a boycott against Wells Fargo Bank. Chávez's presence was significant, for he was hated by the Teamster leadership. The animosity dated back to the grape and lettuce boycotts of the mid 1970s when the Teamsters signed sweetheart agreements with the owners to undercut the UFW (W. Flores 1987c). As Oscar Ríos remembers, "It was like a red flag. Chávez represented everything that the Teamsters hated." Again, the Strike Committee held firm.

In August 1986, nearly one year into the strike, Mort Console filed a petition to decertify the Teamsters. Local 912 then petitioned the National Labor Relations Board for a vote. A special election was called that permitted the scabs as well as strikers to vote. They were to vote for either "no union" or representation by Teamster Local 912.

To inflate the anti-union votes, Console hired scabs on four-hour shifts and doubled the number of workers on some lines (Ríos 1987b). Making matters worse, the vote was held in the cannery and, as Moreno explained, "people did not want to go into the company." Using networks of friends and family, the strikers wrote or phoned strikers, many of whom had returned to Mexico or taken jobs in other cities. Representatives of the International supervised the voting. Gloria Betancourt felt "they were spying on us, they didn't trust us, but they had no choice." Through the efforts of the Strike Committee, the strikers, and numerous volunteers from the Support Committee, almost a thousand workers showed up to vote. As Moreno remembers, "We surprised the company and the union. It was a great moral victory."

The failed decertification bid left Console broke. In September 1986, Watsonville Canning closed down for eleven days and reopened with a new loan of $930,000 from Wells Fargo Bank. Wells Fargo's previous $18 million credit line had required Console and his wife to deed thirteen personal properties worth $10.4 million to the bank. His debts were now in excess of $30 million (Ríos 1987b).

After the second loan, the Strike Committee urged the Teamsters to withdraw all assets from Wells Fargo banks and to encourage Teamster members to cancel bank accounts, something the union was unwilling to do. MEChA, the statewide Chicano student network, called for a boycott of Wells Fargo. In January 1987, students and the Northern California Watsonville Strike Support Committee organized rallies at eight branches of Wells Fargo, including one in the San Francisco financial district.

The strikers contacted other unions for possible support. They received donations from Hotel and Restaurants workers (HERE 2), from the Santa Clara County Labor Council, and from a variety of other unions and caucuses. They talked with workers from other industries who had been on strike. As Gloria Betancourt explained, "we learned from them, what they did, what worked and didn't." They also built alliances with the Hormel P-9 strikers and with flight attendants from TWA who were on strike. They held a joint rally march with workers from P-9 and TWA in San Jose, followed by a rally in Watsonville.

Hit by the high cost of the strike, Console closed the plant in December 1986 for one month. Two months later, he was forced to sell the plant. After bankrolling the strike for eighteen months, Wells Fargo declared Console in default and transferred ownership of the plant to NorCal Frozen Foods, a new firm headed by David Gil, a harvester from King City, south of Watsonville. Gil represented eighteen growers who were owed nearly $20 million by Watsonville Canning. On February 28, 1987, four hundred workers met to elect a negotiating committee, which included Gloria Betancourt.

On Friday, March 6, 1987, Gil made a new offer to the workers that would set wages at $5.85 per hour, the same rate that workers at Richard Shaw had accepted a year earlier. The negotiating committee and union leadership endorsed the offer. Union officials felt that the strike was over. But upon returning to Watsonville, the workers voted to wait one week to review the offer.

Several workers, including Gloria Betancourt, organized a hunger strike to hold out for medical benefits. The next morning, on March 7, David Gil gave the workers an ultimatum to return to work on Monday or lose all seniority rights and any opportunity for rehire. The strikers responded by calling on their network of support.

On Monday, March 9, more than one hundred strikers and supporters showed up in front of the plant. Led by the women, the strikers and supporters passed out leaflets to strikers, urging them to continue the strike, and confronted the cars of anyone who tried to enter the plant. They pounded on the sides of cars and yelled at anyone who dared to enter the company grounds. By the end of the day, only a few dozen workers had entered the plant. As Socorro Murillo explained, "We wanted Gil to know that when he bought the union, he bought the strike too."

The strikers continued to press Gil. Gil was anxious to settle because his spinach crop was rotting in the fields. On Tuesday, strikers held a *manda* (ritual vow) and *peregrinación* (pilgrimage). With banners and other strikers marching in procession, more than twenty women and a few men prayed and then moved slowly on their knees four blocks to the Catholic church where a special mass was held. The priest, Father Raúl Carvajal, urged workers not to return to work until medical benefits were restored. He and other community leaders called on Gil to respect the workers' demands. Finally, Gil agreed to pay up to $81.10 per month for health and welfare coverage of seasonal employees who held seniority prior to the strike (Johnson 1987: 13). At the end of the week the negotiating committee settled on a contract at $5.85 per hour with limited medical benefits. On March 11, 1987, strikers voted 543 to 21 to ratify the contract. As Gloria Betancourt felt, "It was not what we wanted, but it was still a victory. We went back into the plant united and with a stronger voice in the union. We knew we would win, if we could stay together."

The *huelguistas* did win. A few days later they held a victory rally through the streets of Watsonville, chanting, "*El Pueblo Unido Jamás Será Vencido*" ("The People United Will Never Be Defeated"). As striker Margarita Páramo recalled, "It was beautiful, we marched with a long banner and chanted '*Victoria!*' spelling it out for everyone to hear. We knew we had won, and we began to feel that we had won more than the strike. *Ganamos dignidad y un futuro bueno para nuestros hijos* [We won dignity and a good future for our children]."

Dignity, Respect, and Rights

The women's activism was fueled by their anger. They felt violated by the actions of the canning companies. Their loyalty to their company and to their jobs meant nothing. The companies cut their wages and benefits without regard to how their families would survive. As one Mexicana in her late fifties told me, "We worked all these years, gave them our lives, our loyalty, and how do they treat us? *Como perros* [like dogs]. It hurt me deep inside. It was like they were cutting out my heart. We had no choice. We had to strike, *era una cosa de nuestra dignidad* [it was a matter of our dignity]."

Issues of dignity and respect represented a recurrent theme in nearly all of our interviews. The women spoke of *falta de respeto* (lack of respect), *humillación* (humiliation) and *dignidad* (dignity). The women took pride in their jobs and worked conscientiously. As one Mexicana told me, "We are packing food that somebody's family will eat. We have to make sure that we do a good job." The companies' actions displayed contempt for the workers. Instead of acknowledging their contributions to the companies, management treated the workers like objects. In the view of many of the workers, the companies' actions reflected their racist attitudes toward Mexicans. One worker, a man in his mid-fifties, noted, "They think they could get away with this because we're Mexicans. That we have no rights. We wanted to let them know that they were wrong." One woman, who had worked for her plant for nearly thirty years, told me, "I had hoped to work here until I could retire. This company was like a second home to me. My friends are here. Now, what am I going to do? How could they treat us like this? *No somos basura para tirar. Somos seres humanos.* [We are not trash to be thrown out. We are human beings.]"

The companies had stripped them of their humanity by treating them like "dirt," "dogs," and "trash." A woman who worked at Richard Shaw Canning for fifteen years explained her reaction to the cuts: "They were saying we didn't matter. Our families didn't matter, our children, nothing mattered. Only money. That's what made us so mad." Another woman spoke of being *violada* (raped), while a male worker stated "*nos chingaron*" (they fucked us). The metaphor of rape reveals the visceral nature of their pain. The companies had abused them, using their power and the threat that everyone would lose their job to force them into submission. Patriarchical and class structures intertwine. Rape denies women the ability to have control over their own bodies and their sexuality (Leghorn and Parker 1981: 156). The owners' "rape" of them took away their self-respect, leaving them traumatized. But it also made them angry. The strike became a means to fight back.

For Socorro Murillo, the strike provided an opportunity to force the city's white elite to treat Mexicans with respect. She explained, "We didn't want to go on strike. The company forced us. We had to tell them, 'You can't do this.' The strike was our way of doing it—of telling the whole town, 'We are not dirt to be swept away. We are people just like you. We have children who go to school. We go to church. We pay taxes. Treat us with respect!'"

The strike became a means to win back *respeto* (respect) and *dignidad* (dignity). As Mary Castro points out in her analysis of labor union women in Brazil, references to dignity quickly move to discussions of rights. She explains, "'Dignity' in the labor union discourse was equivalent to 'rights' owed to the workers, because they 'deserved' them" (Castro 1994: 12). When the company sped up the lines, reduced wages, and fired workers, it stripped the workers of their dignity, thus violating their rights. By fighting back, the workers reclaimed their *dignidad* and self-respect. As Socorro Murillo explained,

> When this [the strike] began, I only thought about feeding my children and keeping my job. Now, that's not enough. Before the strike they treated us like

> animals [*como animales*]. Never again. We won respect, from the union, from the bosses, even from our husbands and families. It was hardest on them. But, they won too. We all did. But more than that, now I respect myself. I'll never let anyone treat me or my family badly again. We beat Mort Console, now we are starting to take on the schools and the city—so they will respect our children and our families.

The workers feared for their children's future. As one worker explained, "If we let them do this to us, what will our children think? We are fighting for them too. So they can have a better life." Cuca Lomelí linked the economic struggle with a broader struggle for rights and to a future legacy. She explained:

> The strike has shown us a lot of things.... It has shown me to defend my rights against the boss and to fight for what is just. That is why I keep on in the battle.... We are fighting for our rights and our jobs. We have kept fighting because we feel so much anger towards the scabs who cross the picket lines.... When you tell them [the scabs] that it's the future of the children that's at stake, that the only legacy that we will leave the children is the benefits and to win a good salary, the scabs don't understand that. (Ríos 1987a: 6–9)

The women felt they had to strike in order to defend the well-being of their families, since cutting wages and benefits would directly impact the families. Moreover, winning the strike would secure a brighter future for their children. Since the entire family was affected by the outcome of the strike, it seemed only logical to organize families to support it. In doing so, the workers constructed their own political community.

Family and Community

In the years prior to the strike, Mort Console, the owner of Watsonville Canning, and company management often referred to workers and management as "my family." He made it appear that everyone, management as well as workers, suffered together and prospered together. The concept of "family" implied mutual concern and interest. Underlying the appeal was a sense of trust and reciprocity. Workers described their jobs before the strike as "back-breaking" and "hard work." But, as one worker explained, "at least we were paid well back then." The workers expected reciprocity: if they worked hard, they should be paid well. Moreover, Console had promised the workers that he would raise wages once conditions improved, something that never occurred. While the workers sacrificed, Console stockpiled product in preparation for a strike.

Metaphors of "family" are common in companies and obscure the exploitative nature of relations between capital and labor, while inscribing a paternalistic relationship. As Bookman (1988: 164) notes, such analogies assume that the company owner, the father, "knows best." The patriarchal father tells the children what to do in the interests of the family. He makes the decisions that affect the lives of the entire family. Thus, Console treated the workers like children. He forced them to accept the decision of their "father" or suffer punishment.

The leadership of Local 912 facilitated Console's appeal that "everyone sacrifice together." As Gloria Betancourt explained, "They made us feel it was the best we could expect. That if we didn't go along [with wage reductions], Console would close the plant." Oscar Ríos commented, "the old leadership and Mort Console were practically in bed together. They let Console get away with anything he wanted."

Ironically, during the strike the workers, reversing the power of the concept, made their own allusions to family. The meaningful family became the strikers and their supporters. Cuca Lomelí recalled that during the strike many workers felt betrayed by the company and asked, "Why should I go back to work when before we were like one family working in peace?" (Ríos 1987a: 10). Similarly, Gloria Betancourt explained: "We have worked at that company as if we were one single family. We were all united. We all defended ourselves from the boss, from the supervisors, from everybody. So then they treated all of us in the same way and tried to run us out. But that's why we have remained united" (Ríos 1987a: 9).

The strike created a sharp division between the cannery workers and the owners. The workers saw themselves as a family, as brothers and sisters in struggle. Through the course of the strike they built off of family and friendship networks to establish a community of interests bound together in a common purpose. Each relied on the other and drew inspiration from the sacrifices of the other. As Gloria Betancourt, who had worked in the plant for more than twenty years, explained, "I have learned about brotherhood and sisterhood. We all look at each other as brothers and sisters in the struggle. We have tried to help one another. We have struggled together. And the strike has united us" (Ríos 1987a: 10).

A similar sentiment came from Lydia Lerma, a Chicana from Texas, who had worked in the plant for twenty-five years. The strikers, she told me, "became my sisters and my brothers. . . . They are like my family now. We rely on each other to take care of our children. We help each other out. It's a deep feeling of *confianza* [trust]. I know that if there's any kind of problem, I can count on them and they can count on me." Lerma explained that during the strike, it was hard to continue, but she drew inspiration from others to continue her work on the Food Committee. She held out because she was fighting for them as well as herself. The other strikers were part of her extended family. On occasion during the strike she felt like giving up, "but then I think about it again, and I just can't do it, because it's not just myself, but there's thousands of people who are depending on the food" (Ríos 1987a: 20).

The workers sacrificed a great deal to win the strike. Many strikers lost their homes and their cars. But they sacrificed as a family. Some strikers found jobs in nearby cities, but sent donations to the Strike Committee. Mothers took their children to picket lines and union meetings. As the strike progressed, so did the suffering. Socorro Murillo, a Mexicana who had worked in Watsonville Canning for eight years prior to the strike, lost her house as a result of it. For several months, she slept in a van and showered at different houses. Sometimes she would just wash up at the union hall. She described her pain: "It was terrible, so humiliating. I felt dirty. But, I kept my mind on the strike. We had lost everything—our homes, our cars, even husbands or children that had to go back to Mexico. But we supported each other. The whole community became *una familia* [one family], except for the scabs, of course."

Another striker, Margarita Páramo, had to choose between moving back to Mexico or sending her children back to Mexico to survive the strike. She had come to California from Guanajuato, Mexico. Her husband had left her and her children alone, so she worked for a few years and then came to the United States. She had to leave her children behind. Working in the fields and canneries, she would return to Mexico each year in the off-seasons to visit them. After seven years, she sent for the children to come live with her. She said, "I was so happy. Finally, we would all be together." Then came the strike and she decided to send them back to Mexico, except for her smallest child. She explained to me,

> It was the hardest thing I ever had to do. Sending them back. But, we didn't have a choice. *Yo no podía sostenerles con los $55, no podía pagar la renta, nos salimos de la casa . . . estuve en el carro con mi niña, allí nos dormimos como dos or tres meses* [I couldn't sustain them on $55 a week, I couldn't even pay the rent, so we left the house. I stayed in my car with my youngest, where we slept for two or three months].

During the strike, women's forms of organizing, while resisted by many of the men, proved essential to the eventual victory. Sarah Eisenstein argues that women's labor organizing grows out of their "active response both to new conditions of work and working-class life, and to the ideas that were available to them" (1983: 5; cited by Zavella 1988: 203). In Watsonville, the women made use of family and friendship networks to survive the strike and to build support. They relied on family members to build networks of financial support. As Chavelo Moreno commented, "They brought their children to the picket lines. Their sisters and cousins brought food. Pretty soon the whole family was involved."

The networks also circulated word of the strike, which built up strike support and discouraged other Watsonville Mexican residents from scabbing. Donations poured in from families scattered in the neighboring towns of Hollister, Salinas, and San Jose. During the strike as many as 70 percent of the Chicano population worked in the canneries or had at least one family member working in the industry. Oscar Ríos said: "This helped us during the strike. Families and friends gave donations, especially food. It also meant that very few people who lived in Watsonville dared to cross the picket lines. After all, you might be scabbing on your *familia* or your close friends." Making use of the close overlap between community and family proved to be an essential element of the strike's success. As Chavelo Moreno recalled,

> Nearly every Mexican family in the town had somebody who worked in Watsonville Canning or Richard Shaw or one of the other canneries. Not one of the strikers crossed the picket lines to scab, not one. The families helped too with donations or helping a worker who lost a home. It wasn't just the strikers who were on the strike, it was the Mexican community on strike. We realized that if we lost, everybody was going to suffer. So, they [the companies] had to bring in scabs from outside of the city.

Families provided a source of sustenance. But there were also conflicts. Some of the women strikers faced judgmental relatives. As Gloria Betancourt told us, "They said awful things, like, 'What kind of mother are you? You should be taking care of children, not striking!'" Criticism from family members, especially from mothers and mothers-in-law, cut the deepest. It was hard on the children, too, who had difficulty understanding why there was so little food or why they had to wear the same clothes to school. The strikers were unable to buy Christmas or birthday presents for their children. Betancourt elaborated: "We cannot buy them clothes when they need it, nor books they need for certain classes. One of my daughters was taking classes in Salinas . . . in cosmetology. But she had to leave them because I could not give her the money to take the bus every day and other expenses" (Ríos 1987a). Socorro Murillo felt that the children suffered most during the strike. She remembers the complaints of her eleven-year-old son, who tired of dried milk. She recalled, "He couldn't understand why we had to have the food from the food bank. He would say, 'Why can't we get some good milk? I hate this packaged stuff.' "

Many of the children became active members of the strike committees, helping on the picket lines or serving food. As Cuca Lomelí explained, "They got to understand why we were doing it." Through the strike, the children became aware of issues in the community that they had thought about. As a seventeen-year-old girl who joined in the strike said, "It really opened my eyes. I got a lot of respect now for my mom and my aunt. They are really fighters. It makes me glad I was a part of it. It's something I can tell my children about."

Old Ways Die Hard

The women faced a great deal of resistance from the men in their lives: their fathers, brothers, husbands, and sons. As the women took a greater role in the strike, several marriages strained under the pressure. Separation and divorce followed in some cases. Socorro Murillo recalled one case where "one of the strikers almost left his wife, because her sister was a scab." But usually if a man left it was because he could not accept his wife's activism. As Betancourt explained: "Some of the husbands, they want the women to stay home, do the cooking and all that. . . . They didn't like to do so much babysitting. Some of them, they'd lock the door on wives who were picketing. There were a lot of divorces out of this."

Chavelo Moreno said that the men had family problems too, but it was much more severe with the women. He explained, "It was different for me. A man can be involved, but it still causes problems at home. It was hard on my family. But everyone knew we had to do whatever it took to win the strike." He recognized that the women had a different problem. He explained, "In Mexico, the unions are run by men. In politics too. Women are supposed to stay home with the kids. I think a lot of the men felt that. They made it hard on their wives."

Fidelia Carrisosa, a member of the TDU who was a student activist in

Culiacán, Mexico, in the mid 1960s, had different problems. She came to the United States in 1978 with her husband, who picked fruit in the orchards while she worked nights in the canneries and took care of their two children. She explained: "Before the strike the women had to carry the burden of two jobs, at work and at home. For most of them the only thought in the cannery was giving labor to the boss for their wages. When we went out on strike it was to protect our jobs, to put food on the table. We thought it would only be a couple of weeks" (S. Turner 1987: 23).

Neither she nor her husband realized how much the strike would affect their lives together. Several months into the strike, Carrisosa's husband became angry when their three-year-old daughter jumped up in the middle of the living room and began playing *huelguista* (striker). The young girl was walking back and forth in the living room with a clenched fist chanting, "*Huelga sí! Policía no!*" Carrisosa's husband told her not to go to the meeting that night. She described what followed: "My husband says, 'You see? Is that anything to teach a child?' My husband didn't want me to go out at night. 'This strike,' I tell him, 'this is for the children too'" (S. Turner 1987: 23).

The women also faced barriers in the union. As Chavelo Moreno explained, "The union didn't care about the women for many years. But they became the leaders of the strike. That's why we won. While some of the men were complaining or drinking, the women were out on the picket lines." The union hall and even the TDU were perceived by many of the women as male domains. To the men, implicitly, it was their space. At first the women preferred to meet at the picket line or at the house of one of the strikers. As one woman explained, "We could talk there among ourselves and feel comfortable. There were no men there." Their homes became a separate space. Such "woman's space" provides women "an opportunity for developing networks, support and a sense of self-worth" (Leghorn and Parker 1981: 260). Bit by bit, however, the women claimed the union and the union hall as part of their domain.

It took a while for the men to adjust to the women's activism in the union. The women brought their children to the meetings, thus transforming the nature of those meetings. Gloria Betancourt remembers, "At first they [the men] were upset because the women brought their kids. The young ones were crying. Some of the mothers changed diapers or fed the kids on the tables. What did they expect? You have to take care of your children." Over time, the male strikers relented. They recognized that the women had to take an active role in the strike. Some of the husbands took on childcare, "but mainly it was the women and the older daughters who take care of the kids."

Chavelo Moreno was inspired by the role of the women. He felt that they had it much harder. Not all of the men agreed. He explained,

> It was hard for many of the men. You know in our culture women are expected to stay at home, not get out on the picket lines. That was hard for some of the men to take. A lot of the men are very traditional; they wanted their wives at home. I remember some of them got upset because the women brought their children to the union hall. A lot of them thought that the men should run the strike. But the women were the majority of the strikers—why shouldn't they be on the picket lines or in the union hall?

Winning the strike required that women play a leadership role in all phases of the strike, including the Strike Committee and the union. The women stressed the need for all the strikers, men and women, to work together. As Gloria Betancourt explained, "The men were not our enemies. We needed them. The children needed their fathers. The wives needed their husbands. But we were determined to win, even if it meant that some marriages broke up. It was hard, but what choice did we have?"

Eventually many of the men came around. Some who left their wives or lovers returned as the strike progressed or after it was over. Many men also actively supported their wives. Some worked in other jobs or temporarily moved to other towns where they could work and send money to their families. Lydia Lerma's husband, for example, supported her newfound activism. He gave her support, "because he wants me to continue until the strike ends." The struggle within the union was much more problematic.

"Things like that made us stronger"

The Strike Committee provided an important social space for the strikers.[20] Created by them, it operated outside of the union structure. As the daily leadership of the strike, it provided the strike's key leadership with a training ground to take on the union. For the women, the Strike Committee provided a space to develop and test their leadership skills. But they had not originally viewed it in that fashion. In fact, at first, they weren't exactly sure what a Strike Committee was or how it was supposed to function. As Gloria Betancourt recalled, "We sort of made things up as we went along. We spent a lot of time talking to each other. We asked people on the picket lines for their suggestions. But we had to make the decisions."

Gloria Betancourt and Chavelo Moreno had been elected to the Strike Committee at the mass meeting in October 1985. Betancourt recalled: "Some workers questioned the meeting. They said, 'We have a union, let them run the strike. We pay them enough.' I said, 'No. We are on strike. We are the union. We must tell them what we want, to win the strike! And, if they don't listen then we get rid of them.'" Chavelo Moreno explained that being elected to the Strike Committee was exciting, but also intimidating. It meant that he was respected by the rest of the strikers, that they trusted him, Betancourt, and the others to lead the strike. He explained, "I didn't know what it meant. None of us did. But they [the other strikers] had faith in us, so we couldn't let them down. It was our meeting, not the union's. We decided who was going to lead the strike. From that day we began to think of the union as ours and of taking it back."

One month into the strike, the workers formed a slate to run for union office. Gloria Betancourt ran for president of the local, while Sergio López, the lone Chicano in the union leadership, ran for secretary-treasurer. López won, Betancourt did not. Joe Fahey, a white union activist, was also elected. Both Betancourt and Chavelo Moreno felt that the *planilla* (slate) represented a victory and a turning-point in the union. As Moreno explained,

> We weren't prepared. We set up the *planilla* (slate) in a hurry. Besides, we hadn't been involved in the union that long or even in the plant. It was all right though because we got rid of the old ones, like Richard King [former secretary-treasurer], who decided not to run again. We won something. They had to respond to our criticisms. They had never had to do that. All the Mexican workers were involved and they had to listen. So, bit by bit we took over the union.

Betancourt was not deterred by her defeat. Several women had urged her to run. She recalled, "They felt since the women were leading the strike, why couldn't we lead the union? So, I did." Although the workers had had conflicts with López, they felt they could work with him. Moreover, it was the first time a Chicano had ever been elected to the top post of the local. As Betancourt explained, "It meant a lot for us to have one of our own as head of the union. We began to feel like now the union belonged to us too."

Still, the election vividly underscored tensions between the men and the women. In an interview, one male striker who had worked in the plant for more than fifteen years explained why he would not vote for Betancourt:

> If they [the women] win, we'll have to build a beauty salon in the union hall so they can get their hair done. And forget the union meetings, they'll all be brushing their hair and gossiping. Look at Gloria's hair, all dyed. *Como si fuera una rubia* [Like she's a blonde]. What makes them think they can run the union anyway? Sure, they've done a lot, but run the union? No, we need someone with experience.

Betancourt was one of the most visible leaders of the strike. Her example inspired other women. As one Mexicana who had worked ten years in the plant told me, "I know Gloria. She has the same problems that I do. She's got to take care of her kids. But she's there every day, and I know she's making sacrifices for us. I feel bad when I don't show up to the picket line."

A year after the strike, Betancourt made an unsuccessful bid for union trustee. The experience left her bitter and burned out. She withdrew from activism within the union, although she remained active within the plant. One of her co-workers told me, "She had done so much, she feels it's somebody else's turn now." Her defeat underscores the difficulty women face in union elections. It also reflects persistent attitudes about male and female roles. One woman who voted for Betancourt explained, "A lot of the people, including many women, voted for someone else because they think men should be in charge of the union." A man who worked at NorCal explained, "Gloria did a good job during the strike. But being a union official you have to deal with the union leadership. They're all men. It's better for a man to do it. They'll listen to another man."

Underlying her defeat was the notion that union leadership remained a male domain for many workers. The defeat reinscribed a social division of labor, with women working behind the scenes, while men retained the seats of power. The justifications for the vote revealed individuals' efforts to externalize the problem, rather than taking responsibility for their actions. Thus, those who voted for Betancourt's opponent, a man, did so not because Betancourt was incapable, but because other men, the union officials, would not listen to a woman. This transparent rationale masked their own refusal to accept a woman in a position of union authority. As Cuca Lomelí told me, "For a lot of people, it's o.k. for a woman to lead a strike, just not o.k. to lead a union." Still, Betancourt's example sparked the activism of many other women and her bid for union leadership encourages other women to consider running for union office. As Cuca Lomelí explained, "I think the women have learned to develop themselves politically. Right now there are no women representatives in the union. Perhaps in the future there will be. . . . My hope is that in future there will be a woman as a union official representing us" [Ríos 1987a: 21].

Gloria Betancourt's own transformation came in steps. By the end of the strike, she felt comfortable speaking in front of large audiences. She recalls, "I was always afraid of speaking in front of people. Others helped me with my speeches. Finally, it was o.k. Women need to see other women up there on the platform. They need to know that they can do it too." Cuca Lomelí agreed. For her, "the most important experience is learning how to speak in front of different types of people" (Ríos 1987a: 10).

William V. Flores

Becoming Political Subjects

In the course of the strike women emerged as political subjects, in what Cornel West terms a process of "new self-perception, in which persons no longer view themselves as objects of history, but rather as subjects of history, willing to put their own selves and bodies to reconstruct a new nation" (1993: 134).

The strike and the meetings that the workers held in the Strike Committee provided an opportunity for the women to transform their lives. Several of the strikers were arrested repeatedly in their attempts to confront the scabs. Women as well as men threw rocks at the scabs. Betancourt was arrested four times, once for throwing a rock at a van, although she claims that *that* time she was innocent. But other times she did throw rocks at scabs: "The *esquiroles* [scabs] would throw pennies at us, wave their paychecks at us. . . . Sure we threw rocks, wouldn't you? They threw rocks too, and ball bearings. . . . My trouble was I could never hit what I aimed for" (S. Turner 1987: 30).

Another striker who was transformed by the strike was Margarita Páramo. Prior to the strike she had not been involved with the union. But on the first day of the strike she grabbed a sign and joined the picket line. She was afraid of violence, especially from the police. She explained, "I was afraid I would be arrested. Then, who would take care of my daughter?" But as the strike wore on, Páramo became determined to stop the scabs. In an effort to discover its starting point, she and two other women followed the bus. A car followed them and sped up as they approached a narrow bridge. She explained, "We were afraid that the other car was going to try to push us off the bridge. The car just missed us. Then the sheriff came. You can imagine how surprised they were when they found out the car was filled with women."

On another occasion, the police arrested Chavelo Moreno, one of the leaders of the Strike Committee. One striker began throwing rocks at the police and fled into the crowd. Margarita Páramo remembers the day vividly:

> We blocked the way so the police couldn't catch him, because we knew that they would throw him down to the ground and beat him. . . . Later, I saw another cop in a police car with someone he had arrested. And I grabbed my one-year-old daughter [*y llevaba a mi niña en mis brazos*] and stood in the center of the road to block the police car and I told him, "Go ahead and run me over, but I won't let you pass." The cop hit the siren to get me to move, but I stood my ground. When the other strikers saw that I wasn't going to move, they joined me and made a line in front of the cop car. So the police had to turn around and take another route. . . . We headed off to the police station and started chanting to let Chavelo and the others go. We stayed there screaming all night!

In retrospect, Páramo's actions surprised her. She said, "I don't know where I got the courage to stand in front of a car. I just had to do it. The strike did that to people." Páramo felt that she grew during the strike, everyone did, especially the women. The men were more visible at the beginning, especially when it came time to confront the scabs. Several of the men were arrested for throwing rocks or hitting scabs. But as the strike dragged on, they drifted away, sometimes drinking or playing cards at the union hall. Páramo recalled, "We women were there every day. At first the men didn't respect us, but they learned we were serious. We were strong, the majority of us, single mothers. We were doing what we had to do, for our children. That's what gave us strength. That's why we won."

Prior to the strike, Socorro Murillo had not thought of herself as part of the union. But the strike changed that. She began to feel that the union was them, the strikers. She recalled,

> I never went to a union meeting, until just before the strike, when the meetings were being held. When the strike started and I was at the picket lines all the time. I began going to the picket lines every day. On one day we followed a bus of scabs to Salinas. Fifty strikers went and we prevented the bus from leaving. Finally, the bus driver he got out and he ran away. We all started screaming, "*Viva la Huelga!*" It was a great feeling. Things like that made us stronger. We knew we could win, if we could just stay together. That's when I realized that we are the Union *y la unión hace la fuerza* [and there is strength in unity].

These various examples illustrate how women emerged as political subjects. The strike changed their lives. It forced them to take on new roles and develop new voices. It also affected their consciousness.

Cultural Citizenship, Agency, and Empowerment

Documenting the strike was important. Labor victories during the Reagan era were rare. The Watsonville strike coincided with the better-known Hormel strike and the TWA flight attendants strike, both of which received national publicity. Yet the workers at Hormel and TWA lost their strikes, while the less heralded workers in Watsonville won. Moreover, the Watsonville strike was predominantly led by Mexican women. As such, it became a symbol for the struggle of Chicanos and Chicanas for political empowerment and self-determination.

The strike demonstrates the centrality of class, race, and gender for understanding empowerment. These categories create identities that sometimes conflict and collide in the complexities of life. The women sorted out their multiple identities through the course of the strike, wherever possible building unities based on common interests and experiences. Thus, they built support among family members and the community. But to do so also required conflict over existing social roles, particularly gender roles. Their identity shifted as they acquired new roles. The women began to see themselves as active subjects in society, as agents of social change within all aspects of their lives.

Often social scientists refer to the "intersection" of race, class, and gender, as if they momentarily come together and only at one point. The analogy fails to describe the reality of identities that emerge from the simultaneity of race, class, and gender oppression. As Zavella explains, "Women of color experience gender, class, and racial statuses concurrently, and a feminist analysis of labor organizing should focus on the totality of women's experience" (1988: 202). Mary García Castro (1992) terms the interaction of race, class, and gender as a process of "alchemy" that shapes the social construction of political subjects. For the women workers of Watsonville Canning, the strike was the catalyst for such an "alchemy." It transformed them into political subjects, making them not only aware of their social existence, but also determined to change that existence.

The strike cannot be described solely in class terms, as a battle between cannery workers and owners. Nor was it mainly a battle of Latinos against whites, although it clearly underscored the racial segmentation of the city. In fact, much of the support the strikers received came from white labor union activists. Nor should the strike be characterized as a conflict of women against men. Instead, the strike encompassed aspects of each of these broader societal divisions simultaneously. The strikers had to carefully select their battles, keeping in mind the need to build alliances in order to win the strike. The women were not just strikers, but Mexican women strikers who were conscious of their oppression as women, as Mexicans, and as workers. They had to make use of each of these identities to win the strike.

The same was true of their relationship with the union. The old leadership of the Teamsters Union Local served the rule of capital, like the classic aristocracy of labor. The workers paid dues to the International, but had little to show for it. Union officials, after all, had negotiated contracts that lost the workers 30 percent of their wages. The strikers sought to transform the local. Bit by bit the workers claimed the union first by forming the Strike Committee and subsequently by electing some of the strikers to union office. They had good reason to mistrust old-guard union officials, but they needed the support of the Teamsters, particularly the Joint Council and the International.

It was often a difficult tightrope to walk. During a Solidarity Day rally, the strike leaders chanted "*Viva Los Teamsters!*" despite disagreements with the International. As one worker remembered, "It turned my stomach. But we needed their help." Some activists in TDU disagreed with the strategy and criticized the Strike Committee for working closely with the "sellout" union officials (Bardacke 1988). But as Moreno explained, "The strategy paid off. We won the strike and won a say in the union."

In the course of the strike, the workers became increasingly aware that they were battling bigger foes than Mort Console, the plant's owner. They learned of Wells Fargo Bank's $18 million loan to Console and saw the connections to foreclosures on their homes and cars. Oscar Ríos explained,

> It was not just a fight against one company. The banks and other canneries wanted Console to win, to drive down wages in the industry. There hadn't been a strike for thirty years; they wanted desperately to defeat the workers. To use them as an example. They wanted Console to drive down the wages. But it [the strike] proved just the opposite, that workers can win if they are united and have strong support."

The workers did not develop class consciousness—the idea that as workers they are part of a class exploited and oppressed by the capitalist system. Yet the strike made them anti-capitalist, at least in some sense.[21] They spoke of how the banks, ranchers, and large companies control Watsonville and the entire country. They were angry at certain capitalists or specific corporations, such as Mort Console, Green Giant, and Wells Fargo. But they did not view capitalism as the source of their oppression. Their consciousness reflected militant trade unionism, a desire to strengthen their power as workers and to unite with other workers. Thus they identified with and gave support to other striking workers. As Gloria Betancourt said of the Hormel workers, "They're just like us. The company only cares about profits, not the workers or their families. We have to stick together. That's the problem. Workers have stopped supporting each other and the companies can do whatever they want. And the unions have let them. That's why we must get back control of the unions, to work for the workers, not the companies."

The strikers also became aware of a broader movement of women for equal rights. Participation in the strike transformed the lives of the women strikers, who emerged as rank-and-file leaders. Traditional gender roles stood in the way of the strike. But patriarchy is deeply rooted in the society and is not overturned by one event, even a strike. Many of the men would not accept activism from their wives, even while saying they supported the strike. Several divorced or separated from their wives.

Moreover, the women did not develop a "feminist consciousness" that cuts across race or class. Rather, they adopted a working-class feminism that sought to build solidarity with other women whose lives were similar to their own.[22] In fact, most of the women that I interviewed did not consider themselves "feminists." They saw "*feministas*" as middle-class white women who wanted to "be the same as men" or who wanted abortions, something several of the Mexican women opposed. As Luttrell argues, these "perceptions are not to be seen as a rejection of feminism. Rather they reflect concrete class conditions and pressures that shape women's consciousness" (1988: 150).

In fact, the women I interviewed strongly supported women's rights. For example, assisted by the Strike Support Committee, the strikers organized a Women's Day event in March 1987. They sought and received support from the Coalition of Labor Union Women (CLUW). They felt a special affinity toward the struggles of other Latinas, especially of other workers, such as garment workers in Mexico or the Chicana Levi Strauss workers in San Antonio, Texas (whom they met after the Watsonville strike).

Ironically, though the women were the backbone of the strike, men gained most visibly. Sergio López was elected secretary-treasurer and Chavelo Moreno was elected business agent, while Gloria Betancourt was defeated twice in her bid for union leadership. Oscar Ríos was elected to the city council and subsequently as mayor, while another activist, Cruz Gómez, who served as plaintiff in the suit against the city's at-large election system, lost in her bid for city council.[23]

Still, the overwhelming feeling of the women I spoke with was that they had gained from the union elections and had greater representation as a result. In fact, Oscar Ríos attributed his victory to the women who were the backbone of his campaign: "I won because of them. Many of them couldn't even vote, because they are not citizens, but they were there every day working to get me elected."

Similarly, several women felt that the Ríos victory was a victory for cannery workers. Lydia Lerma explained,

> Oscar was always there for us during the strike. He was one of us. When the earthquake hit and the city was doing nothing, Oscar organized people to help the victims. We marched up to city hall and they almost arrested us. But he got aid for the victims. When he won, every Latino in the city won. Now the [city council] meetings are translated. When we have problems, there is someone we can go to. That's what winning the strike meant for us. We all won.

The strikers also developed a national consciousness, becoming aware of the Chicano national movement, although distinguishing themselves from Chicanos. Groups like MAPA, LULAC, MEChA, the Latino Agenda Coalition and others supported the strike. Before the strike, many of the Mexicanos thought of Chicanos as "*pochos*" who couldn't speak Spanish or who were ashamed to be thought of as Mexican. As Margarita Páramo told me, "I am Mexicana, *cien por ciento* [one hundred percent], but my kids are Chicanos. They can barely speak Spanish. But the [Chicano] students supported us. Now, I think we are part of the Chicano movement too, because what we want, they want too—a better place to live, better schools for our children, and being treated with respect."

Similarly, the strike changed how Latinos were viewed in the city. They became active citizens in the city as well. The strike became a symbol of the lack of power and equality that Chicanos and Mexicanos face in Watsonville and in the many small agricultural towns throughout California. Watsonville Canning represented the power of the entire Anglo structure, Wells Fargo, which gave the company a loan to help it survive the strike, the Anglo city council and courts that provided police and injunctions to weaken the strike, and the frustrations of racial tensions in the city. The battle against the company became a symbol to Chicanos throughout California of their own struggle for dignity, respect, and empowerment. Since many Chicanos have roots in the fields and the canneries, the strikers were able to appeal to this special bond and successfully drew support from Chicano community groups throughout California.

Cultural Citizenship and Affirmation

The Watsonville strike demonstrates how cultural citizenship involves agency and affirmation, reflecting the active role of the oppressed in claiming what is their own, of defending it, and of drawing sustenance and strength from that defense. In this instance, the strikers claimed an ever-broadening social sphere that reached into their families, the plant, their union, and the city.

The strike in Watsonville changed the entire community. It dramatically transformed how the workers perceived themselves, what they were capable of, and how they viewed society and their role in it. They became subjects responsible for changing the institutions that affected their lives. They affirmed themselves as human beings deserving of respect and demanded that they be treated as such.

Women who went to church every Sunday and who would chastise their children for using profanity were suddenly confronting police, throwing rocks at scabs, and challenging the union leadership over control of the strike. As a consequence of the strike, the strikers, women and men alike, became active in the union. They claimed the union and forced its leadership to actively fight management as their representatives. For the first time, the workers began to view the union and union hall as "theirs" rather than as something apart from and alien to them. They gained confidence in their abilities and began to expand their sense of what they could accomplish. As they did, their claim to space and what was theirs expanded as well.

Most striking to me was the manner in which the workers gained a sense of ownership in the union and the plant. This was vividly demonstrated in October 1987. At the time, the NorCal plant (formerly Watsonville Canning) was scheduled to package produce belonging to a second company, United Foods of Salinas, that was engaged in a strike. The produce would bear the United Foods label. By coincidence I was in Watsonville at the time and was interviewing Chavelo Moreno and Oscar Ríos. Workers from

United Foods arrived and met with union officials. Moreno and Ríos took me with them into the plant right past the supervisor and the guard. They told workers to shut off the machines and held a series of meetings inside the company lunchroom. Gloria Betancourt urged the workers to vote in favor of a motion to refuse to run the product:

> Remember how it was when we were on strike? We wouldn't have won if we hadn't received support from other cannery workers. They were there for us. Now, they need our support. We had to hold out for so long. Remember what it meant to our families, to our children? We got help from other workers. We can't turn our backs on them now that they need our help.

In a nearly unanimous vote, the workers voted to refuse to run the product from United Foods. This was no small sacrifice for workers who had been on strike for nearly nineteen months. They understood that running the product could mean an additional three months of work. They made it clear to management that they were willing to walk out if necessary. Moreover, meetings called by the workers and held in the plant were unheard of prior to the strike. The workers had claimed the cafeteria as their own space. In their eyes, the plant was as much theirs as it was David Gil's. As one worker explained, "we were here long before he was." The incident also demonstrates how the workers now felt empowered to negotiate over issues that were not covered by their contract and were generally seen as the sole realm of management, that is, what produce would be run and under what label.

An important aspect of cultural citizenship is defining your community and its interests. The strike did that. It delineated sharply the community and its boundaries, those who supported the strike and those who didn't. The scabs were treated as low-life scum. The workers called them "*pinches traidores de su gente y vendidos*" (traitors of their people and sell-outs). When the strikers saw strike-breakers shopping on the street, they would spit at them or cross the street to walk on the other side.

The strikers also claimed the church. At first, the church hierarchy did not support the strike. The cannery owners and large landowners were patrons of the church. One priest who supported the strike was transferred to another parish. But the strikers attended mass, asking for and receiving donations. As the strike wore on, the priests prayed for an end to the strike and urged parish members to lend support. In the last days of the strike, the parish priest openly supported the strikers and when David Gil bought the plant, supported the strikers' hunger strike and *manda* (ritual vow).

Language also evolved during the strike. Words used in everyday language took on special meaning in the context of this community. Thus, workers used the term *destino* in reference to the strike. They tied the outcome of the strike to their "future" as a people and to their "destiny." I often heard the phrase, "*Nuestro destino está en nuestras manos*" (Our destiny is in our own hands). It is common in Mexico and Latin America for strikers to have *lemas* or political slogans associated with their struggle or its aims. This phrase was such a *lema*. Inherent in their use of the term *destino* was the notion that it was *their* destino, one that was in *their* hands and of *their* making, to win the strike, not only for themselves but for future generations. They were also constructing a collective identity with shared interests that went beyond the wage and benefit issues of the strike. The slogans underscored these common bonds and common goals.

Interestingly, when strikers marched through the streets of Watsonville during their rallies and demonstrations, they often raised their clenched fists, challenging the owners to view their determination. They chanted "*Este puño, sí se ve!*" (You will see our fists!), a common political slogan in Mexico and Latin America. Simple words like *puño* took on the meaning of defiance in the face of the company, scabs, police, and court injunctions, while simultaneously signifying the determination of the strikers and community to win the strike, again reflecting that the outcome of the strike was in "*sus propias manos*" (in their own hands). During the Second Solidarity Day Rally, Jesse Jackson stated, "Workers who picked the vegetables will one day pick the President." Borrowing from Jackson, the workers referred to "picking" one of their own for union leadership and as mayor.

They had toiled with their bodies and their backs; now they were reaping the crops.

Cultural citizenship is a process by which excluded groups claim their rights. Over time, they become public citizens of the society, enter the public sphere, make demands on society, and change that society in the process. The workers of Watsonville, particularly the women, clearly transformed themselves and their social world, at least for the duration of the strike. The longterm victories remain less certain, particularly given the flight of the cannery industry to Mexico and other countries. Class, gender, and racial hierarchies remain in Watsonville as they remain in the country as a whole. Nonetheless, the victory of the Watsonville women is a powerful example of how people's lives can change and how victories can be won.

Cultural citizenship represents a broad continuum. It is not one response, but many responses and will vary from community to community. It reflects the various behaviors that result in the affirmation of a people. It may take on the grand scale of combat, as it did in Watsonville, or it may take on the subtle form of cultural resistance, reflected in the nuances of cultural performance and oral traditions. As researchers we must study the many forms and varieties that cultural citizenship takes.

In Spanish we use the term *ánimo* to describe that sense of inspiration that gets people tapping their feet and swaying to the infectious rhythms of salsa, cumbia, and rancheras or that evokes a *grito* (shout). At times, it gets them to organize and fight for their rights. The Watsonville strike filled the Mexican and Chicano workers with *ánimo*. It is the spirit of a people rising.

EPILOGUE

Citizens vs. Citizenry: Undocumented Immigrants and Latino Cultural Citizenship

William V. Flores

IN THE UNITED STATES, discourse on citizenship is too often limited to concepts of "legal" status and formal membership in the nation-state. This country's anti-immigrant hysteria deflects our attention from a simple reality: being a citizen guarantees neither full membership in society nor equal rights. To be a full citizen one must be welcome and accepted as a full member of the society with all of its rights. Unfortunately, full citizenship rights have systematically been denied to Latinos and to other nonwhite racial groups in the United States. In fact, even when Latinos are U.S.-born citizens, they have been treated as second-class or third-class citizens.

This epilogue explores the concept of citizenship from the perspective of citizens as social actors, struggling not only to gain full membership in society, but also to reshape it. I apply here the concept of cultural citizenship (Rosaldo and W. Flores 1987; Rosaldo and W. Flores 1993; W. Flores and Benmayor herein) as a vehicle to better understand community formation and the processes by which rights are claimed by subjugated groups. I also present a case study of Chicano efforts to support claims of undocumented Mexicanos. The case illustrates how Latinos forge community, claim space, and claim rights—all of which are essential elements of cultural citizenship. It also demonstrates how Latino efforts to support immigrants have created space for the political participation of undocumented and legally resident immigrants.

Rights, Citizenship, and Membership

Race, language, and culture are markers of difference that, in this country, have been used as a basis to deny equal rights. It is not uncommon for nonwhites to be mistreated by police or to fear a judicial system that routinely administers harsher sentences to Latinos or African Americans. The brutal beating of Rodney King, an African American, a few years ago and the April 1996 videotaped beatings of undocumented Latino immigrants in Riverside, California, graphically underscore the reality of everyday life, where African Americans and Latinos remain the Other, still denied equality and basic rights. For Latinos and other nonwhites, becoming full citizens is tied to the struggle to obtain rights and to change society.

Latinos have found that the racial, cultural, and linguistic differences that bind them as a group also mark them as different from the dominant society. As Stuart Hall explains, racism constructs "impassable symbolic boundaries [and] . . . constantly marks and attempts to fix and naturalize the difference between belongingness and Otherness" (Hall 1988: 28; cited in Giroux 1994: 37). Alterity appears fixed and permanent. Thus, as Paul Gilroy argues (1987: 61), in the United Kingdom being English and being black are categories that are "mutually impermeable." You can be one or the other, but not both. Sadly, the same holds true in this country, with nonwhite and "American"[1] being equally impermeable.

My own experience growing up in this country is hardly unique. I am third generation. My parents were born in the United States, as was I. But in my elementary school teachers often referred to the white kids as the "Americans" versus the "Mexicans" or "Chinese." The point was not lost on me. I was "Mexican" even though I was born in the United States, had never been to any part of Mexico other than Baja, and spoke very little Spanish.

Homi Bhabha (1993: 49–50) refers to such hybridity as "doubling," as if we are both. Certainly, as Latinos, we have access to two worlds, especially those of us who speak and can read Spanish. We can explore and fully appreciate the richness of Latin American culture. But our hybridity is more complex—we are both and we are neither. Not fully accepted or welcome in either world, the hybridity forces us to claim our own space. The hyphen between Mexican and "American" becomes a space, sometimes of denial, and other times of affirmation. It is a border that both separates and links two worlds and we, with a foot on both sides, are both trapped and liberated, defined by others, yet free to define ourselves.[2]

Theories of citizenship often link membership and rights, with one often defining the other. T. H. Marshall (1950), for example, argues that citizenship is essentially an amalgam of three categories of rights: civic, political, and social. Taken together this ensemble of rights constitutes social membership. But, as Bryan Turner points out, "the Marshall tradition is unsatisfactory because citizenship is an arbitrary or contingent set of rights" (1993: 498). Turner argues that the incorporation of new citizens into the polity may temporarily stabilize the social system, but it can also produce further areas of frustration as these rights are curtailed or unevenly distributed.[3] He explains, "As citizenship institutionalizes social expectations which cannot be satisfied by the state under all circumstances, citizenship entitlements fuel political dissent" (1991: 217).

For nonwhites the link between membership and rights is a critical but vexing one, particularly since both rights and membership are restricted. Kenneth Karst in *Belonging to America* (1991) argues that minorities achieve membership in U.S. society not by assimilation, but through the struggle to claim rights as citizens. Patricia Williams similarly contends, in *The Alchemy of Race and Rights* (1991), that for African Americans the litmus test of being full citizens is obtaining the same rights enjoyed by white Americans. Claiming such rights is, according to Williams, the "marker of citizenship."

In fact, the struggle for full citizenship is not limited to claiming the rights already enjoyed by whites. By struggling to open the doors to society, excluded groups emerge as "new citizens" (Hall and Held 1990). They not only demand existing rights, but create new ones, altering society in the process. Hall and Held refer to "new citizens" as entrants from new social movements, including ecology, peace, and civil rights. Similarly, in this country, the "new citizens" of the social movements of the 1960s and 1970s were not new in terms of length in society. Rather, they were new political subjects, actors who challenged existing power and social relationships while claiming "new rights."

Thus, African Americans fought to desegregate schools, an effort spurred less by a desire to live among whites and more by the strong sense that predominantly minority schools were, as they are now, not separate and equal, but separate and quite unequal—with less space, older buildings, less equipment, less prestige, less money, and more dropouts, drugs, violence, and despair. African Americans fought against poll taxes and at-large elections to ensure the right to vote, something that had been granted under the Fourteenth Amendment, but restricted and denied by Jim Crow laws. The struggles of African Americans and battles won as a result of their struggles opened the doors to the participation of many Americans, especially other minority groups.

But gains were not limited to nonwhites. The new social movements demanded that society be more inclusive. Women, particularly white women, obtained new opportunities for education and employment under affirmative action laws, while also fighting for recognition of gender equality, laws to prohibit sexual harassment, and the right to control their own bodies. The physically challenged demanded and obtained protection under the law to make public and private facilities accessible. Gays won rights to job protection and, more recently, to some city-sanctioned registered domestic partnerships. Each of these groups gained from a door shoved open by the civil rights movements led by minorities, especially by African Americans.

Moreover, their struggles for "new rights" signaled their emergence as social actors and as "new citizens."

Latinos too fought to desegregate schools. As early as 1930, the League of United Latin American Citizens (LULAC) fought "Mexican" schools in Texas (Gómez-Quiñones 1994: 369). A year later, in 1931, Chicano parents in Lemon Grove, California, fought placing their children in a "barnyard" school, rejecting claims by the school district that such segregation was necessary to more effectively "Americanize" them (Alvarez 1987: 153). Similar struggles were waged by Chicanos in San Jose in the 1970s, while in some cities, such as Denver, Chicanos established alternative schools to teach Chicano history, pride, and identity.

Latinos also fought to obtain new rights, particularly language and cultural rights. Along with Chinese and Native Americans, Latinos fought for and won bilingual education. Through court actions, Latinos won the right to speak Spanish on the job and in schools and gained the rights of undocumented immigrants to attend public schools (rights that are currently under attack by both the courts and the Republican-controlled U.S. Congress). The right to vote, bilingual ballots, and the extension of voting rights to the undocumented have been central components of Latino struggles for political empowerment, reflecting the sense that the undocumented are "members" of Latino communities and should have the rights of any other such members. In New York in the 1980s, for example, Dominicans fought for and won the right for parents, whether U.S. citizens or not, to vote for community school board seats, which resulted in the election of a Dominican, Guillermo Linares, to the school board. Since then, other cities and school districts have extended limited voting rights to noncitizens (Sontag 1992).

The battle to extend the right to vote to undocumented immigrants takes on a different light if the issue is seen not from the restrictive context of formal citizenship, the usual determinant of voting eligibility, but rather from other vantage points. For New York Latinos, the issue was not whether the undocumented should have the right to vote, but rather whether all parents, citizens or not, should have the right to have a determination in the governing bodies of their local schools. Moreover, undocumented workers pay taxes without representation. Their taxes contribute to school construction, as does ADA (average daily attendance) money earned by the schools from their children's attendance. Should they as parents not then have the right to vote? In fighting to extend voting rights, Latinos extended both parents' rights and the rights of the undocumented.

Voting rights debates were thus reframed not in terms of formal membership, but actual contributions. Involving the undocumented in local schools, Latinos deposed the limited concept of citizenship as a restrictive category and replaced it with the much more inclusive notion of "citizens" as public actors and as "subjects" of public action. Winning the right to vote in local community school board elections opens the door for great participation in society. Parents who take interest in their school matters are more likely to participate in other local elections and civic issues.

For Latinos generally, and particularly for Chicanos, the protection of the rights of the undocumented is inexorably linked to the rights of all Latinos. After all, during the repatriations of the 1930s, when at least 400,000 Mexicans were sent to Mexico, many U.S.-born citizens of Mexican descent were also deported (Hoffman 1979). Scapegoating and political rhetoric have created an atmosphere of open hostility toward Latino immigrants. California's Proposition 187, to deny basic services to undocumented immigrants, was overwhelmingly supported by whites and even by some Latinos. Politicians from both major parties clamored to "close the border" and to deny public assistance, public education, and health care benefits to the undocumented. California Governor Pete Wilson, just prior to his failed bid for the Republican nomination for President, went further, calling for a constitutional amendment to deny citizenship to U.S.-born children of undocumented parents (Rohter 1993).

Not all Latinos support immigrant rights. Latinos are extremely heterogeneous in their backgrounds and politics.[4] Many working-class Latinos, especially Chicanos living along the border, support restrictions on Mexican immigration, based on real-life competition for jobs and wages. Indeed, a 1992 national political survey of Latinos found that 65 percent of all Latinos and 74 percent of all whites surveyed believed that there were currently too many immigrants coming to the United States. A majority of Puerto Ricans, Mexican Americans, and whites believed that U.S. citizens should be hired over noncitizens (de la Garza 1992: 102).

While the issue of undocumented immigrants sometimes divides Latinos, for the most part Chicano and Latino organizations have defended immigrant rights and opposed denial of rights to the undocumented. Chicanos and other Latinos realize that the border crosses them as well. Each stricture against the undocumented diminishes the rights of all Latinos, because as a group Latinos are targeted. Border patrol officers make few distinctions between Latinos who are born here and those who are not. We are all suspect. This realization fuels the creation of a Latino consciousness. It coincides with a strong desire to create a distinct Latino social space and to claim rights as Latinos. Later, we will examine how Chicanos in one community fought for the rights of the undocumented, shaping their conception in the process.

Cultural Citizenship: Claiming Space and Rights

Developing a sense of belonging to society is a key attribute of active citizenship. Those who feel excluded are less likely to participate in the political arena. Several recent studies of U.S. society discuss the notion of "belonging in America." Robert Bellah (1996) in *Habits of the Heart* and Constance Perin (1988) in *Belonging in America*, for example, portray a social world rooted in the experiences of middle-class whites. Such a world contrasts sharply with daily life in most barrios in the United States. Indeed, the study in chapter 3 of the Latino social world in San Jose, California, reveals a distinct Latino perspective of U.S. society, one replete with stories of racial discrimination—stories which use distinct Latino terms such as *falta de re-*

speto (lack of respect), *humillación* (humiliation), and the desire for *dignidad* (dignity) to describe their treatment by white Americans and their desire for a better world for their children. Thus, the Latino conception of "America" is one that might make whites uncomfortable, for it is far less equitable and less caring than the world described by Bellah or Perin.

Several of us working together have termed the process by which Latinos form community and claim rights as cultural citizenship (Rosaldo and W. Flores 1987; Rosaldo and W. Flores 1993; Flores and Benmayor herein). Cultural citizenship can be thought of as a broad range of activities of everyday life through which Latinos and other groups claim space in society, define their communities, and claim rights. It involves the right to retain difference, while also attaining membership in society. It also involves self-definition, affirmation, and empowerment.

When Latinos claim space they do so not for the purpose of being different, but rather simply to create a place where they can feel a sense of belonging, comfortable, and at home. Typically, claimed space is not perceived by Latinos as a place of difference, although it is often perceived as "foreign" or "exotic" to outsiders. Rather, Latinos develop what we have termed "sacred places" (Rosaldo and Flores herein) that acquire a distinct Latino quality of life, a Latino flavor, *un ambiente Latino*. Claiming such space is a "natural" process that occurs as a group interacts, creates networks, and lives out its daily existence. It is also an essential element of cultural citizenship.

Clearly, Latinos must have a physical space to call their own, whether rented or owned. Struggles to control neighborhood land use and to have public places to hold cultural events are critical parts of how communities bind themselves, define their boundaries, and make their existence known to others. Parks and recreation centers are closed or underfunded, longtime barrios are carved out for freeways or redevelopment, and social halls and nightclubs are cited by police and fire patrols for code violations or heavily patrolled and their patrons arrested for loitering or disturbing the peace. Efforts to maintain such spaces require community organization and political participation.

Community formation and claiming physical space in this country take place in the context of a capitalist society and the dictates of the capitalist market as well as routinized and uncaring political bureaucracies. In essence, there is a tension between the needs of community, use-value, if you will, and the needs of accumulation, exchange-value. As John Mollenkopf notes, "each operates by a distinct, unequal and ultimately opposing logic" (1981: 320). Similarly, Manuel Castells argues that city dwellers must reconstruct a sense of local community (1983: xviii). This is especially true for Latinos, who are often forced to organize on a neighborhood or city-wide basis to retain sacred space and for cultural identity, group survival, and representation.

But space cannot be thought of simply as location, as important as that remains. Rather, as Mark Gottdiener (1985) argues, space includes place and geographic locale but also includes opportunities for creative expression, self-representation, and engagement. Thus, Latinos must have space for the expression of their culture, to be themselves and to develop their own identity as a group. This requires both physical and creative space. Both are contested and restricted by the dominant society.

Claiming space in both senses is a key component of cultural citizenship. Cultural citizenship includes how groups form, define themselves, define their membership, claim rights, and develop a vision of the type of society that they want to live in. It includes how excluded groups interpret their histories, define themselves, forge their own symbols and political rhetoric, and claim rights. It includes how groups retain past cultural forms while creating completely new ones. In the case of Latinos, cultural citizenship involves syncretism of native cultures and lifestyles, those from Latin America and the new experiences of living in this country, such as folkloric dance and Los Pastores, Chicano and Nuyorican art and poetry, salsa, Latin jazz, and Latino rap, as well as political formations to acquire political representation and group empowerment. Thus, cultural citizenship for Latinos involves the creation of a distinct Latino sensibility, a social and political discourse, and a Latino aesthetic, all of which flow out of the unique reality of being Latino in the United States and the desire to express that uniqueness.

Latinos must have a space to think, to create, and to act in a way that reflects their sense of being. Without the ability to express themselves, excluded groups have no ability to "belong," except on someone else's terms, i.e., from the perspective of the dominant culture. The daily life practices, taken together, carve out space that is distinctly "Latino" and an evolving consciousness of being "Latino." The social practices may or may not be oppositional, but they can become oppositional if they are opposed, restricted, resisted, or prohibited by the larger society. Part of this process is the creation of self-representations. Insofar as they contest the dominant culture's view of the world and its political order these self-representations can be seen as counter-hegemonic.

Chicanos and Mexicanos have attempted to overcome these divisions. Based on field research conducted in San Jose, California, I will next explore the emergence of counter-narrative as a component element to community formation and the enunciation of rights.

Claiming Community, Claiming Rights

Three cases from my fieldwork and from twenty-five years of activism in San Jose, California, illustrate the defense of cultural space, rights, self-representation, and the formation of counter-hegemonic social movements. These examples represent concrete efforts to build community between Chicanos and undocumented Mexicanos and to expand and defend the rights of the undocumented. They also demonstrate cultural citizenship as Chicanos and Mexicanos joined together to defend community interests, define for themselves community membership, establish symbols, and claim rights.

The three cases take place in a predominantly Mexican immigrant neighborhood in west central San Jose, California. The barrio, often called "Little Michoacán" (because of the large number of immigrants from that Mexican state), is over 80 percent Mexican. Most of the barrio's residents are Spanish-speaking and many are undocumented. Little Michoacán is one of the poorest neighborhoods in Santa Clara County. In 1990, 21 percent of barrio residents lived at or below the official government poverty level and median family income was only $20,807, while per-capita income was just $6,779. To survive residents share cars and apartments, and help one another locate jobs and avoid detection by the Immigration and Naturalization Service (INS). As high-tech and defense industry displaced agriculture and work in the canneries, Mexican immigrants have been concentrated in the low-paying service sector—in restaurants and hotels, as maids, janitors, and day-laborers.

The barrio and the adjacent downtown area have been frequent targets of INS raids. On several occasions, Chicanos and Mexicanos in San Jose have rallied to defend the rights of undocumented immigrants. These various cases illustrate cultural citizenship through: the claiming of space; the development of a distinct Chicano perspective to unify Chicanos and Mexicanos; and the emergence of Mexican undocumented and legally resident immigrants as political subjects, "new citizens" demanding "new rights."

The first example illustrates how the struggle over rights helped Chicanos and Mexicanos to define their community and its members. In August 1973 a small clinic (referred to here as La Clínica) that serves the barrio received a County Revenue Sharing Grant to provide health care to medically indigent patients in its service area. The county required contracting agencies to determine the residency status of non-citizens and to count "illegal" aliens. Fearing that this would be the first step toward denying services to the undocumented, the clinic staff refused. A broad-based community struggle resulted as Chicano clinic staff and community activists held meetings at La Clínica and at the nearby church hall to map out strategy.

La Clínica and the nearby church grounds represented what Evans and Boyte term "free space"—that is, "environments in which people are able to learn a new self-respect, a deeper and more assertive group identity, public skills, and values of cooperation and civic virtue" (1986: 17). The church and La Clínica provided physical space for community organization and for sanctuary for the undocumented, a space where they could discuss their problems, seek out assistance, and together plan community action.

The lay leaders of the parish Catholic church,[5] many of whom were Mexican immigrants themselves, believed strongly in the philosophy that "Health Care is a Right, Not a Privilege." In fact, this slogan appeared in La Clínica's brochure and its statement of philosophy. The health center was first established as a free clinic with the intent of providing service to the parish poor, particularly to the large immigrant population. It had been built by community volunteers, who raised the money and donated their labor. In their minds, they had more right to say who would be served than did the county. According to Mauricio Ramírez, one of the founders of La Clínica, "We built this clinic, painted it, got it furnished, and got doctors to donate equipment, not the county. We felt we had the right to decide who we would serve, not them." In his opinion, "Sure, a lot of them [the patients] didn't have papers, so what? If a child has a fever, are we supposed to turn him away? No. We felt we should treat that child and we weren't going to ask the parents to show us their I.D."

The issue of membership and rights laced all discussions. On the one hand, the clinic founders felt strongly that health care is a right. The high cost of health care, hospitals, and private physicians and the lack of health care insurance made health care inaccessible for many barrio residents. Founding La Clínica was a self-determined act. The community identified a problem and through their own efforts found a solution. They had thus created a space which was their own to be used to benefit community members. In their view, their labor and their efforts had also earned them the right to decide who would and who would not be served by the clinic. And they were not about to relinquish that power to the county.

Moreover, the county's demand to review documents and to count the undocumented reminded many people of the 1930s repatriation of Mexicans, including U.S.-born citizens, and the roundups and deportation raids of "Operation Wetback" in the 1950s. Lucio Bernabé, a Cannery Workers Committee (CWC) founder, who has since passed away, told me: "It made me sick. I got so angry. I thought, 'Not again. Not again!'" He recalled:

> They [whites] forget we [Mexicans] built this city. . . . In the 1930s, there were thousands of us that marched for jobs and unemployment benefits. They deported a lot of people who were labor leaders just for being Mexican. They didn't care. We were just all seen as the same, as Mexicans. In the union we had a saying, "*Un daño contra uno es un daño contra todos*" [An injury to one is an injury to all]. We can't let them divide us. We must defend each other. Just because someone doesn't have papers, doesn't mean that they don't have rights.

Stories like Bernabé's are part of the collective memory (Halbwachs 1992) that serves group formation and cohesion. They forge collectivity by explaining common history, experiences, and trajectories. Tales of past battles won and lost articulate a collective identity.[6] The past provides powerful symbols and myths that give meaning to the present and visions for the future. Our interpretations of the present are often framed by past experiences and collective memory (Lipsitz 1990). The present helps us to interpret the past, which in turn shapes our understanding of the present and the future. The experiences of immigration and discrimination provide a common bond for many Latinos and frame their understanding of this country and their treatment in it.

By defending the undocumented, the Chicano activists asserted their right to determine who is and who is not part of their community. The community was not limited to U.S. citizens, but included the documented and undocumented alike. Ernestina García, then president of La Confederación de la Raza Unida, feels that Chicanos and Mexicanos are really *una familia* (one family). In her opinion, the city and county officials in those days were "mostly racist." She explained, "To them we were all simply 'Mexicans'— maybe behind our backs they even called us 'wetbacks.' We felt we had to protect them [the undocumented]. That's what being Chicano is all about, protecting your own, protecting your community. And they [the undocumented] are part of our community. They are our *hermanos y hermanas* [brothers and sisters]."

By defending the undocumented, Chicanos and other Latinos claim rights for themselves and erode borders between citizen and noncitizen, between documented and undocumented. Community is self-defined and includes, rather than excludes, the undocumented. The "we" in the stories depicts an inclusive collectivity that must be protected, in counter-discourse—an injury to one becomes an injury to all. The stories frame collective identity and then provide a reason for collective action. They are, of course, at odds with other stories, which include real conflicts and reflect real differences that exist between Chicanos and Mexicanos and between the documented and undocumented—of language, culture, and competition for jobs. Even so, the common story of discrimination and oppression provides a powerful and unifying narrative that can be called upon by Chicano activists and that played an important part in the Chicano ideology of the times.[7]

References to the undocumented as *familia* and as *hermanos y hermanas* reflect the reality that many Latinos who are U.S. citizens have family members who are not. Many Latinos who are now legal residents or even citizens entered the country without papers or have close relatives who did. Thus, the plight of the undocumented is appreciated by Chicanos and has often been lived out by them. *Familia* acts as a metaphor for community. Family members, after all, are to helped. Similarly, the "they" in the stories are those who would divide Chicanos and Mexicanos, denying common bonds of *familia*. Thus, the stories draw clear boundaries between who is and who is not part of the community. Community is self-defined, not imposed by governmental officials.

The stories of past deportations, of the repatriations of the 1930s, and of Operation Wetback told by Bernabé and others provide Chicanos with a counter-narrative. They form a collective memory that engages the present and fuels the struggle for rights and social change. Stories of the past, popular culture, narrative, life histories, and cultural practices contest master narratives and create counter-narratives. The Other emerges as subject, in part, through such contestation.[8]

Chicanos have not only heard the stories many times; they have also lived them: witnessing deportation raids, being called "wetback," getting caught in INS raids, finding themselves as citizens yet nonetheless running out of fear of apprehension and possible injury for being confused with the Other as stranger. They realize that merely being Latino puts them at risk of abuse by the INS.

A second example illustrates cultural citizenship as expressed through performance, and how performance can serve to member and stimulate the claiming of rights. In 1979 community activists working in La Clínica observed school-age Mexican children in yards or playgrounds during school hours. They learned that the children could not register for school without proof of immunization. Yet, parents feared that the county nurses might discover their undocumented status, which could result in the deportation of the entire family. The Chicano activists organized special immunization days at La Clínica and formed an ad hoc committee, the Comité pro Derechos de Los Niños Indocumentados (Committee for the Rights of Undocumented Children).

Many undocumented parents feared what would happen to their children, if they, the parents, were deported. It was common to hear stories of children left alone because their parents were picked up at work or at the bus station. Such children were called *dejados*, those left behind. The Comité organized networks of support to alert families if INS officers were seen in the area and to provide temporary foster homes for children in case parents were arrested and deported.

As in the earlier example, here community activists rallied in support of the undocumented. In this case, parents and children transformed fear of deportation and *dejo* (abandonment) into networks of support. Parents were also informed of the rights of their children and their rights to grieve treatment of their children by school officials. Again, La Clínica and the church served as a "free space" where parents, children, extended family, neighbors, and activists could meet and plan joint action free from fear of arrest or deportation. The experience provided strength for more public collective action.

Together with Mexican undocumented parents and children, community activists wrote a play to present the issues to the community. The Comité held performances after the church mass, in parks, and at a local school. The skit, or *acto*, educated parents on the right of their children to attend school and also their rights as immigrants. Along with the *acto*, two community members sang a *corrido* (ballad) they wrote about immigrant rights.

These cultural forms of expression allowed children and parents to discover new strengths. Performance, according to Victor Turner (1986), serves to "re-member." It re-enacts and reconstitutes community (R. Flores herein). Thus, the undocumented, used to concealing their identities and their status, found sufficient strength to take center stage in an *acto* about their conditions. The skit revealed the complexities of the broader social drama it exemplified—the fear of deportation, anxieties of separation from loved ones, anger at the power of the INS, and the public message that collective action yields the strength to confront the INS. The *acto* provided a space for social inversion, similar to Bakhtin's carnival that "uncrowns power" by its mocking laughter (Lipsitz 1990: 16).

Unlike a carnival, the purpose of the *acto* is to activate, to stimulate what Paulo Freire terms "*concientización*," the process of acquiring critical consciousness and of becoming political subjects. Freire explains that only as the oppressed "grasp the themes [of their oppression] can they intervene in reality instead of remaining mere onlookers" (1973: 4). Through discussions about what issues to present in the play, the parents and children grasped the "themes" of their oppression and became subjects to oppose it. The creation of political subjects is itself a process of social practice. "*Conscientization*

[sic]" is, according to Cornel West, a "new self-perception, in which persons no longer view themselves as objects of history, but rather as subjects of history, willing to put forward their own selves and bodies to reconstruct a new nation" (1993: 134).

In performing the *acto* the activists further elaborated community. They drew the audience into the sketch, by calling on them to join in the singing, and collectively chanting about their rights. By hissing and laughing at the INS, the audience practiced and prepared for real-life confrontations. Their ridicule "uncrowned" the INS, and, by association, the state apparatus of which it is a part. By witnessing and cheering victories on stage, the audience, Mexicans and Chicanos alike, shared common experience. The *acto* allowed them to symbolically practice collective resistance and to prepare for victories in real life. It broke down boundaries between the documented and undocumented, script and spoken words, performer and performed, subject and object, as the undocumented themselves became subjects, agents of change to transform their conditions and the conditions of their children. On several occasions, audience members, many of whom were undocumented, later joined community rallies against deportations. Thus, the *acto* prepared them for later public action. Self-defined representation, then, becomes a vehicle for oppositional action. As Henry Giroux argues,

> Representation . . . gives way to opposition and the struggles over questions of identity, place, and values. Difference in this context brings out the possibility of not only bringing the voices and politics of the "Other" to the centers of power, but also understanding how the center is implicated in the margins. (1991: 26–27)

Through inverting and subverting power in the *acto*, the community related its own story. The children and their parents became collective "heroes," examples to be emulated. By contrast, *La Migra* (INS) and the school officials and police who cooperated with them to turn in parents were booed as villains, who ripped children from their parents' arms. The *acto* served as a broad re-telling of the story of the undocumented, a counter-narrative to evoke collective action.

The third example represented an open attack on immigrants. Again Chicano community groups rallied to their defense. In May 1982, President Ronald Reagan instituted his infamous "Operation Jobs" to arrest undocumented workers holding supposedly well-paying jobs to free up those jobs for U.S. citizens. Latinos represented more than 80 percent of those apprehended, the vast majority of whom were Mexican. Within a few weeks of the raids, most of the U.S. workers had left the jobs because they refused to do the back-breaking, dangerous, and undesirable jobs left vacant by the deportations.

Raza Sí, formed by Chicano activists in 1980, built broad community support against the raids. Several La Clínica staff, including myself, cofounded the group. Both affirmation and negation, the name Raza Sí emerged from Chicano resistive culture, from a call-and-response chant popular at immigration rights rallies: "*Raza Sí! Migra No!*" The concept of "*la migra,*" a vernacular term for the INS and Border Patrol, although unspoken, lay beneath the surface, challenged by the more powerful affirmation of "*Raza Sí.*"[9]

At a meeting organized by La Clínica, the board, staff, and community members voted unanimously to refuse admittance to INS agents. Again, La Clínica became a sanctuary. Raza Sí held a community meeting at the church school to inform residents of their rights. A loose community alert network gathered information on the whereabouts of immigrants and alerted community members, a form, if you will, of the community's own "Border Patrol."

Meanwhile, a city-wide coalition formed, including Raza Sí, La Clínica, the Asian Law Alliance, the Central Labor Council, church groups, community agencies, and student groups. The coalition demanded that city officials order all city employees not to cooperate with INS officials. Blanca

Alvarado, who at the time was the only Chicano on the city council, sported a button at the press conference that read "Illegal Alien," to mock the INS and identify with its victims. In the next few days, church leaders and leaders of community agencies wore similar buttons. Raza Sí printed up its own "green cards" with the words "Raza Sí Member," and distributed hundreds of these throughout San Jose. Councilwoman Alvarado told me, "I was really upset by what Reagan was doing, blaming the undocumented. Wearing the button was our way of fighting back, saying 'Just try to take us!' "

The coalition won an important victory. The city council ordered the police and city employees not to cooperate with the INS raids. Raza Sí and the city-wide coalition joined with statewide and national groups to condemn the raids and to counter Reagan's ideology that the undocumented "steal" jobs. Through these coalitions, Raza Sí joined in national debates around various proposed pieces of immigration legislation that eventually were adopted in 1986 as the Immigration Reform Control Act.[10]

The language of protest produces a powerful counter-discourse. The Chicano activists reversed the symbols of the INS, subverted their meaning, and appropriated their power. The INS, long feared as a source of terror that routinely conducts raids in the canneries and other factories, became, instead, an object of derision. The community alert network, its "border patrol," reversed roles. Thus, the objects of searches, Mexicans and Chicanos, became the subjects conducting their own searches. No longer passive onlookers forced to hide, the undocumented became political subjects acting upon and changing power relationships. Similarly, the community "border patrol" claimed free space. The "borders" of the barrio, protected through collective action, became a sanctuary of safety and political organization. Rejecting false divisions between those born on one side of an arbitrary line and those born on the other, the barrio demarcated its own imagined community forged through mutual interest and action. The church and La Clínica became sanctuaries where the INS were unwelcome.

The community-produced "green cards," while worthless in the eyes of the INS, became sources of power and identity within the community. Chicanos, Mexican legal residents, and undocumented residents all bore the bright "green cards" pinned to their shirts, blouses, and jackets. The "green cards" became markers of membership in a community formed by collective action. Through mass distribution of its cards, Raza Sí undermined and symbolically made worthless the INS Green Cards, which are official sanctions of legal residence. In a similar vein, buttons declaring "Illegal Alien" deposed the concept, stripping it of its pejorative power. By claiming membership in a proscribed group, the bearers eliminated its proscriptive powers. By donning the button, the councilwoman and others declared in words unspoken, "If you are to take them, you must take me first." It shouted defiance to the INS, no small utterance coming from an elected official and church and community leaders.

Similarly, T-shirts, buttons, and placards displayed at rallies included such slogans as "*Somos Un Pueblo—Sin Fronteras!*" (We are One People—Without Borders); "We Didn't Cross the Border—The Border Crossed Us!"; "Who's the Alien?—Pilgrim!"; "E.T.'s an Alien—We're People"; "Land of the Free? What About Raza?"; "The INS Are Criminals—Not Undocumented." Each of these slogans interrogated the notions of border and historicity. The slogans reminded Chicanos that San Jose and in fact the entire Southwest belonged to Mexico until taken through war by the United States. Deposing border ideology, the discourse interjected Chicano notions of affirmation and nationhood.

This counter-ideology transforms Mexicans into migrants returning to their own lands, while Anglos become "illegal aliens" stealing land from the Indians and Mexicans. Criminality is contested and reversed. The INS became criminals for violating rights and separating parents from children. Unjust laws were thus subordinated to broader appeals for justice and *familia.* This counter-discourse moves Chicanos and Mexicanos from the margin to a newly visualized and revisualized center. As the examples demonstrate, Latino groups are constructing counter-discourse and counter-hegemonic ideology that sustain those movements and that contest the dominant discourse.

Cultural Rights and Civil Society

The cases presented in this chapter are not uncommon. Similar struggles have taken place throughout the country. They do, however, illustrate the importance of linking cultural practices to broader struggles for social change. By advocating for and claiming rights, Latinos are also defining their own communities and interests.

To feel as though they belong and are welcome in this society, Latinos must have a social space for expressing their interests and creativity. After all, the Declaration of Independence claims life, liberty, and the pursuit of happiness as basic human rights. Excluded groups, however, may perceive the "pursuit of happiness" differently than dominant groups. Such happiness is impossible if the conditions for attaining it are denied by the dominant society.

Gays, for example, might feel more at home in the Catholic Church if it accepted their way of life and if it allowed gay marriages. Such a claim runs counter to church doctrine and to the opinions of many Latinos. Even so, the efforts of gays to obtain those rights might also open up the claims of other groups, challenging the hierarchy and dominance inherent in the church.

Such claims are potentially counter-hegemonic even when they do not contest state or class rule, but rather contest dominance within social institutions that themselves are part of a cultural hegemony. Although such struggles begin in civil society, they often involve the state. In the late 1960s, for example, Chicanos in Los Angeles, California, formed Católicos por La Raza to force the church to play an activist role in opposing racism and oppression. The state intervened in support of the church by arresting the protesters and charging them with conspiracy. What began as an effort to claim cultural space, in this case within an institution that has immense cultural and ideological influence, was perceived as a threat not only to the church, but to hegemonic relations.

The target of opposition of such movements may not be the state. At the crux of the contestation is the notion of a civil society with all of its diverse institutions that together constitute the cultural domain in which hegemony is enforced. Mechanisms of social and cultural reproduction are never complete. They produce and are met by oppositional elements. What is key is that the cultural practices that compose cultural citizenship are often anti-hegemonic and can become oppositional social movements.

While I do not argue here that cultural citizenship supplants or obviates the need for broader movements that can challenge class or hegemonic rule, I do argue that creating social space and claiming rights can be oppositional and can lead to powerful redressive movements. The cases I have presented of Chicanos and the undocumented joining together to fight for the rights of the undocumented illustrate several points: first, Latinos are creating their own social spaces (both physical and expressive) that knit and compose self-defined communities; second, Latino communities are rejecting the artificial boundaries established by the state to distinguish between citizens and noncitizens; third, by their actions to include both undocumented and legal residents in their social movements, Latinos create social space for immigrants to emerge as subjects joining with U.S.-born Latinos to fight for common interests; fourth, through these movements new citizens and new social actors are emerging, redefining rights, entitlements, and what it means to be a member of this society; and, finally, counter-narratives are emerging that offer alternative visions of U.S. society.

The examples also help us to understand how cultural citizenship operates. Cultural citizenship, as an amalgam of both culture and citizenship, reflects the tensions of each. While citizenship is contested and incomplete, culture is constantly shifting and evolving. The various examples reveal the power of cultural claims in creating new citizens and sustaining social movements that demand new rights. While immigrants are castigated by the dominant society, they are embraced by Latinos who see commonality of history and interests. The undocumented live out their lives in the shadows. Their masks of anonymity conceal their hopes and aspirations to be members of society. Their role as political actors for the most part remains as subterranean as their lives, hidden from public view. But, as the cases demonstrate, they are emerging from the shadows as new subjects with their own claims for rights. These claims are given space by Latino social movements and by counter-ideology that stresses unity between Latino citizens and the undocumented based on commonality rather than difference. Cultural citizenship helps us to better comprehend the relationship between cultural practices and demands for cultural rights and new citizenship movements.

Simply put, Latinos are not only entering society, they are reshaping it, remolding it in their own image. The world that they are seeking to create is neither a replication of the old countries nor an assimilation into the host society; rather, it is a renegotiation of what it means to be a citizen with a distinct Latino infusion into the defining fabric of the United States. Ironically, the world that Latinos envision is more like how "America" views itself than the "America" that exists. It is a society committed to the values of democracy and social justice. As Latinos "imagine" (Anderson 1983) and set out to shape their vision of society, as they create space to live it, claim rights and entitlements based on it, and through their daily life practices construct it, they are not only "imagining" America, they are recreating it. While Latinos may not fully "belong" to "America," their hopes and frustrations do. Their dreams help us conceive of a different "America," a more just and egalitarian one. They offer a potential for reordering, restructuring, and renewal.

Notes

TWO: "THE WORLD WE ENTER WHEN CLAIMING RIGHTS"

This project was begun while the author was a fellow of the Center for Advanced Study in the Behavioral Sciences at Stanford, California. The financial support of Stanford University and the Social Science Research Council is also gratefully acknowledged. The author appreciates the comments and support of Renato Rosaldo, Gerald Lopez, and Charles Lawrence III.

1. We still need to explore fully the significance of the church in the process of cultural affirmation of Latinos in the United States. Latinos feel able to preserve their cultural heritage through religious organizations. Even for the Protestant groups, without direct roots to the Catholic Latin American tradition, church is one of the favorite places to exchange their culture and to sustain their sense of unity.
2. Again the organizers' sense of human rights clashed with the prevalent views, because they claimed to have economic rights and some basic human rights not acknowledged in the American legal system.
3. The norms invoked were viewed as exclusionary by the Latino organizations. Participants felt that the gatherings proposed were similar in character to events in any other community. After all, similar fairs are organized throughout California in the spring and people meet frequently to gain a political space. However, many aspects of the activities—the varied food, garments, music—were considered "alien" by the larger society.
4. In the second part of this essay I will address the assumptions of anti-discrimination law on these matters. For the time being, though, I will assume that anti-discrimination law is prevalent in the American legal system and that the issues involved here are of a different nature.
5. For the purposes of this essay I am referring only to Latinos who are U.S. citizens by birth—in particular, Puerto Ricans and Chicanos.
6. A note of caution in speaking of boundaries: in barrios there is greater diversity than has been recognized in the literature. For years, there has been a sharing of space with other groups.
7. Communities that do not have a well-defined spatial location maintain, nevertheless, a strong sense of cohesion as they make their presence known to themselves through informal focused gatherings. They are emergent communities whose increasing numbers and evolving political forms eventually make them a major political force. The concepts of imagined communities (Anderson 1983) and multidimensional identities are useful in understanding Latinos' construction of the law and the legal system. They liberate us from the need to choose between legal and cultural citizenship. People do cross from one to another, and perhaps we all do, because we tend to move from one identity to the other without necessarily having to choose between them or feeling handicapped or dispossessed by doing so.
8. O'Brien explains that "the protection

of cultural rights is an issue rarely acknowledged, much less squarely dealt with by the United States legal system. The courts have never defined culture and in several instances have offered conflicting conclusions as to the relevance of religion or language to culture. More importantly, the courts have not interpreted the Constitution to include a protection of cultural rights, as they have a protection of privacy" (O'Brien 1987: 354).

9. I use the term "culture rights" rather than cultural rights here, because I want to make a conceptual distinction between the two. Cultural rights often denote in the literature specific claims that minority groups may have to maintain those things by which their culture is identified. Some scholars include religion, language, literature and the arts, food, and folklore among cultural rights. The United Nations Charter acknowledges these claims as rights.

   Culture rights stem from a much broader definition of culture. "Culture lends significance to human experience by selecting from and organizing it. It refers broadly to the forms through which people make sense of their lives, rather than more narrowly to the opera or art museums. It does not inhabit a set-aside domain, as does, for example, that of politics or economics. From the pirouettes of classical ballet to the most brute of brute facts, all human conduct is culturally mediated. Culture encompasses the everyday and the esoteric, the mundane and the elevated, the ridiculous and the sublime. Neither high nor low, culture is all-pervasive" (Rosaldo 1989: 26).

   Therefore, culture rights sustain a claim to be who we are. They change over time: sometimes they are very clearly defined, at others less apparent because rather than being cross-cutting they are multifaceted and complex. In general, culture rights are linked to the centrality that dignity and respect have in human identities.

10. For a discussion of some instances and examples, see Karst 1991, passim.

11. Anti-discrimination law is based on the assimilation model and this particular view of culture. Minorities get the strict scrutiny treatment while they are being assimilated. But the goal of the doctrine is assimilation, because it denies the possibility of cultural citizenship.

12. *Santa Clara Pueblo v. Martinez*, 436 U.S. 49, 71–72 (1978).

13. Pub. L. No. 95-341, 92 Stat. 469 (1978) (codified at 42 U.S.C. § 1996 (1978).

14. Ibid.

15. *People* v. *Woody*, 394 P.2d 813, 40 Cal. Rptr. 69, 61 Cal.2d 716 (1964).

16. Ibid. at 817, 818.

17. Ibid. at 819.

18. Ibid. at 821–22 (emphasis added).

19. *Peyote Way Church of God, Inc. v. Smith*, 556 F. Supp.632. In *Peyote*, the court held that non–Native American members of the Peyote religious organizations were not exempted from drug laws as were the Native Americans.

20. Ibid. at 637.

21. In *New Rider v. Board of Ed. of Ind. Sch. Dist.*, 480 F.2d 693 (10th Cir. 1973) (Lewis, J., concurring), the court reminds us that "hair styles . . . have traditional but variable significance to the Pawnee. . . . Their present contention of religious oppression rises no higher under this record than a desire to express pride in their heritage. . . . Their desire to do so is understandable but not a constitutionally protected right" (at 700–701).

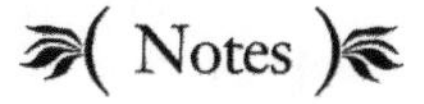

22. Ibid. at 639 (emphasis added).
23. Ibid. at 640.
24. 406 US 205 (1972).
25. Ibid. at 210.
26. Ibid.
27. Ibid. at 211.
28. Ibid. at 216. It is interesting to note that in *Yoder* the court identifies with some of the values that Amish culture represents. In an effort to legitimize its position, the court explains that "this record strongly shows that the Amish community has been a highly successful social unit within our society, even in apart from the conventional 'mainstream.' Its members are productive and very law-abiding members of society; they reject public welfare in any of its usual modern forms. The Congress itself recognized their self-sufficiency by authorizing exception of such groups as the Amish from the obligation to pay social security taxes" (ibid. at 222).

    Later, the court linked the Amish mode of life with Western values by making a comparison of Amish isolation and instances in the Middle Ages. In that time, members of religious orders both isolated themselves from worldly influences and preserved important values of Western civilization.
29. Ibid. at 224.
30. Ibid. at 205. To justify its position, the court explains that "the Amish communities singularly parallel and reflect many of the virtues of Jefferson's ideal of the "sturdy yeoman" who would form the basis of what he considered as the ideal of a democratic society" (ibid. at 225–26).
31. *Santa Clara Pueblo v. Martinez*, at 71–72.
32. Based on *Woody* and *Yoder*, in *Sequoyah v. TVA* (6th Cir 1980) the court concludes that "the overwhelming concern of the affiants appears to be related to the historical beginnings of the Cherokees and their cultural development. It is damage to tribal and family folklore and traditions, more than particular religious observances, which appears to be at stake. . . . Though cultural history and tradition are vitally important to any group of people, these are not interests protected" (at 1165).
33. Just recently the Chair of the U.S. Senate Subcommittee for the Study of the Status of Puerto Rico stated that Puerto Rico could not be a state of two languages.
34. *Meyer v. Nebraska*, 262 U.S. 390 (1923) (emphasis added).
35. *Lau v. Nichols*, 414 U.S. 563 (1973).
36. Ibid. at 564.
37. HEW, 1979, 35 Fed. Reg. 11595.
38. Ibid.
39. *Washington Post*, March 4, 1981.
40. *Soberal-Perez v. Heckler*, 717 F.2d 36 (1983).
41. Ibid. at 42.

THREE: IDENTITY, CONFLICT, AND EVOLVING LATINO COMMUNITIES

1. *Comadre* literally means "co-mother." Traditionally, it is the term of address that a mother uses for her child's godmother. It is commonly used among women to signify a relationship of created kinship that may not involve godparenting.

FOUR: CITIZENSHIP, CULTURE, AND COMMUNITY

1. The number of books, anthologies and articles on citizenship has increased dramatically. See Beiner

(1995); Carens (1995); Hill (1994); Kymlicka (1995a, 1995b); Lowndes (1995); van Steenbergen (1994).

2. A recent study by Valle and Torres (1994) provides an instructive analysis of the Latino eastside of Los Angeles that is organized on an adaptation of Zukin's (1991) notion of landscape.

3. A more in-depth analysis of these changes is provided in Rocco (1996).

4. The report issued by the Latino Coalition for a New Los Angeles (1993) provides a comparative summary of the changing socioeconomic profiles of Anglo, Latino, Asian, and black populations in Los Angeles.

5. For a discussion of how the restructuring process needs to be conceptualized as more than an economic process, see Law and Wolch (1993).

6. These data are from the 1990 census tract-tables.

7. The first part of this study was carried out between 1990 and 1993 by a team of researchers formed to study the processes involved in the creation of emerging Latino communities in the Los Angeles region. The initial phase focused on Southeast Los Angeles and included three components: (1) a structural analysis of the changes in the political economy of the region, (2) ethnographic studies of multiple sites of community activity, and (3) life-histories of households and families. The ethnographies and life-histories were carried out by a team of six researchers based at UCLA. After 1992, the scope of the project was extended to include other sections of Los Angeles undergoing significant growth in Latino communities. We carried out life-history interviews with nearly seventy Latino, mostly Mexican, families and households throughout this region during the last five years and included about twenty households from other Latino groups. In addition to compiling these life-histories, a team of researchers spent hundreds of hours with different families and household members, accompanying them as they went through different aspects of their daily or weekly routines, including sharing meals; attending weddings, baptisms, funerals, dances, parties, "quinceañeras"; shopping with them at different markets and commercial sites; eating at many of the small restaurants and food stands in the area; attending meetings of various cultural organizations as well as rotating credit and burial insurance organizations, PTA meetings, and meetings of a Spanish-speaking parents' organization; and visiting hospitals, doctors' offices, employment offices, and welfare offices.

8. This is not to say that we did not also find significant conflicts and divisions between Latino workers from different countries. This was particularly clear in the case of Salvadoran and Mexican immigrants.

FIVE: AESTHETIC PROCESS AND CULTURAL CITIZENSHIP

1. Poyo and Hinojosa (1991) contains several important essays that contribute significantly to the growing historiography of this period.

2. Various scholars have written about this era from a number of perspectives, including the following: Barrera (1979), De León (1982, 1983), M. García (1981), Montejano (1987), and Weber (1973).

3. In R. Flores 1993, I discuss the relationship between Don Leandro and Tranchese in more detail, highlighting their distinct and contradictory understandings of performance and memory. I argue that Tranchese's editorial

work makes it clear that he was greatly concerned with the orthographic errors and lack of biblical realism of Don Leandro's ledger; he revised, edited, and translated the text of Los Pastores along these lines.

4. During my return visit to San Antonio in December 1993, I found the social characteristics of the performers much as I did between 1987 and 1989. While a few of the faces were different, the social location of the actors remained the same.

5. Our Lady of Guadalupe Church has historically and currently been associated with sponsoring Los Pastores. Such sponsorship, however, at least at the time of my field research, translated into providing space on the school sidewalk for the troupe to practice, and loaning out the bus for transportation when and if it was in working condition. In return, the first official performance of Los Pastores, on Christmas Eve, was undertaken in the church hall, with perhaps one final performance in February.

6. The usual place of performance in the barrio is a driveway or backyard. Such sites offer a nice, elongated, rectangular area in which to perform. The main concern of the performers is having enough room in which to place the *infierno*, or hellmouth, where the devils stay during the performance. Other than this there is little consideration given to any formal stage setting of the area. In some cases families will decorate walls and specially made *altarcitos* (home altars or shrines) with Christmas lights and candles but none of this is required and it is left totally to the discretion of the hosting family.

7. A *promesa* is a ritual vow made to a saint, *el Niño Dios*, or the Virgin for some kind of special need. The *promesa* usually entails some kind of ritual sacrifice or offering as a way of returning the bestowed gift.

8. I have discussed the structural properties of the barrio and mission performance in detail elsewhere (R. Flores 1994). The contextualization narratives of these domains provide further evidence on how these places of performance are quite distinct.

9. Elsewhere (R. Flores 1993, 1995) I describe the mystique of the mission as embedded in the conjunction of memory and place that adds to a romanticized reading of this event.

10. Peter Skerry has recently written a provocative analysis of Mexican-American politics, in which San Antonio and many of the people and organizations listed here are discussed (1993). While I find Skerry's historical and descriptive work commendable, his conclusions concerning Mexican Americans and their place in the larger social order are, in my estimation, quite incorrect and misleading.

SIX: CLAIMING CULTURAL CITIZENSHIP IN EAST HARLEM

This essay has been drawn primarily from two larger studies: *Responses to Poverty Among Puerto Rican Women: Identity, Community, and Cultural Citizenship* (Benmayor et al. 1992), published first as a monographic report to the IUP / Social Science Research Council Joint Committee for Public Policy Research on Contemporary Hispanic Issues; and *Affirming Cultural Citizenship in the Puerto Rican Community: Critical Literacy and the El Barrio Popular Education Program* (Torruellas et al. 1991). Many quotes from life histories that appear throughout this chapter parenthetically refer the reader to these studies, where the quotes were originally published.

The original tapes of these interviews are archived in the Centro de Estudios

Notes

Puertorriqueños Library and Archives. In order to protect the public identity of the interviewees, we have generally used pseudonyms, except in cases where the women themselves chose otherwise, or when citing their writings as published in the Program's yearbooks.

1. In an early insightful article, Antonio Lauria-Perricelli (1964) analyzes the cultural significance to Puerto Ricans of *respeto* and similar cultural concepts.

2. Over the six-year span, the consistent research team was composed of Rosa M. Torruellas, co-director of the Centro Language and Education Task Force and director of the El Barrio Program from 1985 to 1992; Rina Benmayor, director of the Centro's Cultural Studies Task Force; and Ana L. Juarbe, research assistant for the Cultural Studies Task Force. As director, Rosa Torruellas linked the leadership, organizational development, daily administration, and research components of this project. Our research and sustained presence in the El Barrio Popular Education Program came to an end during 1991–92 and coincided with a change in the Program's director, a separation between administration and research, and a move toward greater autonomy from the Centro.

3. We have written and spoken about pedagogical, methodological, and theoretical dimensions of this Program (Torruellas et al. 1991; Benmayor 1991; Benmayor et al. 1992; Torruellas et al. 1996; Benmayor et al. 1997); and other scholars (Gordon 1996; Visweswaran 1994) have noted the ethnographic and feminist dimensions of our work.

4. Carlos Vélez Ibáñez (1983, 1996) speaks of "funds of knowledge," referring to community cultural practices and knowledge among Chicanos and Mexicanos as capital resources.

5. Paulo Freire's now classic work on literacy and empowerment (Freire 1972) continues to inspire many efforts in the United States. Also see Freire and Macedo 1987.

6. Very few men ever enrolled in the Program. The gender composition of the student participants reflected a self-selection process. The El Barrio Program never promoted itself as a "women's program," but it did not make a sustained effort to recruit men. The fact that the Program qualified as an alternative to "workfare" may help explain why more women enrolled, since they are the bulk of welfare recipients. During the life-history gathering phase of the project, only three men were enrolled in the classes. We decided to focus our study on women, since the sample for a comparative reading of gender experience would have been so small.

7. Excerpts were used from the *testimonios* of Nobel Peace Prize winner Rigoberta Menchú (1983); Domitila Barrios de Chungara (1976); the *Memorias de Bernardo Vega* (1977); and Jesús Colón (1982); and a videotape on "las madres de la Plaza de Mayo," the mothers and grandmothers of the disappeared in Argentina.

8. Around this time, increasing enrollments were forcing public schools to have "double enrollment" and "interlocking" systems. What this meant, in effect, was that teachers ended up teaching two sessions a day, with one group of students attending in the morning and another in the afternoon. The same facilities were being used by twice as many students, suggesting that numerical expansion was not accompanied by an increase in physical resources. School retention figures present a dismal picture of the state of public education by the late

1940s. As an illustration, of 19,599 students who entered urban schools in 1935, only 4,330, or 22 percent, reached twelfth grade by 1946. The statistics for rural areas present an even worse situation: only 9 percent of children enrolling in first grade reached eighth grade, and none of them graduated from high school. See Osuna (1949) for a complete account of education in Puerto Rico through the 1940s.

9. Geographic concentration of poverty, poverty over long periods, loose connection with the labor market, and "dysfunctional" behavior are all characteristics associated with "underclass" status in population samples (*Focus* 1989). Moreover, the term "underclass" itself has become loaded with pejorative implications. Even though the usefulness of this terminology has been questioned by its originator, William Julius Wilson (1987), "the underclass" is still very much a part of media, political, and policy parlance (Lemann 1991). For an effective critique of the concept, see Moore and Pinderhughes 1993.

10. Under the provisions of "workfare," women had the choice of taking on menial, dead-end jobs for no pay or going to school. The El Barrio Popular Education Program was accredited as an educational program option under the "workfare" system in New York City. Many of the women came to the Program on the recommendation of a caseworker.

11. Educational opportunities in Puerto Rico were scarce at the time many of these women were growing up, especially in rural areas. Some spoke of one-room schoolhouses, where all grades were integrated. Many of these schools were also at a considerable distance from their homes. Universalization of schooling was not achieved until the late 1950s and early 1960s on the island.

12. Torruellas et al. (1991) includes a more extensive description of the pedagogical methods used in the Program.

13. *Casitas* are small wooden houses, typical of the Puerto Rican countryside, constructed on empty lots in the urban barrios of New York. They are mini Puerto Rican environments that often include vegetable and flower gardens, chickens and roosters, and music. In good weather, neighbors congregate at a *casita* to socialize, have cookouts, play live and taped music, and party. They are social clubs, but they are also visible statements of Puerto Rican and Latino identity in the migration context (González 1990).

14. When we began this research, attention to spirituality in Latino studies was just beginning to emerge on academic agendas. Because of our limited knowledge of the field of religion and spirituality, we did not actively investigate the significance of these networks in the women's lives. As we delved more deeply into analyzing the life histories, we came to realize that there is a crucial need to understand how spirituality functions in Puerto Rican/Latino communities. The IUP seeded an important Working Group on religion and spirituality that now has a strong voice in national Latino research.

15. From the translated transcript of a live television interview on "Portada," Univisión, November 6, 1990.

16. This is true, despite the fact that forms of strike participation and support by women have a long historical tradition among the working class in Puerto Rico and other Latin American countries, and among Latinos in the

United States. Oral history and community histories of Puerto Ricans in New York also evidence the significant role of women in public political actions (Benmayor et al. 1987).

17. While the women recognize the liberating effects of self-revelation, they are also highly sensitive to the dangers of entrusting personal information to the wrong people. Protecting oneself from becoming the subject of idle gossip is part of the traditional cultural code of social interaction. More important, the high degree of economic and social vulnerability in which they live has taught the women that survival hinges in part on their ability to strategically control the flow of personal data into the public institutional sphere.

18. Patricia Hill Collins (1991) resituates the cultural and political debates that presuppose single, unified centers around which all others are marginal. By arguing that black women speak from their own organic and historical "center," she acknowledges the real processes of organization and historical empowerment that take place in communities.

SEVEN: MUJERES EN HUELGA

Research for this article was made possible by a California State University grant for Research and a mini-grant from the Stanford Center for Chicano Research.

1. Chicanas are generally U.S.-born Mexican descendants. Throughout the article I distinguish between Chicanos, Mexicanos (Mexican-born immigrants), and Latinos (used as a generic designation to refer to immigrants and their descendants from Latin America and the Caribbean). The majority of the cannery workers I interviewed were Mexican immigrants. Some of their children were born in Mexico, but raised in the United States and speak English. Although they too are "Mexican" by nativity, several of them identify as Mexican Americans and/or Chicanos.

2. During the early 1970s, however, César Chávez and the UFW were sharply criticized for their attacks on undocumented immigrants. The UFW viewed undocumented workers as potential strike-breakers and advocated patrols along the border to apprehend undocumented immigrants. Several Chicano activist groups met with the UFW. As a result, Chávez changed his position (see Acuña 1988).

3. The film was a target of the red scare of the McCarthy era. Several people associated with the film were blacklisted and Rosa Revueltas, its star, was deported. The film was unique in that it used the strikers themselves to recreate their own story (Wilson and Rosenfelt 1978).

4. While she believes families adopt survival strategies, Baca Zinn (1987) cautions us against romanticizing or overstating the capacities of families to oppose racial and class oppression. In her view, such culture of resistance arguments run the risk of ignoring the sexual division of labor or of understating the social costs to women of protecting their families.

5. While Latino families were once characterized in social science literature as "macho-dominated," pathological, and sources of a "culture of poverty," several studies in the past two decades have contested these characterizations (Mirandé 1977, 1985; Baca Zinn 1979; Segura and Pierce 1993). Ybarra (1982) has argued that egalitarianism increases for Latina wives as their percentage of household income rises. Moreover, there is some evidence that

Chicano men play more of a role in caring for their children than Anglo counterparts (Lamphere, Zavella, and Gonzáles 1993). The rise in families headed by single women, blended families (resulting from second and third marriages), blended households (with two or more families residing in the household), and extended families, combined with Latina labor force participation rates in 1990 of nearly 51 percent, force us to reconsider the character of Latino families.

6. Chicana feminists have also had disagreements with white feminism that tends to view the family as a primary source of women's oppression. As Pesquera and Segura (1993: 99) explain, "Although Chicanas recognized the need to struggle against male privilege in the Chicano community, they were reluctant to embrace a feminist position that appeared anti-family. Caught between two incompatible positions, Chicanas developed their own discourse reflecting their multidimensional sources of oppression and validation."

7. Estela Mejía, a Chicana graduate student from Watsonville, assisted me in the interviews. Her interviews were particularly helpful. As a woman and a member of the community, she was able to speak with the women about their personal lives in ways that I could not. Moreover, she provided a woman's perspective in analyzing some of those interviews. Estela and I conducted structured interviews in the summer of 1988. I made several further visits and conducted interviews following the October 17, 1989, earthquake and again in 1991 and 1992. Impressions during the strike are based on my observations, notes, and discussions with workers, union leaders, and community members. Unless otherwise indicated in the text, direct quotations have been taken from these interviews.

8. In 1950, Latinos represented less than 10 percent of the city's 11,000 inhabitants. Ten years later, the percentage of Latinos had doubled to 17 percent. By 1980 Latinos made up just under 50 percent of the city's population, which had grown to nearly 24,000 inhabitants (Cruz Takash 1990). In 1993 Latinos represented over 60 percent of the town's 33,000 residents.

9. By the year 2020, Latinos are expected to be this country's largest minority with a projected population of 51.2 million, or 15.7 percent of the U.S. population. By that time, California will have 47.9 million people ("Americans in 2020").

10. To this day, a sign welcoming visitors to Watsonville proudly bears this slogan.

11. In 1980, mean family income for Mexican residents of the city was only $16,899, 20 percent less than the city as a whole, while nearly 17 percent of the city's Mexican population lived in poverty and more than 20 percent of the Mexican labor force was unemployed for more than fifteen weeks (Cruz Takash 1990: 95).

12. Between 1980 and 1985 per-capita canned fruit consumption in the United States declined by nearly 50 percent from 16.2 pounds to 8.9 pounds. California's share of the nation's broccoli crop dropped from 90 percent to under 80 percent, while imports of frozen broccoli from Mexico tripled to 100 million pounds (Segal 1988a: 4; Wise 1985). From 1978 to 1987, Mexico's total share of the U.S. broccoli market rose by 700 percent.

By 1988, Mexican produce claimed 22 percent of the U.S. broccoli market and 27 percent of the U.S. cauliflower market (Bardacke 1988).

13. Between 1964 and 1975, U.S. agricultural firms in Mexico reaped a 16.7 percent rate of profit, twice that of the United States (Arizpe and Aranda 1986).

14. Ruiz describes how food processing workers mark time by the product season: "For instance, the phrase 'We met in spinach, fell in love in peaches, and married in tomatoes' indicates that the couple met in March, fell in love in August, and married in October" (1990: 266).

15. The "joy" of work must, however, be tempered with recognition of the exploitative relations that women face, particularly in jobs that are segmented along racial and gender lines. Lourdes Arizpe and Josefina Aranda argue that women working in strawberry plants in Zamora, Michoacán, express joy at "being allowed to leave the narrow horizons of their villages. . . . At the same time, salaries and working conditions at these plants are dismally exploitative." Moreover, since the industry "requires submissive and docile workers, it reinforces patriarchal and authoritarian structures. Since it benefits from a constant turnover of workers, it does not oppose machismo that confines women to home and marriage" nor does it lessen physical abuse (1986: 192).

16. The TDU chapter gained some credibility for its defense of Juan Parra, a Watsonville Canning worker, who was charged with assault with a deadly weapon after he hit a white racist foreman who harassed many of the Mexican workers. During the trial the INS arrested three workers who had agreed to testify on Parra's behalf. Eventually the case was thrown out of court. (See Bardacke 1988: 158.)

17. Zavella (1987) describes even more stringent constraints in her study of cannery workers in the Santa Clara Valley. There a union member had to have attended all but two of the union meetings within the previous two-year period to qualify for union office. This rule effectively excluded the participation of seasonal workers.

18. The rally included a significant delegation of labor activists from throughout Northern California, including a large contingent from the United Farmworkers Union. However, TDU, which consisted of several anarchists and white radicals, maintained tight control of the rally. Chavelo Moreno remembers, "The TDU organized a solidarity Day. We [the strikers] worked with them, but they wanted to control the rally. They didn't even let one striker speak. That's when we knew we couldn't trust them."

19. There were tensions between two groups, the Northern California Watsonville Strike Support Committee and the Watsonville Strike Support Committee, based on differences within the left and disagreements on strategy. The Watsonville TDU and Watsonville Strike Support Committee were led by an "amorphous grouping of radicals and militants working together with the Communist Party (CP)," while the League of Revolutionary Struggle (LRS) worked closely with the Northern California Watsonville Strike Support Committee and the Strike Committee (Bardacke 1988: 173). Bardacke argues that the LRS and the Strike Committee advocated a "united front" with some of the Teamster leadership, particularly Sergio López, while the TDU and Watsonville Strike Support Commit-

tee urged the workers to "spread the strike to the other frozen food plants and the fields" (ibid.: 177). Oscar Ríos disagrees, "They [TDU] wanted a general strike, but there was no basis for that. To them all the union leaders were 'sold-out.' They didn't understand that the workers needed broad support, including the Teamsters."

20. Sara Evans defines social space as an area where "members of an oppressed group can develop an independent sense of worth in contrast to their received definitions as second-class or inferior citizens" (1980: 219). Similarly, Evans and Boyte define free space as "settings between private lives and large-scale institutions where ordinary citizens can act with dignity, independence, and vision" (1986: 17). They argue that "democratic action depends upon these free spaces, where people experience a schooling in citizenship and learn a vision of the common good in the course of struggling for change" (ibid.: 18).

21. Chavelo Moreno, who is not a Marxist or socialist, learned to respect socialist ideas. He explained, "I have noticed that socialist ideas are those that benefit more the working class, the working people and not the rich, like for example the Reagan administration" (Ríos 1987a: 22). Similarly, Cuca Lomelí commented, "I came to realize that there is a need to get along with people with socialist ideals or other ideals. I am also grateful for the support that we have gotten. It doesn't matter where the support comes from" (ibid.: 23).

22. Pesquera and Segura argue that "analyses of feminist consciousness should attend to the dynamics of each social location in framing women's experiences. It is theoretically possible and likely that Chicanas' multiple sources of group identification conflict at times with one another, rendering the development of a group consciousness based on the privileging of one social location over the others ahistorical and untenable. The interplay of the multiple axes of class, race-ethnicity, and gender informs a unique Chicana perspective or world view that guides their assessment of the relevancy of feminism. This cross-positioning motivates a distinct Chicana feminism grounded in the experience of being female and Mexican from largely working-class backgrounds" (1993: 97).

23. Several of the women I interviewed felt that Gomez's defeat was in large part due to her attacks on Ríos during the strike and her lack of a strong base within the Mexican community.

EPILOGUE: CITIZENS VS. CITIZENRY

1. I use the terms "American" and "America" in quotations to reflect the fact that the United States appropriates for itself the name of two entire continents. Nonetheless, the terms are commonly used in this country in debates about nationality and nationhood.

2. In the 1960s, Mexican-American activists adopted the term "Chicano" to affirm the existence of a separate identity with distinct claims and rights, including the call for self-determination, interpreted alternatively as community control and the right to political secession or regional autonomy.

3. Even the meaning of citizenship is contested. Roberto Alejandro terms citizenship a "mask carried by particular individuals [while denied to others. . . .] This tension constitutes an arena of latent and open conflicts. Citizenship is a sign of membership, while

some individuals may feel excluded from crucial descriptions and purposes of their society" (1993: 2).

4. Although dominant groups often perceive Latinos as homogeneous, Latinos are in fact, quite diverse, including various nationalities, political perspectives, racial types, and classes. Some are monolingual Spanish-speaking, while others are bilingual or only monolingual English-speaking. Some are immigrants, while others are U.S.-born. Some came here to escape death squads and political persecution, while others came seeking jobs and better living conditions. Politically, Latinos range from conservative Republicans to liberal Democrats and socialists.

5. Until 1985, La Clínica was housed in the old rectory of the parish church which itself was a sanctuary for political refugees from Chile and Central America, and a host to a variety or organizations, including the Cannery Workers Committee (CWC), a caucus within the Teamsters Union, and, for a brief period, CASA, an immigrants' rights organization. The proximity of the various groups, all housed on the church grounds, reinforced networks of mutual support. Thus, during the cannery closures the church held special masses for the cannery workers. Members of La Clínica's mental health staff jointly sponsored community forums with the CWC to fight plant closures and to demand benefits for displaced workers and their families (W. Flores 1987a).

6. As Homi Bhabha explains, "There are no stories . . . only the ghosts of other stories" (1993: 307). Telling the stories, according to Frederic Jameson, "invokes . . . [the] notion of 'situational consciousness' or national allegory, 'where the telling of the individual story and the individual experience cannot but ultimately invoke the whole laborious telling of the collectivity itself' " (cited in Bhabha 1993: 292).

7. In fact, one organization active in the community at the time, of which I was a member, the Center for Autonomous Social Action (CASA), strongly believed in Chicano-Mexicano unity. Its main slogans were "*Chicano-Mexicano Somos Un Pueblo*" (Chicano-Mexican We Are One People), "*Somos Un Pueblo Sin Fronteras*" (We Are One People Without Borders), and "*Un Daño Contra Uno Es un Daño Contra Todos*" (An Injury to One Is an Injury to All). CASA had a small office in one of the church buildings and organized a march on behalf of the undocumented in downtown San Jose in the summer of 1973.

8. As Ramón Saldívar explains, "the subject exists as a mirror reflection of an *other* subject and becomes a subject itself in the recognition and reflection of and in the other" (1991: 16).

9. The name "Raza Sí", literally meaning "Race Yes" derives from, among others, "*La Raza Cósmica*," a concept of Mexican revolutionary intellectual José Vasconcellos that transformed *mestizaje*, the mixture of races and cultures resulting from colonialism, into a source of pride. The concept of the "Cosmic Race" envisions a world where barriers between nations and races become meaningless. Thus, the group's name evokes pride, empowerment, and self-determination. It appeals to a mythical past while indicating a possible future.

10. As opposed to "amnesty," which implied forgiveness for past crimes, Raza Sí argued that the undocumented contribute to society and should receive immediate unconditional residency.

Bibliography

ACUÑA, RODOLFO. 1988. *Occupied America: A History of Chicanos.* 3d ed. New York: Harper and Row.

Adultos hacia el futuro. 1990. Yearbooks 5 and 6. New York: El Barrio Popular Education Program.

AGNEW, JOHN A., AND JAMES S. DUNCAN, eds. 1989. *The Power of Place: Bringing Together Geographical and Sociological Imaginations.* New York: Unwin Hyman.

ALEJANDRO, ROBERTO. 1993. *Hermeneutics, Citizenship, and the Public Sphere.* Albany, N.Y.: State University of New York Press.

ALVAREZ, ROBERT A., JR. 1987. *Familia: Migration and Adaptation in Baja and Alta California, 1800–1975.* Berkeley: University of California Press.

"Americans in 2020: Less White, More Southern." 1994. *New York Times,* April 22.

ANDERSON, BENEDICT. 1983. *Imagined Communities: Reflections on the Origin and Spread of Nationalism.* London: Verso.

ANZALDÚA, GLORIA. 1987. *Borderlands/*La Frontera: *The New Mestiza.* San Francisco: Aunt Lute Books.

Aprender a luchar, luchar es aprender. 1988. New York: Oral History Task Force, Centro de Estudios Puertorriqueños, Hunter College.

ARIZPE, LOURDES, AND JOSEFINA ARANDA. 1986. "Women Workers in the Strawberry Agribusiness in Mexico." In *Women's Work: Development and the Division of Labor by Gender,* ed. Eleanor Leacock, Helen I. Safa, et al., pp. 174–93. South Hadley, Mass.: Bergin & Garvey.

ARONOWITZ, STANLEY. 1992. *The Politics of Identity: Class, Culture, Social Movements.* New York: Routledge.

AZIZE, YAMILA. 1985. *La mujer en la lucha.* Río Piedras, Puerto Rico: Editorial Cultural.

BACA ZINN, MAXINE. 1979. "Chicano Family Research: Conceptual Distortions and Alternative Directions." *Journal of Ethnic Studies* 7: 59–71.

———. 1987. "Structural Transformation and Minority Families." In *Women, Households and the Economy,* ed. Lourdes Benería and Catharine R. Stimpson, pp. 155–71. New Brunswick, N.J.: Rutgers University Press.

BARDACKE, FRANK, 1988. "Watsonville: A Mexican Community on Strike." In *Reshaping the U.S. Left: Popular Struggles in the 1980's,* The Year Left Series vol. 3, ed. Mike Davis and Michael Sprinker, pp. 149–82. New York: Verso.

BARRERA, MARIO. 1979. *Race and Class in the Southwest: A Theory of Racial Inequality.* Notre Dame: University of Notre Dame Press.

BARRIOS DE CHUNGARA, DOMITILA. 1976. *Si me permiten hablar . . . :Testimonio de Domitila, una mujer de las minas de Bolivia.* Mexico City: Siglo XXI.

BAUMAN, RICHARD, AND CHARLES BRIGGS. 1990. "Poetics and Performance as Critical Perspectives on Language and Social Life." *Annual Review of Anthropology* 19: 59–88.

Beiner, Ronald. 1995. *Theorizing Citizenship*. Albany: State University of New York Press.

Bellah, Robert N., et al. 1996. *Habits of the Heart: Individualism and Commitment in American Life*. Rev. ed. Berkeley, Los Angeles, London: University of California Press.

Benmayor, Rina. 1991. "Testimony and Empowerment in Community-Based Research." In *Women's Words: Oral History and Feminist Methodology*. Ed. Sherna Berger Gluck and D. Patai. New York: Routledge.

Benmayor, Rina, Ana Juarbe, Celia Alvarez, and Blanca Vazquez. 1987. *Stories to Live By: Continuity and Change in Three Generations of Puerto Rican Women*. New York: Centro de Estudios Puertorriqueños, Hunter College. Revised in *Oral History Review* 16:2 (Fall 1988); and in *Myths We Live By*, ed. Paul Thompson and R. Samuels, London: Routledge, 1988.

Benmayor, Rina, Rosa M. Torruellas, and Ana L. Juarbe. 1992. *Responses to Poverty Among Puerto Rican Women: Identity, Community, and Cultural Citizenship*. New York: Centro de Estudios Puertorriqueños, Hunter College.

———. 1997. "Education, Cultural Rights, and Citizenship." In *Women Transforming Politics: An Alternative Reader*, ed. Cathy Cohen, Kathleen Jones, and Joan Tronto. New York: New York University Press.

Benmayor, Rina, and Andor Skotnes, eds. 1994. *Migration and Identity: International Yearbook of Oral History and Life Stories*, vol. 3. Oxford and New York: Oxford University Press.

Bennett, William J. 1992. *The Devaluing of America: The Fight for Our Culture and Our Children*. New York: Touchstone.

Bhabha, Homi K. 1993. "DissemiNation." In *Nation and Narration*, ed. Homi K. Bhabha, pp. 291–322. New York: Routledge.

Bonfil Batalla, Guillermo. 1990. *México profundo: Una civilización negada*. Mexico City: Grijalbo.

Bonilla, Frank, and Ricardo Campos. 1986. *Industry and Idleness*. New York: History Migration Task Force, Centro de Estudios Puertorriqueños, Hunter College.

Bookman, Ann, and Sandra Morgen. 1988. *Women and the Politics of Empowerment*. Philadelphia: Temple University Press.

Brimelow, Peter. 1996. *Alien Nation: Common Sense about America's Immigration Disaster*. New York: HarperPerennial.

Brown, Martin L. 1981. "A Historical Analysis of the Wage Structure of the California Fruit and Vegetable Industry." Ph.D. diss., University of California, Berkeley.

Browning, R., D. Marshall, and D. H. Tabb. 1984. *Protest Is Not Enough: The Struggle of Blacks and Hispanics for Equality in Urban Politics*. Berkeley: University of California Press.

Bruner, Edward M. 1986. "Experience and Its Expressions." In *The Anthropology of Experience*, ed. Victor Turner and Edward Bruner, pp. 3–30. Urbana: University of Illinois Press.

Bibliography

BUELL, FREDRICK. 1994. *National Culture and the New Global System.* Baltimore: Johns Hopkins University Press.

Buscando un futuro mejor. 1988. Yearbook 3. New York: El Barrio Popular Education Program.

CANNING, KATHLEEN. 1994. "Feminist History After the Linguistic Turn: Historicizing Discourse and Experience." *Signs* 19: 368–404.

CÁRDENAS, G., J. CHAPA, AND S. BUREK. 1993. "The Changing Economic Position of Mexican Americans in San Antonio." In *Latinos in a Changing U.S. Economy,* ed. Frank Bonilla and Rebecca Morales, pp. 160–83. Newbury Park, Calif.: Sage Publications.

CARENS, JOSEPH H. 1995. "Aliens and Citizens: The Case for Open Borders." In *The Rights of Minority Cultures,* ed. Will Kymlicka, pp. 331–49. Oxford and New York: Oxford University Press.

CASTELLS, MANUEL. 1983. *The City and the Grassroots.* Los Angeles: University of California Press.

CASTRO, MARY. 1992. "The Alchemy Between Social Categories in the Production of Political Subjects: Class, Gender, Race and Age in the Case of Domestic Workers Union Leaders in Salvador-Bahia, Brazil." Unpublished manuscript. Brazil.

———. 1994. "The Sexual Division of Power: Women in Labor Unions in Brazil." Unpublished manuscript. Centro de Estudios Puertorriqueños, Hunter College, City University of New York.

CAULFIELD, MINA D. 1974. "Imperialism, Family and Cultures of Resistance." *Socialist Revolution* 29: 67–75.

CERVANTES, LORNA DEE. 1981. *Emplumada.* Pittsburgh: University of Pittsburgh Press.

CHAMBERS, IAIN. 1994. *Migrancy, Culture, Identity.* New York: Routledge.

CLEANING UP SILICON VALLEY COALITION. 1991. *The Rich, the Poor, and the Forgotten . . . in Silicon Valley.* San Jose, Calif.

CLIFFORD, JAMES. 1988. *The Predicament of Culture: Twentieth Century Ethnography, Literature, and Art.* Cambridge, Mass.: Harvard University Press.

COHEN, LAURIE, GAIL HERSHATTER, AND EMILY HONIG. 1980. "Women at Farah: An Unfinished Story." In *Mexican Women in the United States,* ed. Magdelena Mora and Adelaida del Castillo. Los Angeles: UCLA Chicano Studies Research Center Publications.

COLÓN, JESÚS. 1982. *A Puerto Rican in New York and Other Sketches.* New York: International Publishers.

CORWIN, MILES. 1986. "Cannery Workers' Bitter Strike Devastates Lives, Economy of Watsonville." *Los Angeles Times,* September 14.

CRUZ TAKASH, PAULE. 1990. "A Crisis of Democracy: Community Responses to the Latinization of a California Town Dependent on Immigrant Labor." Ph.D. diss., University of California, Berkeley.

DAGNINO, EVELINA. 1991a. "Some Ideas about the Concept of Cultural Citizenship." Notes presented to IUP Cultural Studies Working Group.

———. 1991b. "Social Movements and Politics in the Building of Democracy in Brazil." Paper published at the Symposium on Portuguese Traditions, UCLA, Los Angeles, April 20–21.

———. 1994. "On Becoming a Citizen: The Story of Dona Marlene." In *Migration and Identity: International Yearbook of Oral History and Life Stories*, ed. Rina Benmayor and A. Skotnes, 3:69–84. Oxford and New York: Oxford University Press.

DAVIS, MIKE. 1990. *City of Quartz: Excavating the Future of Los Angeles.* New York: Verso; and 1992, London: Vintage.

DE LA GARZA, RODOLFO, ET AL. 1992. *Latino Voices: Mexican, Puerto Rican, and Cuban Perspectives on American Politics.* Boulder, Col.: Westview Press.

DE LEÓN, A. 1982. *The Tejano Community, 1836–1900.* Albuquerque: University of New Mexico Press.

———. 1983. *They Called Them Greasers: Anglo Attitudes toward Mexicans in Texas, 1821–1900.* Austin: University of Texas Press.

DEPALMA, ANTHONY. 1993. "Vague Mexico Wage Pledge Clouds Free Trade Accord." *New York Times*, September 29.

DICKEY, JIM. 1986. "Misery in Watsonville Strike: Evictions Mount as Cannery Walkout Goes into Sixth Month." *San Jose Mercury News*, February 11.

DUANY, LUIS, 1991. "Puerto Rican Welfare Recipients in New York City: Effective Service Delivery to Those Most in Need." Manuscript. New York State Department of Social Services.

DURHAM, EUNICE RIBEIRO. 1984. "Movimentos Sociais, a Construção da Cidadania." *Novos Estudos* 10 (October). São Paulo: Novos Estudos Cebrap.

ECKSTEIN, SUSAN, ED. 1989. *Power and Protest: Latin American Social Movements.* Berkeley: University of California Press.

EISENSTEIN, SARAH. 1983. *Give Us Bread But Give Us Roses.* London: Routledge and Kegan Paul.

ESCOBAR, ARTURO, AND SONIA E. ALVAREZ, eds. 1992. *The Making of Social Movements in Latin America: Identity, Strategy, and Democracy.* Boulder, Col.: Westview Press.

ETZIONI, AMITAI. 1993. *The Spirit of Community: The Reinvention of American Society.* New York: Simon and Schuster.

EVANS, SARA M. 1980. *Personal Politics.* New York: Basic Books.

EVANS, SARA M., AND HARRY C. BOYTE. 1986. *Free Spaces: The Sources of Democratic Change in America.* New York: Harper and Row.

FAGEN, RICHARD. 1973. *The Transformation of Political Culture in Cuba.* Stanford, Calif.: Stanford University Press.

FAHEY, JOE. 1987. "Victory in Watsonville: Not a Single Defector in 18 Months!" *Labor Notes* 98 (April): 1ff.

FLORES, RICHARD R. 1992. "The *Corrido* and the Emergence of Texas-Mexican Social Identity." *Journal of American Folklore* 105: 166–82.

———. 1993. "History, 'Los Pastores,' and the Shifting Poetics of Dislocation." *Journal of Historical Sociology* 6(2): 164–85.

———. 1994. "'Los Pastores' and the Gifting of Performance." *American Ethnologist* 21(2): 270–85.

———. 1995. *Los Pastores: History and Performance in the Mexican Shepherds' Play of South Texas*. Washington, D.C.: Smithsonian Institution Press.

Flores, William V. 1973. "Mexico and Runaway Shops." *Regeneración* 2(3): 11–12.

———. 1987a. *The Dilemma of Survival: Organizational Dependence, Conflict and Change in a Chicano Community*. Unpublished Ph.D. diss., Stanford University.

———. 1987b. "The Notion of Cultural Citizenship." Unpublished manuscript. Stanford Center for Chicano Research, Stanford, Calif.

———. 1987c. *Viva La Huelga! UFW Celebrates 20 Years*. Oakland, Calif.: Unity Publications.

———. 1988. "Cultural Citizenship and Empowerment." Paper presented at the IUP Conference on Latino Cultural Citizenship, May 10–11. University of California, Los Angeles.

———. 1990. "The Watsonville Cannery Strike: Lessons in the Dialectics of Cultural Citizenship and Change." Paper presented at the Annual Meeting of the American Studies Association, Nov. 1–4. New Orleans.

———. 1992a. "Chicano Empowerment and the Politics of At-Large Elections in California: A Tale of Two Cities." In *Community Empowerment and Chicano Scholarship*, ed. Mary Romero and Cordelia Candelaria, pp. 181–200. Berkeley: National Association for Chicano Studies.

———. 1992b. "Cultural Citizenship, Collective Memory and the Social Construction of Community—Downtown Redevelopment and Chicanos in San Jose." Paper presented at the 20th Annual National Association for Chicano Studies Conference, March 25–28. San Antonio, Texas.

———. 1993. "Claiming the Past, Envisioning the Future: Collective Memory and Chicano Cultural Citizenship." *Boletín* Centro de Estudios Puertorriqueños 6 (Spring).

———. 1994. "Rethinking Borders: Health Care Rights and the Undocumented." Paper presented at the Colloquium on Health Care, Media and the Nation, New York University, April 16.

Focus. 1989. "Special Issue: *Defining and Measuring the Underclass*." 12(1).

Foucault, Michel. 1977. *Discipline and Punishment: The Birth of the Prison*. London: Allen Lane.

Freire, Paulo. 1972. *Pedagogy of the Oppressed*. New York: Herder and Herder.

———. 1973. *Education for Critical Consciousness*. New York: Seabury.

Freire, Paulo, and D. Macedo. 1987. *Literacy: Reading the Word and the World*. South Hadley, Mass.: Bergin and Garvey.

Friedmann, John. 1992. *Empowerment: The Politics of Alternative Development*. Cambridge, Mass.: Blackwell.

Fuentes, Carlos. 1988. "Images of Latin America." Lecture, California State University Fresno, April 30. Fresno, Calif.

———. 1992. "The Mirror of the Other." *The Nation* (March 30): 408–411.

Ganguly, Keya. 1992. "Migrant Identities: Personal Memory and the Construction of Selfhood." *Cultural Studies* 6(1): 51–72.

García, Alma. 1990. "The Development of Chicana Feminist Discourse: 1970–

1980." In *Unequal Sisters: A Multicultural Reader in U.S. Women's History*, ed. Ellen Carol DuBois and Vicki L. Ruiz, pp. 418–31. New York: Routledge.

García, M. 1981. *Desert Immigrants: The Mexicans of El Paso, 1880–1920*. New Haven: Yale University Press.

García, R. 1991. *Rise of the Mexican American Middle Class*. College Station, Tex.: Texas A&M University Press.

García Canclini, Néstor. 1989. *Culturas híbridas: Estrategias para entrar y salir de la modernidad*. Mexico City: Grijalbo.

———. 1995a. *Consumidores y Ciudadanos: Conflictos multiculturales de la globalización*. Mexico City: Grijalbo.

———. 1995b. *Hybrid Cultures: Strategies for Entering and Leaving Modernity*. Minneapolis: University of Minnesota Press.

Garreau, Joel. 1991. *Edge City: Life on the New Frontier*. New York: Doubleday.

Gilroy, Paul. 1987, 1991. *There Ain't No Black in the Union Jack: The Cultural Politics of Race and Nation*. London: Unwin Hyman; 1991, Chicago: University of Chicago Press.

Giroux, Henry A. 1991. "Modernism, Postmodernism, and Feminism: Rethinking the Boundaries of Educational Discourse." In *Postmodernism, Feminism, and Cultural Politics: Redrawing Educational Boundaries*, ed. Henry A. Giroux, pp. 1–59. Albany: State University of New York Press.

———. 1992. *Border Crossings: Cultural Workers and the Politics of Education*. New York: Routledge.

———. 1994. "Living Dangerously: Identity Politics and the New Cultural Racism." In *Between Borders: Pedagogy and the Politics of Cultural Studies*, ed. Henry A. Giroux and Peter McLaren, pp. 29–55. New York: Routledge.

Gittell, Marilyn, M. Schenhl and C. Fareri. 1990. *From Welfare to Independence: The College Option*. A Report to the Ford Foundation. Graduate School and University Center of the City University of New York: Howard Samuels State Management and Policy Center.

Gluck, Sherna, and Daphne Patai, eds. 1991. *Women's Words: The Feminist Practice of Oral History*. New York: Routledge.

Gómez-Quiñones, Juan. 1994. *Roots of Chicano Politics, 1600–1940*. Albuquerque: University of New Mexico Press.

González, David. 1990. "Las Casitas: Oases or Illegal Shacks?" *New York Times* (September 20): B1.

González, Lydia Milagros. 1990. *Una puntada en el tiempo*. Santo Domingo: Centro de Estudios de la Realidad Puertorriqueña and Centro de Investigación para la Acción Femenina.

Gordon, Deborah A. 1995. "Border Work: Feminist Ethnography and the Dissemination of Literacy." In *Women Writing Culture*, ed. Ruth Behar and Deborah A. Gordon. Berkeley: University of California Press.

Gottdiener, Mark. 1985. *The Social Production of Urban Space*. Austin: University of Texas Press.

Bibliography

Halbwachs, Maurice. 1992. *On Collective Memory*. Ed. and trans. Lewis A. Coser. Chicago: University of Chicago Press.

Hall, Stuart. 1988. "New Ethnicities." In *ICA Document* 7, pp. 27–31. London: Institute for Community Arts (ICA).

———. 1993. "What Is That 'Black' in Black Popular Culture?" *Social Justice* 20 (Spring/Summer): 104–114.

Hall, Stuart, and David Held. 1990. "Citizens and Citizenship." In *New Times: The Changing Face of Politics in the 1990s*, ed. Stuart Hall and Martin Jacques, pp. 173–88. London: Verso.

Harding, Vincent. 1987. "Toward a Darkly Radiant Vision of American's Truth." *Cross Currents* 37(1): 1–16.

Harvey, David. 1989. *The Condition of Postmodernity*. Cambridge, Mass.: Basil Blackwell.

Hazle, Maline. 1991. "Census Shows Shift in S.J. Ethnic Mix." *San Jose Mercury News*, February 27.

Herrnstein, Richard J., and Charles A. Murray. 1994. *The Bell Curve: Intelligence and Class Structure in American Life*. New York: Free Press.

Hill, Dilys M. 1994. *Citizens and Cities: Urban Policy in the 1990s*. London: Harvester Wheatsheaf.

Hill Collins, Patricia. 1990. *Black Feminist Thought: Knowledge, Consciousness and the Politics of Empowerment*. Boston: Unwin Hyman.

Hiss, Tony. 1990. *The Experience of Place*. New York: Vintage Books.

History Task Force, Centro de Estudios Puertorriqueños. 1979. *Labor Migration under Capitalism: The Puerto Rican Experience*. New York and London: Monthly Review Press.

Hoffman, Abraham. 1979. *Unwanted Mexican Americans in the Great Depression: Repatriation Pressures: 1929–1939*. Tucson: University of Arizona Press.

Hondagneu-Sotelo, Pierrette. 1994. *Gendered Transitions: Mexican Experiences of Immigration*. Berkeley. University of California Press.

IUP Cultural Studies Working Group. 1987. "The Concept of Cultural Citizenship." Unpublished working concept paper no. 1. Los Angeles: UCLA Chicano Studies Research Center, Los Angeles, Calif.

———. 1988. "Draft Concept Paper on Cultural Citizenship." Unpublished working concept paper no. 2. Stanford, Calif.: Center for Chicano Research.

———. 1989. "Draft Concept Paper on Cultural Citizenship." Unpublished working concept paper no. 3. New York: Centro de Estudios Puertorriqueños, Hunter College.

———. 1991. "The Concept of Cultural Citizenship." Unpublished revision by Richard Flores. Madison: University of Wisconsin.

Jelín, Elizabeth. 1990. *Women and Social Change in Latin America*. London: Zed Books Ltd.; Switzerland: United Nations Research Institute for Social Development.

Johnson, Bob. 1987. "Unity and Victory: How Watsonville Strikers Won Their Strike." *Santa Cruz Sun* 1(28), March 26.

KARST, KENNETH. 1991. *Belonging to America.* New Haven: Yale University Press.

KASINITZ, PHILIP, AND JUDITH FREIDENBERG-HERBSTEIN. 1992. "The Puerto Rican Parade and West Indian Carnival: Public Celebrations in New York City." In *Caribbean Life in New York City: Sociocultural Dimensions,* ed. Constance R. Sutton and Elsa M. Downey, pp. 305–325. New York: Center for Migration Studies.

KONDO, DORINNE K. 1990. *Crafting Selves: Power, Gender, and Discourses of Identity in a Japanese Workplace.* Chicago: University of Chicago Press.

KYMLICKA, WILL. 1995a. *Multicultural Citizenship: A Liberal Theory of Minority Rights.* Oxford: Clarendon Press.

———, ed. 1995b. *The Rights of Minority Cultures.* Oxford and New York: Oxford University Press.

LAMOTT, ANNE. 1994. *Bird by Bird: Some Instructions on Writing and Life.* New York: Anchor.

LAMPHERE, LOUISE. 1985. "Bringing the Family to Work: Women's Culture on the Shop Floor." *Feminist Studies* 11(3) (Fall): 519–40.

———, ed. 1992. *Structuring Diversity: Ethnographic Perspectives on the New Immigration.* Chicago: University of Chicago Press.

LAMPHERE, LOUISE, PATRICIA ZAVELLA, AND FELIPE GONZÁLES, WITH P. EVANS. 1993. *Sunbelt Working Mothers: Reconciling Family and Factory.* Ithaca: Cornell University Press.

LATINO COALITION FOR A NEW LOS ANGELES. 1993. *Latinos and the Future of Los Angeles.* Los Angeles: Latino Futures Research Group.

LATINO ISSUES FORUM OF SANTA CLARA COUNTY. 1989a. *The Latino Workforce in Santa Clara County: The Dilemmas of High Technology Change on a Minority Population.* Report prepared by Dr. Edward J. Blakeley and Susan Sullivan, Latino Issues Forum, January. San Jose, Calif.

———. 1989b. *Political Empowerment Task Force Report.* Report prepared by Joaquín Avila, Latino Issues Forum, January. San Jose, Calif.

LAURIA-PERRICELLI, ANTONIO. 1964. "*Respeto, Relajo* and Interpersonal Relations in Puerto Rico." *Anthropological Quarterly* 37: 53–67.

———. 1992. "Towards a Transnational Perspective on Migration: Closing Remarks." In *Towards a Transnational Perspective on Migration: Race, Class, Ethnicity and Nationalism Reconsidered,* ed. H. G. Schiller et al. Annals of the New York Academy of Sciences 645 (July): 251–53.

LAW, ROBIN M., AND JENNIFER R. WOLCH. 1993. "Social Reproduction in the City: Restructuring in Time and Space." In *The Restless Urban Landscape,* ed. Paul L. Knox, pp. 165–206. Englewood Cliffs, N.J.: Prentice-Hall.

LEBLANC, BRIGITTE. 1991. "San Jose: Capital of Silicon Valley." *Fortune,* Special Advertising Supplement, April 22.

LEGHORN, LISA, AND KATHERINE PARKER. 1981. *Women's Worth: Sexual Economics and the World of Women.* Boston: Routledge and Kegan Paul.

LEMANN, NICHOLAS. 1991. "The Other Underclass." *Atlantic Monthly.* December.

LIMÓN, J. E. 1974. "El Primer Congreso Mexicanista de 1911: A Precursor to Contemporary Chicanismo." *Aztlán* 5: 85–117.

LINDSEY, ROBERT. 1986. "Who Wins and Who Loses in Trend to Fresh Food." *Los Angeles Times*, February 19.

LIPSITZ, GEORGE. 1990. *Time Passages: Collective Memory and American Popular Culture.* Minneapolis: University of Minnesota Press.

LOWNDES, VIVIEN. 1995. "Citizenship and Urban Politics." In *Theories of Urban Politics*, ed. David Judge, Gerry Stoker, and Harold Wolman, pp. 160–80. Thousand Oaks, Calif.: Sage Publications.

LUTTRELL, WENDY. 1988. "The Edison School Struggle: The Reshaping of Working-Class Education and Women's Consciousness." In *Women and the Politics of Empowerment*, ed. Ann Bookman and Sandra Morgen, pp. 136–56. Philadelphia: Temple University Press.

MCCORMACK, DAN, AND ALLEN KANDA. 1991. *Santa Clara County, '91.* Martinez, Calif.: McCormack's Guides.

MARSHALL, T. H. 1950. *Citizenship and Social Class.* Cambridge: Cambridge University Press.

MELVILLE, MARGARITA B., ed. 1988. *Mexicans at Work in the United States.* Houston: University of Houston Press.

Memorias de Bernardo Vega. 1977. Ed. César Andreu Iglesias. Río Piedras, Puerto Rico: Ediciones Huracán.

MENCHÚ, RIGOBERTA. 1983. *Me llamo Rigoberta Menchú y así me nació la conciencia.* Barcelona: Ed. Argos Vergara.

MILLER, DONALD. 1985. "The Strike: How It Happened: Industry Executive Blames Watsonville Canning." *Santa Cruz Sentinel*, November 18.

MIRANDÉ, ALFREDO. 1977. "The Chicano Family: A Reanalysis of Conflicting Views." *Journal of Marriage and the Family* 39: 747–56.

———. 1985. *The Chicano Experience.* Notre Dame: University of Notre Dame Press.

MOLLENKOPF, JOHN H. 1981. "Community and Accumulation." In *Urbanization and Urban Planning in Capitalist Society*, ed. Michael Dean and Allen J. Scott, pp. 319–37. New York: Methuen.

MOLLENKOPF, JOHN H., AND MANUEL CASTELLS, eds. 1991. *The Dual City: Restructuring New York.* New York: Russell Sage Foundation.

MONTEJANO, DAVID. 1987. *Anglos and Mexicans in the Making of Texas, 1836–1986.* Austin: University of Texas Press.

MONTOYA, JOSÉ. 1972. "El Louie." In *Aztlán: An Anthology of Mexican American Literature*, ed. Luis Valdez and Stan Steiner, pp. 333–37. New York: Vintage.

MOORE, JOAN W., AND RAQUEL PINDERHUGHES, eds. 1993. *In the Barrios: Latinos and the Underclass Debate.* New York: Russell Sage Foundation.

MORA, MAGDALENA. 1981. "The Role of Mexican Women in the Richmond Tolteca Strike." In *Mexican Immigrant Workers in the U.S.*, ed. Antonio Ríos-Bustamante, pp. 111–18. Los Angeles: UCLA Chicano Studies Research Center Publications.

MORA, MAGDALENA, AND ADELAIDA DEL CASTILLO, eds. 1980. *Mexican Women in the United States.* Los Angeles: UCLA Chicano Studies Research Center Publications.

MORALES, REBECCA, AND FRANK BONILLA, eds. 1993. *Latinos in a Changing U.S. Economy.* Newbury Park, Calif.: Sage Publications.

Bibliography

MUÑÓZ, CARLOS. 1988. *Youth, Identity, Power: The Chicano Movement.* New York: Verso.

NORTHERN CALIFORNIA WATSONVILLE STRIKE SUPPORT COMMITTEE (NCWSSC). 1987. "Strike Chronology." Watsonville, Calif.: Cannery Worker Service Center.

Nuestras vidas: Recordando, luchando, y transformando. 1987. Yearbook 2. New York: El Barrio Popular Education Program.

O'BRIEN, SHARON. "Cultural Rights: A Conflict of Values." *Law and Inequality* 5 (1987): 267–354.

OCHOA, MAYDA. 1991. "En Peligro Programa Educación Popular El Barrio." *Noticias del mundo,* June 3.

OLDENBURG, RAY. 1989. *The Great Good Place.* New York: Paragon House.

ONG, AIWHA. 1992. "Limits to Cultural Accumulation: Chinese Capitalists on the Pacific Rim." In *Towards a Transnational Perspective on Migration: Race, Class, Ethnicity and Nationalism Reconsidered,* ed. N. G. Schiller et al. Annals of the New York Academy of Sciences 645 (July): 125–43.

ONG, PAUL, ET AL. 1993. "Poverty and Employment Issues in the Inner Urban Core." In *South Central Los Angeles: Anatomy of an Urban Crisis,* ed. Allen J. Scott and Richard Brown, pp. 1–20. The Lewis Center for Regional Policy Studies, Working Paper Series, no. 6.

OSUNA, JUAN J. 1949. *A History of Education in Puerto Rico.* Río Piedras, Puerto Rico: University of Puerto Rico Press.

PARDO, MARY. 1990. "Mexican American Women Grassroots Community Activists (Mothers of East Los Angeles)." *Frontiers* 11(1): 1–7.

Paso a paso: Luchando por nuestro futuro. 1989. Yearbook 4. New York: El Barrio Popular Education Program.

PERIN, CONSTANCE. 1977. *Everything in Its Place: Social Order and Land Use in America.* Princeton, N.J.: Princeton University Press.

———. 1988. *Belonging in America: Reading Between the Lines.* Madison: University of Wisconsin Press.

PESQUERA, BEATRIZ M., AND DENISE M. SEGURA. 1993. "There Is No Going Back: Chicanas and Feminism." In *Chicana Critical Issues,* ed. Norma Alarcón et al., pp. 95–115. Berkeley: Third Woman Press.

PHILLIPS, BRENDA D. 1991. *Post-Disaster Sheltering and Housing of Hispanics, the Elderly and the Homeless.* Final report submitted to the National Science Foundation, August.

PHILLIPS, BRENDA D., AND MELINDA HUTCHINS. 1991. "Living in the Aftermath: Blaming Process in the Loma Prieta Earthquake." Unpublished research report.

PORTELLI, ALESSANDRO. 1991. "'The Time of My Life': Functions of Time in Oral History." In *The Death of Luigi Trastulli and Other Stories: Form and Meaning in Oral History,* ed. A. Portelli. Albany, N.Y.: SUNY Press.

POYO, G. E., AND G. M. HINOJOSA, eds. 1991. *Tejano Origins in Eighteenth-Century San Antonio.* Austin: University of Texas Press.

PRATT, MARY LOUISE. 1992. *Imperial Eyes: Travel Writing and Transculturation.* London and New York: Routledge.

¡Progresando en español! . . . porque es nuestro idioma. 1991. Yearbook 7. New York: El Barrio Popular Education Program.

REINHOLD, ROBERT. 1993. "A Welcome for Immigrants Turns to Resentment." *New York Times*, August 25.

Revista do Patrimônio Histórico e Artístico Nacional. 1996. Antonio A. Arantes, ed. No. 24. Cidadanía Brasilia: Ministério da Cultura.

RINGER, BENJAMIN B. 1983. *We the People and Others: Duality and America's Treatment of Racial Minorities.* London and New York: Tavistock with Methuen.

RÍOS, OSCAR. 1987a. "Roundtable Discussion with the Watsonville Workers." *Forward* 7(1) (January): 3–23.

———. 1987b. "Watsonville: Historic Victory in Cannery Strike." *Unity*, March 16, 1ff.

ROBERTS, BRYAN R. 1995. *The Making of Citizens: Cities of Peasants Revisited.* London: Arnold.

ROCCO, RAYMOND. 1996. "Latino Los Angeles: Reframing Boundaries/Borders." In *The City: Los Angeles and Urban Theory at the End of the Twentieth Century*, ed. Edward Soja and Allen J. Scott, pp. 365–89. Berkeley: University of California Press.

ROHTER, LARRY. 1993. "Revisiting Immigration and the Open-Door Policy." *New York Times*, September 19.

ROMO, RICARDO. 1977. "The Urbanization of Southwestern Chicanos in the Early 20th Century." In *New Directions in Chicano Scholarship*, ed. Raymund Paredes and Ricardo Romo, pp. 183–207. University of California, Santa Barbara, Center for Chicano Studies.

———. 1983. *East Los Angeles: History of a Barrio.* Austin: University of Texas Press.

ROSALDO, RENATO. 1985. "Assimilation Revisited." Stanford Center for Chicano Research. Working Paper Series no. 9 (July), Stanford, Calif.

———. 1989. *Culture and Truth: The Remaking of Social Analysis.* Boston: Beacon Press.

———. 1990. "Re-Imagining National Communities." Paper presented at the Shelby Cullon Davis Center for Historical Studies, Princeton, N.J., September 28. Also published in *Decadencia y auge de las identidades: Cultura nacional, identidad cultural y modernización*, ed. José Manuel Valenzuela, pp. 191–201. Tijuana, Mexico: El Colegio de la Frontera Norte.

———. 1993. "Ciudadanía cultural en San José, California." Paper presented at the International Colloquium "From Local to Global Culture: Anthropological Perspectives," Universidad Autónoma Metropolitana-Iztapalapa, Mexico City, March 29–31.

———. N.d. "Assimilation Revisited." Paper presented at the faculty seminar at the Stanford Center for Chicano Research.

ROSALDO, RENATO, AND WILLIAM V. FLORES. 1987. Notes on Cultural Citizenship. Unpublished manuscript. Stanford Center for Chicano Research. Stanford, Calif.

———. 1993. "Identity, Conflict, and Evolving Latino Communities: Cultural Citizenship in San Jose, California." Research Report No. G5-90-5, Fund for Research on Resolution, National Institute for Dispute Resolution. Washington, D.C.

ROWE, MARSHA, ed. 1992. *Sacred Space*. New York: Serpent's Tail.

RUIZ, VICKI L. 1987. *Cannery Women, Cannery Lives: Mexican Women, Unionization, and the California Food Processing Industry, 1930–1950*. Albuquerque: University of New Mexico Press.

———. 1990. "A Promise Unfulfilled: Mexican Cannery Workers in Southern California." In *Unequal Sisters: A Multicultural Reader in U.S. Women's History*, ed. Ellen Carol DuBois and Vicki L. Ruiz, pp. 264–74. New York: Routledge.

RUIZ, VICKI L., AND SUSAN TIANO, eds. 1987. *Women on the U.S.-Mexico Border: Responses to Change*. Boston: Allen and Unwin.

SACKS, KAREN BRODKIN. 1984. "Generations of Working-Class Families." In *My Troubles Are Going to Have Trouble with Me: Everyday Trials and Triumphs of Women Workers*, ed. Karen Sacks and Dorothy Remy, pp. 15–33. New Brunswick, N.J.: Rutgers University Press.

———. 1989. "Toward a Unified Theory of Class, Race, and Gender." *American Ethnologist* 16(3): 534–50.

SALDÍVAR, RAMON. 1991. "Narrative, Ideology and the Representation of American Literary History." In *Criticism in the Borderlands: Studies in Chicano Literature*, ed. Héctor Calderón and José David Saldívar, pp. 11–20. Durham, N.C.: Duke University Press.

SÁNCHEZ, GEORGE J. 1993. *Becoming Mexican American: Ethnicity, Culture, and Identity in Chicano Los Angeles, 1900–1945*. New York: Oxford University Press.

SAN JOSE, CITY OF. 1989. *San Jose: A Commitment to Housing*. Final Report of the Mayor's Task Force on Housing. San Jose, Calif.

———. 1992. "San Jose Fact Sheet." Department of City Planning. San Jose, Calif. San Jose Metropolitan Chamber of Commerce. 1991. *Economic Fact Book*. San Jose, Calif.

SAN MIGUEL, GUADALUPE, JR. 1987. *"Let All of Them Take Heed": Mexican Americans and the Campaign for Educational Equality in Texas, 1910–1981*. Austin: University of Texas Press.

SASSEN, SASKIA. 1988. *The Mobility of Labor and Capital: A Study in International Investment and Labor Flow*. New York: Cambridge University Press.

———. 1991. *The Global City: New York, London, Tokyo*. Princeton, N.J.: Princeton University Press.

———. 1992. "Why Migration?" *Report on the Americas* 26(1): 14–19.

SCHILLING, R. 1987. "Study Dramatizes Food Industry Plight." *Watsonville Register-Pajaronian*, March 19, p. 1.

SCHLESINGER, ARTHUR. 1991, 1992. *The Disuniting of America*. Knoxville: Whittle Direct Books; 1992, New York: W. W. Norton.

SCOTT, ALLEN J. 1993. *Technopolis: High-Technology Industry and Regional Development in Southern California*. Berkeley: University of California Press.

SEGAL, WILLIAM. 1987. "Victory in Watsonville." *Labor Center Reporter* (Center for

Labor Research and Education, University of California, Berkeley, Institute of Industrial Relations) 210 (April): 1–2.

———. 1988a. "California's Frozen Food Industry: Who Controls It? Where Is It Going?" Presentation to the Cannery Workers Conference, Watsonville, January 23. Watsonville, Calif.: Centro José H. López Para Los Trabajadores de Canería.

———. 1988b. "Economic Dualism and Collective Bargaining Structure in Food Manufacturing Industries." Ph.D. diss., University of California, Berkeley.

Segura, Denise A., and Jennifer L. Pierce. 1993. "Chicana/o Family Structure and Gender Personality: Chodorow, Familism, and Psychoanalytic Sociology Revisited." *Signs* 19: 62–91.

Shklar, Judith N. 1991. *American Citizenship: The Quest for Inclusion.* Cambridge, Mass.: Harvard University Press.

Silvestrini Pacheco, Blanca. 1980. "The Needlework Industry in Puerto Rico, 1915–1940: Women's Transition from Home to Factory." Paper presented at the 12th Conference of Caribbean Historians. Trinidad, W.I.

Skerry, Peter. 1993. *Mexican Americans: The Ambivalent Minority.* New York: Free Press.

Slater, David, ed. 1985. *New Social Movements and the State in Latin America.* Amsterdam: CEDLA.

Smith, Michael Peter, and Joe R. Feagin, eds. 1987. *The Capitalist City: Global Restructuring and Community Politics.* New York: Basil Blackwell.

Soja, Edward W. 1987. "Economic Restructuring and the Internationalization of the Los Angeles Region." In *The Capitalist City: Global Restructuring and Community Politics,* ed. Michael Peter Smith and Joe R. Feagin, pp. 178–89. New York: Basil Blackwell.

———. 1989. In *Postmodern Geographies: The Reassertion of Space in Critical Social Theory.* New York: Verso.

Sommer, Doris. 1988. "Not Just a Personal Story: Women's 'Testimonios' and Plural Self." In *Life/Lines: Theorizing Women's Autobiography,* ed. B. Brodski and C. Schenck. Ithaca: Cornell University Press.

Sontag, Deborah. 1992. "Noncitizens and the Right to Vote." *New York Times,* July 31.

Sorkin, Michael, ed. 1992. *Variations on a Theme Park: The New American City and the End of Public Space.* New York: Noonday Press.

Teamsters (International Brotherhood of Teamsters). 1987. "Watsonville Strike Settled: An 18-Month-Long-Struggle Ends—Courage and Determination Pays Off." *The Teamster* (April): 1–4.

Tilly, L. A. 1978. "Women and Family Strategies in French Proletarian Families." University of Michigan, Michigan Occasional Papers no. 4 (Fall).

Torruellas, Rosa M. 1995. " '*Mi sacrificio bien pago*': Puerto Rican Women on Welfare and Family Values." In *The Anthropology of Lower Income Urban Enclaves: The Case of East Harlem,* ed. Judith Freidenberg, pp. 177–87. New York: New York Academy of Sciences.

Torruellas, Rosa M., Rina Benmayor, Anneris Goris, and Ana Juarbe. 1989. "Testimonio, Identity and Empowerment." *Centro Boletín* 11 (Summer): 6.

———. 1991. *Affirming Cultural Citizenship in the Puerto Rican Community: Critical Literacy and the El Barrio Popular Education Program.* New York: Centro de Estudios Puertorriqueños, Hunter College. Also in *Literacy as Praxis: Culture, Language and Pedagogy*, ed. Catherine E. Walsh. Norwood, N.J.: Ablex.

Torruellas, Rosa M., Rina Benmayor, and Ana Juarbe. 1996. "Negotiating Gender, Work, and Welfare: *Familia* as Productive Labor among Puerto Rican Women in New York City." In *Puerto Rican Women and Work: Bridges in Transnational Labor*, ed. Altagracia Ortiz, pp. 184–208. Philadelphia: Temple University Press.

Tranchese, Carmelo, S.J. 1949. Foreword. In *Los Pastores: A Christmas Drama of Old Mexico*, ed. Carmelo Tranchese S.J. and Leandro Granado. San Antonio: Treviño Brothers.

Trounstine, Philip J., and Terry Christensen. 1982. *Movers and Shakers: The Study of Community Power.* New York: St. Martin's Press.

Turner, Bryan. 1990. "Outline of a Theory of Citizenship." *Sociology* 24(2): 189–217.

———. 1991. "Further Specification of the Citizenship Concept: A Reply to M. L. Harrison." *Sociology* 25(2): 215–18.

———. 1993. "Outline of a Theory of Human Rights." *Sociology* 27(3): 489–512.

Turner, Steve. 1987. "Strike Town, U.S.A." *IMAGE* (June 7): 23–35.

Turner, Victor. 1986. "Dewey, Dilthey, and Drama: An Essay in the Anthropology of Experience." In *The Anthropology of Experience*, ed. Victor Turner and Edward Bruner, pp. 33–44. Urbana: University of Illinois Press.

Twine, Fred. 1994. *Citizenship and Social Rights.* Thousand Oaks, Calif.: Sage Publications.

Valle, Victor, and Rodolfo D. Torres. 1994. "Latinos in a 'Postindustrial' Disorder: Politics in a Changing City." *Socialist Review* 23(4): 1–28.

van Steenbergen, Bart, ed. 1994. *The Condition of Citizenship.* Thousand Oaks, Calif.: Sage Publications.

Vélez Ibáñez, Carlos. 1983. *The Cultural Systems of Rotating Credit Associations among Urban Mexicans and Chicanos.* New Brunswick, N.J.: Rutgers University Press.

———. 1993. "U.S. Mexicans in the Borderlands: Being Poor Without the Underclass." In *In the Barrios: Latinos and the Underclass Debate*, ed. Joan Moore and Raquel Pinderhughes, pp. 195–220. New York: Russell Sage Foundation.

———. 1996. *Border Visions: Mexican Cultures of the Southwest United States*, pp. 163, 159–67. Tucson: University of Arizona Press.

Visweswaran, Kamala. 1994. *Fictions of Feminist Ethnography.* Minneapolis and London: University of Minnesota Press.

Watsonville, City of. 1989. *Watsonville: 2005—A Guide for Orderly Community Development.* Planning Department, Watsonville, Calif.

Watsonville Strike Support Committee. 1987. "Chronology on Wells Fargo."

Weber, D.J., ed. 1973. *Foreigners in Their Native Land.* Albuquerque: University of New Mexico Press.

WEST, CORNEL. 1993. *Prophetic Thought in Modern Times.* Monroe, Minn.: Common Courage Press.

WIEBE, ROBERT H. 1976. *The Segmented Society: An Introduction to the Meaning of America.* London: Oxford University Press.

WILLIAMS, PATRICIA. 1991. *The Alchemy of Race and Rights.* Cambridge, Mass.: Harvard University Press.

WILLIAMS, RAYMOND. 1977. *Marxism and Literature.* Oxford: Oxford University Press.

WILSON, MICHAEL, AND DEBORAH SILVERTON ROSENFELT. 1978. *Salt of the Earth.* Old Westbury, N.Y.: Feminist Press.

WILSON, WILLIAM JULIUS. 1987. *The Truly Disadvantaged: The Inner City, the Underclass and Public Policy.* Chicago: Chicago University Press.

WISE, DEBORAH. 1985. "Where Frozen Food Wages Are a Burning Issue." *Business Week* (November 25): 44.

YBARRA, LEA. 1982. "When Wives Work: The Impact on Chicano Families." *Journal of Marriage and the Family* 44(1): 169–78.

ZAVELLA, PATRICIA. 1985. "'Abnormal Intimacy': The Varying Work Networks of Chicana Cannery Workers." *Feminist Studies* 11(3) (Fall): 541–58.

———. 1987. *Women's Work and Chicano Families: Cannery Workers of the Santa Clara Valley.* Ithaca: Cornell University Press.

———. 1988. "The Politics of Race and Gender: Organizing Chicana Cannery Workers in Northern California." In *Women and the Politics of Empowerment,* ed. Ann Bookman and Sandra Morgen, pp. 202–224. Philadelphia: Temple University Press.

———. 1989. "The Problematic Relationship of Feminism and Chicana Studies." *Women's Studies* 17: 25–36.

ZUKIN, SHARON. 1991. *Landscapes of Power: From Detroit to Disney World.* Berkeley: University of California Press.

———. 1995. *The Cultures of Cities.* Oxford: Blackwell.

Contributors

RINA BENMAYOR is professor of literature, oral history, and cultural studies at California State University at Monterey Bay. She chairs the department of Human Communication and is founder of the Oral History and Community Memory Institute and Archive. Formerly, she directed the Cultural Studies Task Force at the Centro de Estudios Puertorriqueños, Hunter College, CUNY. She is author of *Romances judeo-españoles de Oriente*, a book on Sephardic ballads, and co-editor of *Migration and Identity*, a special issue of the *International Yearbook of Oral History and Life Stories* (Oxford University Press). She has published on Puerto Rican women in the garment industry, Hispanic and Latina literatures, Cuban popular music, and oral history and community empowerment.

RICHARD FLORES is associate professor of anthropology and Mexican American studies at the University of Texas, Austin, where he teaches performance theory, Mexican-American culture and folklore, and critical cultural theory. He is the author of *Los Pastores: History and Performance in the Mexican Shepherds' Play of South Texas*, published by the Smithsonian Institution Press, and editor of a new edition of *History and Legends of the Alamo*, by Adina de Zavala (Recovering the U.S. Hispanic Literary Heritage project, Arte Público Press). He has a book forthcoming on the cultural history of the Alamo.

WILLIAM V. FLORES is dean of the College of Social and Behavioral Sciences at California State University, Northridge. He received and M.A. in political science at Stanford University, spent many years working with community organizations and nonprofit agencies, and returned to complete a Ph.D. in social theory and public policy at Stanford in 1987. He has taught at Santa Clara University and California State University, Fresno, and has published on community empowerment, voting rights, and the relationship between culture and political action. In 1987–88, at Stanford, he served as associate director of the Inter-University Program for Latino Research, where he helped to organize the Cultural Studies Working Group that produced this book; in 1993, he was a Rockefeller Humanities Scholar-in-Residence at the Centro de Estudios Puertorriqueños, where the co-editing of this book began.

Contributors

Ana L. Juarbe is a senior health educator in New York City. She is completing a master's degree in public health in the Community Health Education Program at Hunter College. Born in Isabela, Puerto Rico, she was raised on the Lower East Side. From 1983 to 1993, she was a researcher in the Oral History and Cultural Studies research teams at the Centro de Estudios Puertorriqueños.

Raymond Rocco is a professor of political science at the University of California, Los Angeles. His research focuses on the transformation of Latino communities in the United States, particularly on the process of economic, political, and cultural restructuring and its effects in reshaping policy agendas around issues of citizenship.

Renato Rosaldo is Lucy Stern Professor in the Social Sciences at Stanford University, where he served as director of the Center for Chicano Research and chair of the anthropology department. He is author of *Ilongot Headhunting, 1883–1974: A Study in Society and History*, and *Culture and Truth: The Remaking of Social Analysis.*

Blanca G. Silvestrini is professor of history at the University of Puerto Rico at Río Piedras, and vice president for Academic Affairs for the UPR system. She has published extensively on Caribbean social history, women's transition from home work to factory, and on Puerto Rican history. More recently, she has devoted most of her research and writing to the construction of cultural rights. In 1987, she was a fellow of the Center for Advanced Studies in the Behavioral Sciences at Stanford University, and from 1988 to 1990 taught as visiting professor at the Stanford Law School. She holds a Ph.D. in History and a J.D. (UPR) and a J.S.M. (Stanford).

Rosa M. Torruellas, who passed away in 1993, was the founding director of the Programa de Educación Popular del Barrio (El Barrio Popular Education Program) in East Harlem (1985–1991), and associate director of the Language and Education Task Force at the Centro de Estudios Puertorriqueños, Hunter College, CUNY. She received her Ph.D. in anthropology from New York University. Her dissertation on language politics is titled "Class, Identity, and Ideology: Learning English in Three Private Schools in Puerto Rico." Her subsequent research and publications focused on gender and Puerto Rican community empowerment. At the time of her death she was involved in a research project on Puerto Rican women, welfare, and the state.

Acknowledgments

Like all projects, this was a collective endeavor of many who gave inspiration, vision, and support—*comadres* and *compadres*, *madrinas* and *padrinos*, *madres*, *padres*, *hijos* and *ahijados*, *panas*, *cuates*, created families and communities. This work would not exist without you. *Gracias*,

first and foremost, to the communities—from El Barrio to Watsonville, *pasando por* San Antonio, San Jose, y Los Angeles—who welcomed us into neighborhoods and homes, and entrusted us with their life stories;

to the many student collaborators who contributed to the research, some of whom are now professors in their own right: Laura Gómez, who assisted Blanca Silvestrini, Renato Rosaldo, and William Flores in San Jose, and who has since joined the faculty of the School of Law at the University of California, Los Angeles; Susana Gallardo, also of the San Jose project and currently teaching at Occidental College; Gilbert and Reyna Ramírez, who helped conduct interviews in San Jose; Martín Valadez, who interviewed undocumented Mexican day workers; Quynh Tran, who interviewed Vietnamese residents of San Jose; Fátima Rodríguez, now a doctoral student at Purdue, who conducted library and field research; Estela Mejía, who assisted with interviews and transcriptions in the Watsonville project; William de la Torre, a professor at California State University, Northridge, who conducted field research in the Los Angeles project; in New York, Eric Quiñones Maurás, who transcribed every word of our Mini-Conference back in 1988; and Alicia Díaz Concepción, expert transcriber, literacy tutor in the El Barrio Program, budding ethnographer, and dancer extraordinaire;

to the Inter-University Program for Latino Research (IUP), for creating a national space for Latino comparative research in all fields and for generously seeding and nurturing our particular collaboration; to Frank Bonilla, second executive director of IUP, who has always believed in forging linkages, building community across borders, and lending steadfast support, as he has to our work; to Al Camarillo, first IUP executive director, who encouraged the formation of our Working Group in Culture; to David Hayes Bautista and Rodolfo de la Garza, then IUP Center directors at the University of California, Los Angeles, and the University of Texas, Austin; to our academic and administrative colleagues at our respective IUP-affiliated Centers; and to Charlene Aguilar-Fraga (Stanford), María Chacón and Ana LoBiondo (New York), who gave sustained administrative support to all the IUP projects, including ours;

to the foundations who funded many of the projects beyond the IUP: the Social Science Research Council/IUP Joint Committee for Public Policy Research on Hispanic Issues for partially supporting research in San Jose and New York; the Rockefeller Humanities Residency Program for enabling William Flores to spend a year at the Centro de Estudios Puertorriqueños, writing his pieces and beginning the co-editing process for this book; the Fund for Research on Dispute Resolution and the National Institute for Dispute Resolution for research in San Jose; California State University, Fresno, and the Stanford Center for Chicano Research for minigrants to support research in Watsonville; and the Centro de Estudios Puertorriqueños, Hunter College, for much in-kind support in the New York research;

to our scholarly *familia*—Gregorio Mora, professor of Chicano Studies at San Jose State University, who identified several key families for interviews and who provided a family history of downtown San Jose; Dr. Antonio Lauria-Perricelli for sustained feedback on the research in El Barrio, for venues at the New York Academy of Sciences, and for *mucha solidaridad*; Evelina Dagnino, professor of political science at the Universidade Estadual de Campinas, Brazil, for her valuable theoretical interventions and commentary and for participation in our group during her sabbatical year in the United States; to our other bridge to Brazil, Mary García Castro of the Universidade Federal de Bahia, for reviewing and critiquing various essays in this book during her Rockefeller fellowship year at the Centro; and to Camille Rodríguez (president, Puerto Rican Studies Association), Nélida Pérez (head librarian, Centro Library and Archives), and Iraida López (founding director of the CUNY–Caribbean Exchange Program), *comadres* and solid bridge-builders who supported the idea of this book and what it stands for;

to our brave editor at Beacon Press, Andrew Hrycyna, who took on the arduous task of getting us to final manuscript, pursuing us across the country, and gifting us with his trust and perseverance when life-threatening illnesses loomed large; and to Nancy Evans of Wilsted & Taylor Publishing Services, a truly sharp and most knowledgeable copy editor, who tamed our unruly sourcing practices.

This book has been shaped by all these contributors. It has also been marked with sadness and danger. In 1993, our beloved colleague and friend Rosa Torruellas died of cancer at the age of thirty-six. While we dedicate the book to her, enough cannot be said of her courage. Even though in considerable pain, she came to our last group meeting at Stanford in 1992, such was her commitment to new research on Latino communities. She was an inspiration to all of us and greatly influenced our conceptualization of cultural citizenship. We thank her husband, Lucas Andino, and her son, Eduardo José, for unselfishly sharing her with us. Deep gratitude also goes to William and Velia Flores, and to Antonio and Diana Flores, who stayed by their son and father's side, giving him comfort and support to successfully fight cancer and a stroke in 1995. If it were not for them and their love, the introduction and epilogue of this book would not have been completed. Ironically, just before this book went to copyediting, Renato Rosaldo also suffered a stroke. He was able to return to writing and complete his essay for this book, his first intellectual endeavor since his trauma, thanks to his caring family, Mary Louise Pratt, Olivia, Manuel, and Sam Rosaldo. This book, then, owes its deepest gratitude to the rock-solid support of our most immediate *familias*. We hope they will find themselves reflected herein.

Rina Benmayor and William Flores
March 1997

Index

Absorption, 9, 15
Acculturation, 9
Acto (skit), 270–72
Acuña, Rodolfo, 102, 211
Affirmation, 13; contexts for, 159–67; of cultural rights, citizenship as, 201–9; and Watsonville cannery strike, 251–54
Affirmative action, 4, 5, 34
AFL-CIO, 226
African Americans, 5, 29, 92, 94; citizenship for, 257, 258; concept of rights for, 58; contributions made by, 5; electoral violence against, 34; in Los Angeles, 106; in Los Angeles County, 103; in San Jose, 66, 71, 72
Afro-Brazilians, 208
Agency, 12–13; and Watsonville cannery strike, 246–50
Agnew, John A., 76
Alamo, Battle of the, 127, 128
Alinsky, Saul, 149
Alvarado, Blanca, 272–73
Alvarez, Robert A., Jr., 259
Alvarez, Sonia E., 122
American Anthropological Association, 14
American Folklore Association, 14
American Me (film), 6
American Studies Association, 14
Amish, 50–51
Anderson, Benedict, 208, 277; *Imagined Communities*, 73, 93
Antislavery movement, 96
Anzaldúa, Gloria, 53
Aprender a luchar, luchar es aprender (Learning to Struggle, Struggle Is Learning), 158, 163
Aranda, Josefina, 216
Arango, Alfredo, 155–56
Arizpe, Lourdes, 216
Aronowitz, Stanley, 147
Asian Americans, 29, 94; electoral violence against, 34; in Los Angeles County, 103; in San Jose, 66, 68, 71, 72
Asian Law Alliance, 272
Assimilation, 9, 15, 201; false assumptions about, 11–12; and Native American culture, 49–50
Autobiography, 158; autobiographical writing, 185
Ayala, Mrs. Carmen, 168, 194
Azize, Yamila, 160

Bardacke, Frank, 215, 220, 221, 223, 247
Barrio, 72, 78; in Los Angeles, 104; performance of Los Pastores in, 135–37. *See also* Community(ies)
Bauman, Richard, 142
Bellah, Robert, 81, 262; et al., *Habits of the Heart*, 15–16, 261
Belonging, 15–16, 58, 81
Benmayor, Rina, 12, 255, 262; "Claiming Cultural Citizenship in East Harlem," 20–21, 152–209
Bennett, William J., 4, 10
Bentham, Jeremy, 86
Bernabé, Lucio, 267, 268
Betancourt, Gloria, 220, 221, 248, 252; and cannery strike, 225, 228, 229, 230, 234; and concept of family, 234–35, 237; defeat of, as union leader, 226, 241, 242, 249; on effect of women's activism on men, 240; as political subject, 244; and Strike Committee, 241, 242–43
Bethlehem Steel, 111–12
Bhabha, Homi, 257
Bilingual education, 3, 17, 52, 259
Bilingualism, opposition to, 32
Bird's Eye, 215, 216
Black Power movement, 207–8
Blades, Rubén, 5

Index

Bonfil Batalla, Guillermo, 92
Bonilla, Frank, 160
Bookman, Ann, 234
Border, U.S.-Mexico, violence at, 33, 36
Border Patrol, U.S., 4, 272
Boyte, Harry C., 265
Briggs, Charles, 142
Brimelow, Peter, 4, 9
Brown, Martin L., 222
Browning, R., 67
Bruner, Edward M., 125
Buchanan, Pat, 98
Burek, S., 127, 129
Buscando un futuro mejor, 163, 168, 173

"California Civil Rights Initiative (CCRI)," 4, 34
California Processors and Growers (CPG), 220, 224
California State University, Northridge, 12
Campbell's, 215
Campinas, Universidade Estadual de, 14
Campos, Ricardo, 160
Campos, Tony, 217–18
Canneries, 63, 65, 83
Cannery strike (Watsonville, CA), 210–11; brief chronology of, 225–31; cultural citizenship, agency, and empowerment from, 246–50; cultural citizenship and affirmation from, 251–54; and dignity, respect, and rights, 231–33; emergence of women as political subjects during, 244–46; impact of, on family and community, 233–38; impact of women's activism in, on men, 238–40; and life in canneries, 218–19; significance of, 211–14; and Teamsters Union, 220–24; Watsonville as "Frozen Food Capital of the World," 214–18
Cannery Workers Committee (CWC), 267
Canning, Kathleen, 218
Cárdenas, G., 127, 129
Carrisosa, Fidelia, 238–39
Carvajal, Father Raúl, 230
Castells, Manuel, 16, 65, 164, 263; *The Dual City* (with J. Mollenkopf), 162
Castro, Mary García, 232, 246
Catholic church, 79–80, 145, 230, 252–53, 266, 270, 275
Católicos por La Raza, 275
Caulfield, Mina D., 212
Central Americans, 7, 8
Central Labor Council, 272; of Santa Clara, 226
Centro de Estudios Puertorriqueños, 12, 153, 155
Cervantes, Lorna Dee, 37–38
Chabrán, Richard, 12
Chapa, J., 127, 129
Chávez, César, 211, 228
Chicanos, 31–32, 48; claiming community and rights for, 264–74, 276; in Los Angeles, 275; political activism of, 8; in San Jose, 87–92, 264–74. *See also* Cannery strike
Christensen, Terry, 62, 64
Chrysler Credit Corporation, 111
Churches, performance of Los Pastores in, 137–39
Cinco de Mayo, 67
Cisneros, Henry, 8, 149
Citizenship, 27–32; as affirmation of cultural rights, 201–9; cultural understanding of, 166; and culture and oppositional politics in Los Angeles, 115–23; and ethnographic grounding in Los Angeles, 110–15; new politics of, 95–96; traditional legal definition of, 11; for undocumented immigrants, 256–61. *See also* Cultural citizenship
Civic membership, crisis of, 16
Civil rights movement, 96
Civil society, for undocumented immigrants, 275–77
Cleaning Up Silicon Valley Coalition, 66
Clemente, Mrs. Carmen, 187
Clifford, James, 45–46, 48
Clinton, Bill, 8
Coalition of Labor Union Women (CLUW), 249

Index

Cohen, Laurie, 211
Collazo, Mrs. Rosario, 187–88
Collective identity: and building community, 182–201; and group rights, 196–201
Collective memory, 154; identities, 195, 198; solidarity, 189, 191–92; meanings, and personal transformation, 167–82
Colombians, 105–6
Colonialism, 153, 159, 185, 202
Comité pro Derechos de Los Niños Indocumentados (Committee for the Rights of Undocumented Children), 269–70
Communities Organized for Public Service (COPS), 149–50
Community(ies), 15–17; building, and collective identity, 182–201; and cannery strike, 233–38; changing notions of, 72–73; imagined, and social gatherings, 73–75, 93, 208; national to local, 81–83, 92–94; for undocumented immigrants, 264–74
Console, Mort, 224, 225, 228, 229, 233–34, 248
Console family, 220
Constitution, U.S., 29, 96; culture rights and, 46–53
Contextualization: defined, 142; and politics of "re-membering," 142–46
Cortés, Felix, 155–56
Cortez, Ernesto, 149
Corwin, Miles, 224, 225
Cossío, Mrs., 169, 176–77, 197
Coto, Celestino, 155–56
County Revenue Sharing Grant, 265
Crocetti, *see* J. J. Crocetti
Cruz Takash, Paule, 214, 215, 217, 218
Cubans, 7, 105
Cultural citizenship: culture and, 40–46; defined, 57; affirmation of, 164, 175, 182, 191; in El Barrio Program, 189–96; Rosaldo and W. Flores on concept of, 59–61; site for claiming, 189–96; struggle for, 153; for undocumented immigrants, 261–64; and Watsonville cannery strike, 246–54. *See also* Citizenship
Cultural rights: citizenship as affirmation of, 201–9; and entitlement, 167; struggle for, 154; for undocumented immigrants, 275–77. *See also* Cultural citizenship, Human rights
Culture, 32–38; and citizenship and oppositional politics in Los Angeles, 115–23; and cultural citizenship, 40–46; rights and Constitution, 46–53
Culture Clash, 5
CUNY, 192, 194, 198

Dagnino, Evelina, 14, 204, 205, 208
Davis, Mike, *City of Quartz: Excavating the Future in Los Angeles*, 84–86
Declaration of Independence, 275
de la Garza, Rodolfo, 261
del Castillo, Adelaida, 211, 212
De León, A., 127
Del Mar, 215
DePalma, Anthony, 216
Día de San Juan, 67, 68, 74
Dial Corporation, 112
Dignity (*dignidad*), concept of, 152, 166, 203; issue of, 231–33
Dole, Robert, 34
Dominicans, 7–8, 259
Dornan, Bob, 8
Downtown redevelopment (San Jose), 89–92
Duany, Luis, 165
Duncan, James S., 76
Durham, Eunice Ribeiro, 208

Eckstein, Susan, 122
Eisenstein, Sarah, 236
El Barrio Popular Education Program (East Harlem), 152–54; citizenship as affirmation of cultural rights in, 201–9; collective identity and building community in, 182–201; contexts for affirmation in, 159–67; description of, 154–59; fulfilling long-deferred dream in, 169–75; personal transformation and collective meanings in, 167–82; postscript to,

Index

205–9; recreating *familia* in, 182–89; shifting priorities and new goals in, 176–82; site for claiming cultural citizenship in, 189–96
Elisalde, Angie, 224–25
El Norte (film), 6
Empowerment, 12; and education, 153, 155; and Watsonville cannery strike, 246–50
English as a Second Language (ESL) class, 155
English language, 52–53
Enlightenment, 27, 29
Escobar, Arturo, 122
Estefan, Gloria, 5
Ethnographic grounding and citizenship in Los Angeles, 110–15
Etzioni, Amitai, 16
Evangelical Christians, 34, 36
Evans, Sara M., 265

Fagen, Richard, 210
Fahey, Joe, 241
Family, *familia*: attack on, 194; and cannery strike, 233–38; recreating, at El Barrio Popular Education Program, 182–89, 192; references to undocumented as, 267–68; survival of, 199, *valores de*, 187, 203
Farah strike, 211
Feagin, Joe R., 107
Federal Welfare Reform Act (1996), 3
Fed Mart, 111
Feminist movement, 96
Firestone Tires, 111
First Amendment, 50
Flores, Richard R., 12, 270; "Aesthetic Process and Cultural Citizenship: The Membering of a Social Body in San Antonio," 19–20, 124–51
Flores, William V., 12, 16; "Citizens vs. Citizenry: Undocumented Immigrants and Latino Cultural Citizenship," 22–23, 255–77; "Identity, Conflict, and Evolving Latino Communities: Cultural Citizenship in San Jose, California," 18, 57–96, 261–62; "*Mujeres en Huelga*: Cultural Citizenship and Gender Empowerment in a Cannery Strike," 21–22, 210–54
Food Committee (Watsonville), 226, 235
Food, Tobacco, Agricultural and Allied Workers (FTA-CIO), 220
Forces, global to local, 83–87
Ford Motor Company, 65
Foucault, Michel, 86
Fourteenth Amendment, 50
Free Associated State, 160
Freidenberg-Herbstein, Judith, 74
Freire, Paulo, 156, 174, 208, 270
Friedmann, John, 99–100
Fuentes, Carlos, 98
Funds of knowledge, 153, 160–61, 174–75

García, Alma, 213
García, Andy, 6
García, Ernestina, 267–68
García, R., 128
García Canclini, Nestor, 14, 61, 92
Garment workers, 160–61
Gay rights, 275
GED class, 172
Gender, 28–29; claim for cultural respect, 166; and cultural citizenship, 210–254; exploitation, 172; gendered ideologies, 158; and national community, 166; solidarity, 191–92
General Foods, 216
General Motors, 65, 111, 112
Gil, David, 229–30, 252, 253
Gilroy, Paul, 95, 256; *There Ain't No Black in the Union Jack*, 16
Giroux, Henry A., 256, 271
Gittell, Marilyn, 179
Gold Rush, 62, 214
Gómez, Cruz, 249
Gómez-Quiñones, Juan, 259
Gonzalez, Henry B., 149
González, Lydia Milagros, 160
González, Mrs., 169–70, 171–72, 175, 197–98, 201–2
González, Robert, 102

Index

Gottdiener, Mark, 15, 263
Granado, Don Leandro, 129–30, 148
"Green cards," 273–74
Green Cards, INS, 274
Green Giant, 215, 216, 248
Guadalupe Hidalgo, Treaty of, 94, 127, 214
Guerrero, Natalia, 177
Gulf War, 33

Haagen, Alexander, 86
Halbwachs, Maurice, 267
Hall, Stuart, 14, 30, 95, 256, 258
Harding, Vincent, 81
Hazle, Maline, 67
Held, David, 14, 30, 95, 258
Hernández, Mrs., 152, 191, 200
Herrnstein, Richard, *The Bell Curve* (with C. Murray), 5
Hiss, Tony, 76
History Task Force, 160
Hoffman, Abraham, 260
Hormel strike, 229, 246, 248
Hotel and Restaurant Workers (HERE 2), 229
Huerta, Dolores, 211
Huertas, Esther, 163–64, 178, 180
Human rights, notions of, 14–15, 203; and cultural rights, 196
Hunter College, 9, 12, 153, 191–92
Huntington Park Vendor's Association (HPVA), 119
Hutchins, Melinda, 215

Idar, Nicasio, 128
Immigration and Naturalization Service (INS), 4, 221, 265, 269–74
Immigration Reform Act (1996), 3
Immigration Reform Control Act (1986), 273
Indian Religious Freedom Act (1978), 48–49
Industrial Areas Foundation (IAF), 149
Intermarriage, assimilation and, 11
International Monetary Fund, 108
International Women's Day, 211
International Workers Day, 211
Inter-University Program for Latino Research (IUP), 12–13, 205, 210

Jackson, Jesse, 227–28, 253
Jelín, Elizabeth, 208
Jesús, Mrs. Luz de, 168
J. J. Crocetti, 215, 224, 227
Johnson, Bob, 230
Jovellanos, Mrs., 165–66, 179–80, 200, 208–9
Juarbe, Ana, 12, 156; "Claiming Cultural Citizenship in East Harlem," 20–21, 152–209
Julia, Raul, 6

Kanda, Allen, 63, 66
Karst, Kenneth, 46, 47, 48, 58; *Belonging to America*, 257
Kasinitz, Philip, 74
Kearney, Michael, 13
King, Martin Luther, Jr., 4
King, Richard, 220, 226, 242
King, Rodney, 2, 256
Kymlicka, Will, 114

La Bamba (film), 6
La Clínica, 265–66, 269, 270, 272, 273
La Confederación de la Raza Unida, 267
Lamott, Anne, 37
Lamphere, Louise, 218
Language, importance of issue of, for Latinos, 52–53
"Language deficiency," 52–53
La Raza Unida Party, 211
Latin American Studies Association, 14
Latino Agenda Coalition, 227, 250
Latino Cultural Studies Working Group, 1, 6–7; concept paper of, 12, 44–45; Inter-University Program (IUP), 13, 44
Latino Issues Forum of Santa Clara County, 65–66
La Tolteca tortilla workers' strike, 211
Lauria, Antonio, 12, 13
Lau v. Nichols, 52–53
Law and Society, 14
League of United Latin American Citizens (LULAC), 217, 227, 250, 259

Index

LeBlanc, Brigitte, 65
Leghorn, Lisa, 212, 232, 239
Lerma, Lydia, 235, 240, 249–50
Levi Strauss, 249
Life histories, collection of, 158–59, 160, 169
Limón, J. E., 128
Linares, Guillermo, 8, 259
Lindsey, Robert, 216
Lipsitz, George, 267, 270
Literacy, 154–193; critical, 157
Little Michoacán, 264–65
Loma Prieta earthquake, 215
Lomelí, Cuca, 233, 234, 238, 243
López, Sergio, 220, 225, 226, 241, 242, 249
Los Angeles, 7; citizenship, culture, and oppositional politics in, 115–23; citizenship and ethnographic grounding in, 110–15; Davis' analysis of, 84–86; global economics and local restructuring in, 107–10; Latino population of, 8, 102–3, 104; reconfiguration of Latino, 100–107; riots and rebellion (1992), 2
Los Angeles Street Vendor's Association (AVALA), 119
Los Lobos, 5
Los Pastores (San Antonio nativity play), 124–26, 129–30; conjunction of performance and politics in, 146–51; contextualization and politics of "re-membering" in, 142–46; negotiated spaces for performances of, 134–42; performance of, 132–34; performance of, in the barrio, 135–37; performance of, in churches, 137–39; performance of, at San Jose Mission, 139–42; performers of, 130–32
Luttrell, Wendy, 249

McCormack, Dan, 63, 66
Macedo, D., 156, 174
Marshall, T. H., 122–23, 257
Martínez, Esther, 186
MEChA, 229, 250
Melville, Margarita B., 212
Membership: crisis of civic, 16; for undocumented immigrants, 256–61
Mexican(s): claiming community and rights for, 264–74; immigrants, 93–94; in Los Angeles, 8, 85, 102, 103, 105, 106; in New York City, 7; in San Antonio, 8, 126–30 (*see also* Los Pastores); in San Jose, 84, 89–92, 264–74. *See also* Cannery strike
Mexican American Legal Defense and Educational Fund (MALDEF), 103, 149
Mexican American Political Association (MAPA), 217–18, 227, 250
Mi Familia (film), 6
Migration, Puerto Rican, 153, 159, 161
Mini-Conference on Cultural Citizenship, 13
Mirandé, Alfredo, 212
Molina, Bea, 227
Mollenkopf, John H., 65, 164, 263; *The Dual City* (with M. Castells), 162
Monoglot citizens, 82, 83
Montejano, David, 128
Montoya, José, 82
Moore, Joan W., 98
Mora, Greg, 77
Mora, Magdalena, 211, 212
Moreno, Chavelo, 249, 251–52; arrest of, 244–45; and cannery strike, 225–28, 236–40, 247; and Strike Committee, 241–42, 244
Moreno, Luisa, 211
Multiculturalism, 4, 9
Muñóz, Carlos, 212
Murillo, Socorro, 230, 232–33, 235–36, 237–38, 245
Murray, Charles, *The Bell Curve* (with R. Herrnstein), 5
Music, explosion of clubs and restaurants promoting Latino, 121
Mutual aid (*ayuda mutua*), concept of, 152, 158

National Association for Chicano Studies, 14
National identity, Puerto Rican, 184
National Labor Relations Board, 228

Index

Native Alaskans, 49
Native Americans, 29, 92, 94; cultural rights of, viewed by courts, 48–50, 52; electoral violence against, 34
Native Hawaiians, 48, 49
Navarro, José Antonio, 127
New West, 215
New York Board of Education, 191
New York City, Latino population of, 7
Nicaraguans, 105
NorCal Frozen Foods, 215, 229, 243, 251
North American Free Trade Agreement (NAFTA), 216
Northern California Watsonville Strike Support Committee, 213, 227, 228, 229, 249
Nuestras vidas, 187

Obledo, Mario, 227
O'Brien, Sharon, 48, 49, 51
Ochoa, Mayda, 193
Oldenburg, Ray, 76
Olmos, Edward James, 6
"Operation Jobs," 272
"Operation Wetback," 266–67, 268, 269
Oral History Association, 14
Ortiz, Bethzaida, 174
Oscar Mayer, 112
Our Lady of Guadalupe Church (San Antonio), 130, 141, 148, 150

Páramo, Margarita, 230–31, 236, 244–45, 250
Pardo, Mary, 213
Parker, Katherine, 212, 232, 239
Parsons, Lucy Gonzáles, 211
Paso a paso: Luchando por nuestro futuro, 168, 175, 186, 192, 194
Pedraza, Pedro, 12, 155
People v. Woody, 49
Performance: and politics, conjunction of, 146–51; sociohistorical base of, 126–30
Perin, Constance, 45, 58, 81, 262; *Belonging in America*, 16, 261
Personal transformation, and collective meanings, 167–82
Peruvians, 105, 106
Peyote Way Church of God, Inc. v. Smith, 49
Phillips, Brenda D., 215
Pierce, Jennifer L., 212
Pillsbury, 215
Pinderhughes, Raquel, 98
Pizaña, Aniceto, 128
Pluralism, 9–10; cultural, 15
Politics: conjunction of performance and, 146–51; oppositional, and citizenship and culture in Los Angeles, 115–23; of "re-membering," contextualization and, 142–46
Polyglot citizens, 82–83
Popular education, 7, 153
Portelli, Alessandro, 169
Pratt, Mary Louise, 92
Primer Congreso Mexicanista, 128
Progresando en español porque es nuestro idioma (Progressing in Spanish, Because It Is Our Language), 174, 187, 193–94, 199
Proposition 187, 2–4, 32, 33–34, 98, 260
Proposition 209, 4, 34
Public squares, gathering of citizens in, 28–29
Puerto Ricans: cultural and political identity of, 3, 17; discrimination against, 3, 11; in New York City, 7; in San Jose, 8, 40–42. *See also* El Barrio Popular Education Program (East Harlem)
Puerto Rican Studies Association, 14
Puerto Rico, University of, 12

Quetzalcóatl, unveiling of statue of, 34–35, 36
Quiroz, Mrs., 176

Ramírez, Mauricio, 266
Raza Sí, 272–74
Reagan, Ronald, 53, 70, 246, 272, 273
Redevelopment, downtown, in San Jose, 89–92

Index

Reinhold, Robert, 59
"Re-membering," contextualization and politics of, 142–46
Respect (*respeto*), concept of, 69–71, 152, 166, 172, 179, 203, 231–33
Resto, Mrs. Belén, 179, 181
Restructuring, in Los Angeles, global economics and, 107–10
Richard Shaw Canning, 220, 224, 225, 226, 229, 232
Rights, 15; citizenship as affirmation of cultural, 201–9; claiming, 58; group, and collective identity, 196–201; issue of, 231–33; reproductive, 165; right to have, 204, 208; for undocumented immigrants, 256–61, 264–77. *See also* Cultural rights
Ringer, Benjamin, *We the People and Others*, 10
Ríos, Ana, 199
Ríos, Mrs. Minerva, 186–87
Ríos, Oscar, 220, 251–52; and cannery strike, 225, 226, 228, 233–35, 237, 243, 248; election of, to Watsonville City Council, 218, 249–50
Roberts, Bryan, 99–100
Rocco, Raymond, 12; "Citizenship, Culture, and Community: Restructuring in Southeast Los Angeles," 18–19, 97–123
Rodríguez, Clara, 13
Rodríguez, Eladia, 186
Rodríguez, Richard, 35–36; *Hunger of Memory*, 32
Rodríguez, Sylvia, 13
Rohter, Larry, 260
Rolón, Mrs., 181–82
Romero, Mrs., 170–71, 176, 197
Romo, Ricardo, 102
Ronstadt, Linda, 5
Rosa, Luis de la, 128
Rosaldo, Renato, 1, 12, 16, 255; "Assimilation Revisited," 11; "Cultural Citizenship, Inequality, and Multiculturalism," 17, 27–38; *Culture and Truth*, 11, 43; "Identity, Conflict, and Evolving Latino Communities: Cultural Citizenship in San Jose, California," 18, 57–96, 261–62
Rowe, Marsha, 76
Rubalcalva, Luis, 12
Ruiz, Vicki L., 211, 212, 218–19, 220, 221

Sacks, Karen Brodkin, 143–44, 212
Sacred places, 76–79, 262–63
Salt of the Earth (film), 211
Salvadorans, 105
San Antonio: Mexican-American community in, 126–30; political center for Latinos in, 8. *See also* Los Pastores
San Antonio Conservation Society, 135, 139, 140, 141, 145–46
Sánchez, Loretta, 8
San Fernando Vendor's Association (SFVA), 119
San Jose: Latinos in, 8, 45; Puerto Ricans in, 8, 40–42; unveiling of statue of Quetzalcóatl in, 34–35, 36. *See also* San Jose project on cultural citizenship
San Jose Metropolitan Chamber of Commerce, 63, 64, 65
San Jose Mission, performance of Los Pastores at, 139–42
San Jose project on cultural citizenship, 57–61; changing notions of community in, 72–73; Chicanos and Vietnamese in, 87–89; claiming space in, 71–72; downtown redevelopment and Chicano/Mexicano community in, 89–92; global to local forces in, 83–87; imagined communities and social gatherings in, 73–75, 93; national communities to local communities in, 81–83, 92–94; new politics of citizenship in, 95–96; research phases of, 67–68; research site for, 62–67; and respect, 69–71; sacred places in, 76–79; shared vision in, 79–81
San Jose State University, 64
San Miguel, Guadalupe, Jr., 129
Santa Anna, Antonio López de, 127

Index

Santa Clara County and Valley, 62–64
Santa Clara County Labor Council, 229
Santa Clara University, 213
Santos, Cecilia, 173
Sassen, Saskia, 107, 108–9
Scabs, 225, 228, 233, 238, 252
Schilling, R., 216
Schlesinger, Arthur, 4, 10
Scott, Allen J., 107
Segal, William, 215, 220
Seguin, Juan, 127
Segura, Denise A., 212
Selena, 5
Shame (*vergüenza*), concept of, 152
Shaw, David, 220
Shopping malls, 86–87
Silicon Valley, 8, 62, 63, 64–65, 66, 75; political economy of, 83
Silvestrini, Blanca G., 12, 74, 160, 198; "'The World We Enter When Claiming Rights': Latinos and Their Quest for Culture," 17–18, 39–53
Simplot, 215
Simpson, O. J., 2
Skerry, Peter, 121
Slater, David, 122
Smith, Michael Peter, 107
Smits, Jimmy, 6
Soberal-Perez v. Heckler, 53
Social gatherings and imagined communities, 73–75
Social Science Research Council, 13
Soja, Edward W., 106, 107–8
Solidarity Day, 225, 247; Rally, Second, 253
Sommer, Doris, 181
Sontag, Deborah, 259
South Americans, 7, 8
Southwest Voter Registration Education Project (SVREP), 149
Space, 15–16
Spanish language, 32–33, 35
Stand and Deliver (film), 6
Stanford University, 12, 66
Statehood movement, 3
Street vendors, 119–21
Strike Committee (Watsonville), 213–14, 225, 227–29, 235, 240, 247; importance of, as social space for strikers, 241–43, 244
Supreme Court, U.S., 50, 51, 52
Supreme Court of California, 49

Tavárez, Mrs., 162–63
Teamsters, International Brotherhood of (IBT), 220–21, 223–24; and cannery strike, 225–30, 247; Joint Council of, 226–27, 247
Teamsters for a Democratic Union (TDU), 221, 225, 238, 239, 247
Teamsters International Convention, 227, 247
Teatro Campesino, 5
Tennayuca, Emma, 211
Testimony (*testimonio*), 153, 158, 170, 185
Texas, University of, at Austin, 12
Texas Rangers, 128
Tiano, Susan, 212
Tilly, L. A., 212
Torres, María, 13
Torruellas, Rosa, 12, 155; "Claiming Cultural Citizenship in East Harlem," 20–21, 152–209
Toyota, 65
Tranchese, Carmelo, 130, 148
Trounstine, Philip J., 62, 64
Trust (*confianza*), 172–74
Turner, Bryan, 257
Turner, Steve, 239, 244
Turner, Victor, 130, 142, 270
TWA strike, 229, 246

UCLA, 13; Center for Chicano Research at, 12
Underclass, issue of, 15, 164, 201
Undocumented immigrants, 255–56; claiming community and rights for, 264–74; cultural citizenship for, 261–64; cultural rights and civil society for, 275–77; rights, citizenship, and membership for, 256–61
United Cannery Agricultural Packers and Allied Workers of America (UCAPAWA), 211, 220

Index

United Farmworkers Union (UFW), 211, 227, 228
United Foods, 215, 251–52
U.S. Border Patrol, 4, 272

Velásquez, Willie, 149
Velázquez, Mrs., 172
Velázquez, Nydia, 7
Vélez, Mirtha, 191–92
Vélez-Ibáñez, Carlos, 13, 175, 213
Vendors, street, 119–21
Vietnamese, 87–89
Vietnam War, 33
Vision, shared, 79–81
Voting Rights Act, 8
Voting to express prejudices and fears, 33–34, 36

Waldinger, Roger, 162
Walsh, Bill, 226
War of 1848 (United States and Mexico), 31, 62, 94, 127, 128, 214
Watsonville cannery strike, *see* Cannery strike (Watsonville, CA)
Watsonville Canning, 215, 220, 223, 235, 250; sale of, 229; strike at, 224–27, 228, 246–47, 251
Watsonville City Council, 217–18, 249, 250
Watsonville High School, 217
Watsonville Service Center, 217
Weiser Lock, 111
Welfare, issue of, 165–66, 190, 200
Wells Fargo Bank, 225, 228–29, 248, 250
West, Cornel, 244, 270–71
Wiebe, Robert H., 47
Williams, Patricia, 58; *The Alchemy of Race and Rights*, 257
Williams, Raymond, 80
Wilson, Pete, 59, 260
Wilson, R., 127
Wisconsin v. Yoder, 50, 51
Women's suffrage movement, 96
World Bank, 108

Zavala, Lorenzo de, 127
Zavella, Patricia, 13, 63, 212, 213, 218, 246; and Watsonville cannery strike, 221, 222, 223, 236
Zentella, Ana Celia, 13
Zoot Suit (film), 5–6
Zukin, Sharon, 100, 107